FROM
HOMER
TO
HARRY
POTTER

FROM
HOMER
TO
HARRY POTTER

A HANDBOOK *on* MYTH *and* FANTASY

MATTHEW T. DICKERSON & DAVID O'HARA

BrazosPress
Grand Rapids, Michigan

© 2006 by Matthew T. Dickerson and David O'Hara

Published by Brazos Press
a division of Baker Publishing Group
P.O. Box 6287, Grand Rapids, MI 49516-6287
www.brazospress.com

Printed in the United States of America

Library of Congress Cataloging-in-Publication Data
Dickerson, Matthew T., 1963–
    From Homer to Harry Potter : a handbook on myth and fantasy / Matthew Dickerson and David O'Hara.
      p.   cm.
    Includes bibliographical references and index.
    ISBN 1-58743-133-5 (pbk.)
    1. Fantasy literature—History and criticism. I. O'Hara, David, 1969– II. Title.
PN56.F34D53 2006
809′.915—dc22   2005031195

To our children (in order of birth): Thomas Dickerson, Anastasia O'Hara, Mark Dickerson, Michael O'Hara, Peter Dickerson, and Matthew O'Hara, in hopes that they will never make the mistake of thinking that fairy tales are only for the young.

And to our fantastic wives who continue to enchant us.

CONTENTS

ACKNOWLEDGMENTS

There's something funny about this kind of book, where we get to tell the stories of other stories. Obviously, we could not have written this one if we had not been heirs to a long tradition of those who have created, preserved, and re-told great tales. More important, we owe a debt to those who not only thought the stories were important but who also taught us to think about them. In both categories, C. S. Lewis and J. R. R. Tolkien have been our unparalleled masters. We also owe personal gratitude to Thomas Howard, Peter Kreeft, Tom Shippey, Robert Siegel, and Walter Wangerin Jr.

We are also thankful to the many students and colleagues at Middlebury College in Vermont, The Pennsylvania State University, and Augustana College of South Dakota, who have read and discussed the stories with us and helped to sharpen our thinking.

Finally, we would be remiss if we failed to acknowledge our debts to our teachers over the years, who introduced us to the stories, inspired our continued reading, and aided our understanding: the late Professor Robert T. Farrell (1939–2003) taught Matthew Dickerson Old English, helped him translate *Beowulf,* and gave him his first opportunity to teach a course on Tolkien at Cornell University. Eve Adler, who died in 2004, taught at Middlebury College for a quarter century beginning in 1977. Dave witnessed her excellence as a teacher in 1990–1991 when she taught him to read Greek and to *sing* Homer. None could call Greek a dead language while she taught it. Now that Dave teaches college Greek he has seen with new eyes how well she loved her craft and her students alike. She was a model of scholarship and pedagogy for the faculty at Middlebury College, including Matthew Dickerson who started teaching there in 1989. Greg Vigne taught Dave the importance of loving God with one's mind. Greg's love of the best stories continues to inspire his students. Matthew Davis at St. John's College in Santa Fe, New Mexico, gave Dave an example of what St. Augustine would consider the piety of asking the right questions. Douglas R. Anderson patiently guided Dave through his dissertation at The Pennsylvania State University, and continues to show his students the best of Achilles and the best of Odysseus, while embodying none of their faults. These teachers may not have said or thought the same things we have written in this book, and so we cannot blame them for our mistakes, but we can thank them for spurring our thought.

We are grateful to Rodney Clapp and Rebecca Cooper and the entire team of editors and artists at Brazos Press for their help and hard work, and the opportunity to collaborate with them and with each other on this book.

Matthew Dickerson and Dave O'Hara
October 16, 2005

Abbreviations
for Frequently Cited Sources

For frequently cited sources, we use the abbreviations given below. Since there are so many editions (with different page numberings) of *The Lord of the Rings*, we follow T. A. Shippey's convention and give only the book number (in uppercase Roman numerals) and chapter number (in lowercase Roman numerals); e.g., the reference "IV/iii" would be to the third chapter of the fourth book (the chapter titled "The Black Gate Is Closed," found in *The Two Towers*). Note that *The Fellowship of the Ring* contains books I and II, and *The Two Towers* contains books III and IV, and *Return of the King* contains V and VI. Similarly, for references to the seven books in C. S. Lewis's *Chronicles of Narnia*, we cite the abbreviation for the book name along with a chapter number (in lowercase Roman numerals) as in *Nephew*/xiv for the fourteenth chapter of *The Magician's Nephew*.

Citations from C. S. Lewis

OnSF   "On Science Fiction," in *Of Other Worlds: Essays and Stories*, ed. Walter Hooper (New York: Harvest, 1966), 59–73.

Preface   "Preface," in *George MacDonald: An Anthology*, ed. C. S. Lewis (New York: Macmillan, 1947), xxi–xxxiv.

Sometimes   "Sometimes Fairy Stories May Say Best What's to Be Said," in *Of Other Worlds: Essays and Stories*, ed. Walter Hooper (New York: Harvest, 1966), 35–38.

Battle   *The Last Battle* (New York: Collier Books, 1970).

11

Caspian	*Prince Caspian* (New York: Collier Books, 1970).
Hideous	*That Hideous Strength* (New York: Collier Books, 1965).
Horse	*The Horse and His Boy* (New York: Collier Books, 1970).
Lion	*The Lion, the Witch, and the Wardrobe* (New York: Collier Books, 1970).
Nephew	*The Magician's Nephew* (New York: Collier Books, 1970).
Silver	*The Silver Chair* (New York: Collier Books, 1970).
Voyage	*The Voyage of the Dawn Treader* (New York: Collier Books, 1970).

Citations from J. R. R. Tolkien

Essay	"On Fairy-Stories" in *Tree and Leaf* (Boston: Houghton Mifflin, 1989), 9–73.
Foreword	Foreword to the second edition of *The Lord of the Rings* (Boston: Houghton Mifflin, 1954).
Gawain	*Sir Gawain and the Green Knight*, trans. J. R. R. Tolkien (New York: Ballantine, 1975).
Hobbit	*The Hobbit* (Boston: Houghton Mifflin, 1938).
Homecoming	"The Homecoming of Beortnoth, Beorthelm's Son," in *Tree and Leaf, Smith of Wootton Major, and The Homecoming of Beortnoth, Beorthelm's Son* (London: Allen and Unwin, 1975), 147–75.
Letters	*The Letters of J. R. R. Tolkien*, selected and edited by Humphrey Carpenter with the assistance of Christopher Tolkien (Boston: Houghton Mifflin, 1981).
Monsters	"Beowulf: The Monsters and the Critics," in *The Monsters and the Critics and Other Essays* (Boston: Houghton Mifflin, 1984).
MR	*Morgoth's Ring: The Later Silmarillion, Part 1, The Legends of Aman.* The History of Middle-Earth, vol. 10, ed. Christopher Tolkien (New York: Houghton Mifflin, 1993).
Niggle	"Leaf by Niggle," in *Tree and Leaf* (Boston: Houghton Mifflin, 1989), 75–95.
Silm	*The Silmarillion* (New York: Houghton Mifflin, 1977).
Smith	*Smith of Wootton Major*, in *Smith of Wootton Major and Farmer Giles of Ham* (New York: Ballantine, 1969).

Citations from Other Authors: Story

Compass	Philip Pullman, *The Golden Compass* (New York: Alfred A. Knopf, 1995).
Complete	George MacDonald, *The Complete Fairy Tales of George MacDonald* (New York: Schocken Books, 1977).

Cow	Walter Wangerin Jr., *The Book of the Dun Cow* (New York: Harper and Row, 1978).
Edda	Snorri Sturluson, *The Prose Edda,* trans. Jean I. Young (Berkeley: University of California Press, 1954).
Foul	Stephen Donaldson, *Lord Foul's Bane* (New York: Del Ray, 1977).
Goblet	J. K. Rowling, *Harry Potter and the Goblet of Fire* (New York: Arthur A. Levine, 2000).
Goblin	George MacDonald, *The Princess and the Goblin* (Middlesex: Puffin, 1964).
Grimm's	*The Complete Grimm's Fairy Tales* (New York: Pantheon Books, 1944).
Heliand	*The Heliand: The Saxon Gospel,* trans. G. Ronald Murphy, S.J. (New York: Oxford University Press, 1992).
Knife	Philip Pullman, *The Subtle Knife* (New York: Alfred A. Knopf, 1997).
Order	J. K. Rowling, *Harry Potter and the Order of the Phoenix* (New York: Arthur A. Levine, 2003).
Prisoner	J. K. Rowling, *Harry Potter and the Prisoner of Azkaban* (New York: Arthur A. Levine, 1999).
Secrets	J. K. Rowling, *Harry Potter and the Chamber of Secrets* (New York: Arthur A. Levine, 1999).
Shore	Ursula K. Le Guin, *The Farthest Shore* (New York: Bantam, 1972).
Spyglass	Philip Pullman, *The Amber Spyglass* (New York: Alfred A. Knopf, 2000).
Stone	J. K. Rowling, *Harry Potter and the Sorcerer's Stone* (New York: Arthur A. Levine, 1998).
Tombs	Ursula K. Le Guin, *The Tombs of Atuan* (New York: Bantam, 1971).
Wizard	Ursula K. Le Guin, *A Wizard of Earthsea* (New York: Bantam, 1968).

Citations from Other Authors: Essay and Criticism

Auden-1	W. H. Auden, "Introduction" to *Tales of Grimm and Andersen* (New York: Modern Library, 1952), xiii–xxi.
Auden-2	W. H. Auden, "In Praise of the Brothers Grimm," *New York Times,* Nov. 12, 1944.
Blackburn	F. A. Blackburn, "The Christian Coloring in the *Beowulf,*" from *An Anthology of Beowulf Criticism,* ed. Lewis E. Nicholson (Notre Dame, IN: University of Notre Dame Press, 1963).
Bultmann	Rudolf Bultmann, *Jesus Christ and Mythology* (New York: Charles Scribner's Sons, 1958). Citations are from chap. 1, "The Message of Jesus and the Problem of Mythology," 11–21.
Campbell	Joseph Campbell, "Folklorist Commentary," in *The Complete Grimm's Fairy Tales* (New York: Pantheon Books, 1944), 833–64.

Dickerson   Matthew Dickerson, *Following Gandalf: Epic Battles and Moral Choices in* The Lord of the Rings (Grand Rapids: Brazos Press, 2003).

Duriez   Colin Duriez, "About George Macdonald," in *The Golden Key and Other Stories* (Elgin, IL: Chariot, 1978).

Drout   Michael Drout, "Tolkien and Beowulf: Medieval Materials for the Modern Audience," lecture presented at a colloquium, J. R. R. Tolkien: Fantasist and Medievalist, on March 6, 2003.

Eliot   T. S. Eliot, "Introduction" in Charles Williams, *All Hallows Eve* (Grand Rapids: Eerdmans, 1991).

Fickett   Harold Fickett, *Conversations with Jesus: Unexpected Answers to Contemporary Questions* (Colorado Springs: Piñon Press, 1999).

Howard   Thomas Howard, *An Antique Drum* (Philadelphia: Lippincott, 1969). This book has been reprinted under the title *Chance or the Dance?: A Critique of Modern Secularism* (San Francisco: Ignatius Press, 1989).

Kaske   R. E. Kaske, "The Governing Theme of Beowulf," in *Beowulf: A Norton Critical Edition,* ed. Joseph Tuso (New York: Norton, 1975).

Keyes   Dick Keyes, *Beyond Identity* (Ann Arbor: Servant Books, 1984).

Kreeft   Peter Kreeft, *Heaven: The Heart's Deepest Longing* (San Francisco: Ignatius Press, 1989).

Le Guin   Ursula K. Le Guin, *Language of the Night: Essays on Fantasy and Science Fiction,* rev. ed. (New York: HarperCollins, 1989).

Murphy   G. Ronald Murphy, S.J. "Introduction to the Translation," from *The Heliand* (New York: Oxford University Press, 1992).

Shippey   Tom Shippey, *J. R. R. Tolkien: Author of the Century* (London: HarperCollins, 2000).

Wangerin   Walter Wangerin Jr., *The Orphean Passages* (Grand Rapids: Zondervan, 1986).

AUTHORS' NOTE

This book spans the literature of fantasy over many centuries. The table of contents shows chapters on ancient biblical narrative, Greek myth, medieval legend and romance, and fairy tales from the nineteenth century and earlier. Given a limitless amount of time (both ours and our readers), it would be easy to expand the scope of the book even further to include such examples of fantasy, fairy tale, and myth as Norse mythology, Native American myths, African fairy tales, etc. Indeed, the more we worked on this book, the more we wanted to include (or saw that we *ought* to include).

When we originally conceived of this project, however, our purpose was *only* to provide a guide to *modern* fantasy literature. In particular, our initial goals were: (1) to suggest a few general principles for how to think about and understand the genre of fantasy; and (2) to illustrate those principles by exploring some specific *characteristic examples* (i.e., selected works of a few well-known fantasy authors of the last few decades). This was motivated in part by a comment from author Tom Shippey, who at the start of his book *J. R. R. Tolkien: Author of the Century* writes: "The dominant literary mode of the twentieth century has been the fantastic." Despite the truth of Shippey's words, not enough critical attention has yet been given to fantasy as a literary genre.[1] We set out to write a book that would explore this dominant literary mode *as a mode*.

---

1. There is no shortage of books on some important fantasy authors (especially J. R. R. Tolkien and C. S. Lewis), but there are very few book-length works that take modern fantasy seriously as a literary genre and address the issues of the roots and sources of the genre and how to understand and think about works of that genre as a whole (and not just one or two important authors).

However, modern fantasy literature, especially the deeper and better kind, is steeped and rooted in ancient myth, medieval heroic legend, and fairy tale. To put it differently, "modern fantasy"—by which we mean the fantasy literature of the late twentieth and early twenty-first centuries, or more specifically fantasy in the post–J. R. R. Tolkien era—is in many ways not so modern! If we follow the thinking of J. R. R. Tolkien—and we do—myth, fairy tale, romance,[2] and fantasy can and ought to be understood as different aspects of the same category: what Tolkien calls *Faërie*. Thus, any exploration of modern fantasy should by rights begin with a study of its predecessors. For this reason, not long after the book was conceived, its scope grew considerably to encompass this broader category of Faërie[3]—to provide a background and set of principles that would give the reader not only a guide to modern fantasy, but also an introduction to understanding myth and heroic legend, medieval romance, and fairy story, especially in light of their importance and influence on their modern literary relative. Indeed, accomplishing the former goal would not be possible without some success at the latter.

Of course, the study of myth is an ambitious goal, even if we focus only on a subset of Western myth. Much has been written on the subject: reference guides, adaptations, psychoanalytic explorations of symbolism in myth, etc.[4] For the serious student, the brevity of our chapters will be woefully inadequate. The same goes for medieval romance and fairy tale. There is a variety of literature on these subjects. We seek to provide only an introduction and some background that will enable readers to understand the importance and influence of an important part of our literary culture.

Another point should also be made. Though there has been some very helpful commentary and criticism of myth and fairy story, much of what

2. By "romance" we—and Tolkien—are using the term in a historical sense, referring broadly to medieval romance (especially what is known as Arthurian romance) and to the nineteenth-century romantic movement in literature, and not to the modern romance or romantic novel.

3. The word *Faërie* comes from *Fay-Ry*, meaning: "the realm of the Fay." The word *Fay* itself is an older word for *fairy* and refers to a broad range of magical or supernatural creatures of myth and folklore, including elves, dwarves, goblins, and the like. Thus, for example, the famed *Morgan le Fay* from Arthurian legend is literally Morgan the Fairy. Today there are several derivatives and variants of the word *Fay*. Throughout this book, we use the modern word *fairy* to refer to all Fay creatures, and *fairy story* to refer to the narrow genre of *traditional* fairy tales such as the nineteenth-century collections of the Brothers Grimm and Andrew Lang. We use the more archaic *Faërie* (sometimes written *Faery*) to refer both to the *realm* of the Fay and to the *entire* broad body of literature dealing with that realm (myth and fantasy as well as traditional fairy tale).

4. At the end of the book, a suggested reading list is given for the reader interested in further study.

has been written is either reference guides that help the reader find some myth they once read, or books that intend to dismiss myth as outdated, unimportant, dangerous, or merely symbolic. We'd like to offer an alternative point of view, though not a novel one:[5] myth and fantasy are rich and important elements in our literary lives and moral imaginations, and offer profound insights into truth.

Of course as soon as we mention exploring "characteristic examples" of modern fantasy, every reader will wonder which books and authors we have in mind as "characteristic." One of the things we realized from the start was that whatever authors we choose to *include* would also (by virtue of space limitations) result in other authors being *omitted*. And probably every reader of this book will feel that some vitally important author has been unfairly left out. We make no claim that the authors we've included are either the best or even the most important modern authors of fantasy literature. Our decisions have partly to do with taste and familiarity; we are unapologetic about the fact that we know and like some authors better than others. But the most important consideration was to find a broad range of characteristic works that will best illustrate the principles we present. Indeed, our goal is to help our readers to become more discerning and understanding readers, to help them to learn to understand fantasy literature, and not to tell them what to think about specific works. To that end, it is far better that we omit important authors so that our readers can apply the principles on their own.

There are two exceptions to this approach. Those glancing through our table of contents will notice no chapters on J. R. R. Tolkien or C. S. Lewis, arguably the two most important authors of fantasy in the twentieth century, and who will likely remain the most influential fantasy authors through the twenty-first. The reason for this omission is twofold. First, unlike with the genre of fantasy in general and most of the authors we explore in particular, there is already an abundance (some would say even a glut) of critical work on these two authors. Some of this work is very fine scholarship, much of it is accessible to a general audience, and some of it even achieves both of these qualities. (Readers seeking to explore more thoroughly the writings of Tolkien and Lewis are encouraged to see the recommended reading list at the back of this book.) Second, and more centrally, the ideas of Tolkien and Lewis permeate our writing. One of the things we have done in this book is taken critical ideas about myth and fairy stories scattered throughout the writings of these two luminar-

---

5. In fact, the point of view we offer is very old indeed.

ies, ordered and structured them in a single place, and then applied the ideas to a new body of literature that did not exist when they wrote, and that has come into existence largely as a result of their pioneering work. Put another way, we didn't need a *separate* chapter on Lewis and Tolkien because the entire book bears their fingerprints.

PART 1

The Literature
of Faërie
and the Roots
of Modern Fantasy

1

Introduction: From Cosmogony to Fairy Tale

The dominant literary mode of the twentieth century has been the fantastic.

Tom Shippey

In the foreword to his book *J. R. R. Tolkien: Author of the Century*, Tom Shippey makes a startling and important observation about the importance of fantastic literature to modern culture. Though Shippey rightly includes science fiction and horror along with fantasy as the "Literature of the Fantastic," his own book focuses specifically on fantasy literature, which claims at least an equal share with science fiction as the "dominant literary mode of the twentieth century." As one of the leading philologists of our time, and one who has served on the English faculty at Oxford, as the chair of English Language and Medieval Literature at Leeds, and currently as an English professor at St. Louis University, Shippey has strong credentials to make such a judgment. Whatever personal taste one may or may not have for fantasy literature, it is difficult to gainsay Shippey's assertion. The literary genre of fantasy has blossomed in the twentieth century and continues to flourish into the twenty-first.

But what do we make of this genre? How should one read and understand a modern work of fantasy? Can works of fantasy really have anything important to say to us? Should we take it as a serious literary form, or just dismiss it as a passing (and perhaps embarrassing) trend?

In some ways, the answer to the first two of those questions is straightforward. The best way to "understand" a work of fantasy is simply to read it as story, and enjoy it as story. If we have anything to say in this book, it is this: don't seek to reduce Story, especially that of Faërie, to mere moral platitudes or philosophical propositions. Fantasy doesn't work propositionally; if it works at all, it works as story. Having said that, there is much that can be said about fantasy as story, and about understanding it in this context. For if there is an error in the one extreme of trying to reduce myth or fairy tale to a single, easily digestible platitude, moral, or allegorical meaning, there is danger in the other extreme of missing its meaning and significance altogether—of equating myth with falsehood, fantasy with escapism, and fairy tale with the nursery. Before saying anything about understanding either myth or fantasy, however, we should first address the task of clarifying both of these terms. Clarifying our understanding of what the literature of Faërie *is* will go a long way toward understanding what it *does*.

What Is Myth?

We might start by trying to define *myth* and *fairy story*. This is a more challenging endeavor than it may first appear. In his important essay "On Fairy-Stories," J. R. R. Tolkien sets out to explain what a fairy story is. While he says many things that fairy stories are *not*—he excludes, for example, beast-fables, travelers' tales, and anything explained away as mere dream—he provides no succinct *definition* of *fairy story* other than that "Most good 'fairy-stories' are about the *adventures* of men in the Perilous Realm [Faërie] or upon its shadowy marches" (*Essay*, 38). Even were this not qualified with "most" and "good," this definition is not helpful *until* one understands something about "*Faërie:* the Perilous Realm itself, and the air that blows from that country" (38). However, Tolkien immediately goes on to say, "I will not attempt to define that, nor to describe it directly. It cannot be done. Faërie cannot be caught in a net of words; for it is one of its qualities to be indescribable, though not imperceptible" (38). Thus, we are left at something of a loss in our search for a definition of fairy story.

In some ways, the lack of a definition for fairy tale is appropriate. The nineteenth-century romantic movement that brought about the resurgence of fairy tale (demonstrated by the broad success of nineteenth-century collectors and authors, including Jacob and Wilhelm Grimm, Andrew Lang, Hans Christian Andersen, and George MacDonald) was in many ways a response to (or reaction against) the Enlightenment. The Enlightenment was the age of the encyclopedia, like those of d'Alembert, Diderot, and, later, Hegel. It was an age that wanted to write definitions and provide *encyclopedic* information—that is, to capture the whole truth of a thing rationally and scientifically. The fairy tale, by contrast, defied definition. It succeeded, in part, on the notion that there are things that must be known through the imagination and not merely through deductive arguments or empirical science. The great twentieth-century poet T. S. Eliot recognized this when he wrote his introduction to Charles Williams's[1] fantastic novel *All Hallows Eve:* "What it is, essentially, that [Wiliams] had to say, comes near to defying definition. It was not simply a philosophy, a theology, or a set of ideas: it was primarily something imaginative" (Eliot, xiii).

Likewise, many scholars have attempted to define myth, and while some have made keen insights into the value of myth to society and the understanding of various specific mythologies, it is difficult to find a single satisfactory and universally accepted definition. One popular modern dictionary defines myth as follows:[2]

myth n
1. a traditional story about heroes or supernatural beings, often explaining the origins of natural phenomena or aspects of human behavior
2. myths considered as a group or a type of story
3. a character, story, theme, or object that embodies a particular idea or aspect of a culture
4. somebody or something whose existence is or was widely believed in, but who is fictitious
5. a story that has a hidden meaning, especially one that is meant to teach a lesson

1. Charles Williams was a friend and contemporary of Lewis and Tolkien, and a member with them of the famous literary guild known as the *Inklings*. In addition to various plays and works of Arthurian poetry, Williams also wrote a handful of novels that—while not traditional fairy tales—belong within the literature of the fantastic.

2. Encarta® World English Dictionary © 1999 Microsoft Corporation. All rights reserved. Developed for Microsoft by Bloomsbury Publishing Plc.

One can see that this definition is not especially helpful. Definition 2 is self-referential and thus only provides a definition of myth if one already knows what myths are. Definition 3 might also be true of any number of stories that are not mythical. A typical modernist novel, for example, embodies a particular idea or aspect of the culture in which it was written. Definition 4 is certainly common usage; as in the phrase "urban myth." When somebody says "That's just a myth," they usually mean "That's not true." However definition 4 may be the furthest from what we as the authors mean by the word. Indeed, we will argue that myths may be fundamentally true, often so at many layers; the better the myth, the more true it is. Definition 5 is as unhelpful as definition 3. Myths usually have meaning, and may well teach a lesson, but so do many other types of stories, and the "meaning" of a myth is not necessarily any more or less "hidden" than that of any type of story.

Definition 1 comes only a little closer to what we mean. However, even this definition falls short. What does it mean that a myth often explains "natural phenomena or aspects of human behavior"? The writers of that definition probably had in mind the narrow sort of myths, often called "nature myths" and taught to elementary school children, that provide an explanation (commonly assumed to be fictional) of something like where thunder comes from, or why raccoons have masks, or how tigers got stripes, or why we have lunar eclipses. The schoolchildren may find the story fun (or funny), but they don't in general accept the story's explanation as real history. In "On Fairy-Stories," Tolkien describes nature myths and responds to the common notion that they were the original myths from which later myths and fairy tales derived.

> At one time it was a dominant view that all such matter [fairy-stories] was derived from "nature-myths." The Olympians were *personifications* of the sun, of dawn, of night, and so on, and all the stories told about them were originally *myths* (*allegories* would have been a better word) of the greater elemental changes and processes of nature. Epic, heroic legend, saga, then localized these stories in real places and humanized them by attributing them to ancestral heroes, mightier than men and yet already men. And finally these legends, dwindling down, became folk-tales, *Märchen*, fairy-stories—nursery-tales.
>
> That would seem to be the truth almost upside down. The nearer the so-called "nature myth," or allegory, of the large processes of nature is to its supposed archetype, the less interesting it is, and indeed the less is it of a myth capable of throwing any illumination whatever on the world. (*Essay*, 49–50)

Tolkien here is not only denying the notion that nature-myths provide the source matter for fairy tale, but is going even further, suggesting that so-called nature-myth isn't even real myth. He says it ought instead to be called allegory (a term that for him is usually derogatory). If we do include it as myth, it is a myth of a much lower kind, not at all capable of illuminating the world. The implication, of course, is that real myth *is* capable of throwing illumination on the world—a notion to which we shall return. In any case, this definition of *myth* usually makes myth out to be a story that is useful only in a prescientific culture, implying that we, in our scientific age, have outgrown myths. Thus, definition 1 leads back to definition 4 and the emphasis on "fictitious," except perhaps that in the case of "nature-myths" the explanation isn't even "widely believed" (at least not any more). And whether the myth is believed or not, the suggestion that a myth's main value and purpose is merely to explain something—or worse, that myths may be little more than disguised sermons—diminishes their real significance and has a similar flaw to that of definition 5.

Of course we shouldn't be surprised that an off-the-shelf dictionary would have a less than satisfactory definition of such a complex idea. In "On Fairy-Stories," Tolkien made the same complaint about the *Oxford English Dictionary* (OED). The OED didn't even have an entry for the combination *fairy story* except in the supplement, where the third definition (as with the above definition of *myth*) was simply "a falsehood." For Tolkien, the lack of a satisfying definition was symptomatic of a deeper problem, which is that England lacked its own indigenous myth, fairy stories, or "heroic legends on the brink of fairy-tale and history." He describes himself as "grieved by the poverty of [his] own beloved country; it had no stories of its own (bound up with its tongue and soil), not of the quality that [he] sought" (*Letters,* 144). He acknowledges the heroic legend associated with the "Arthurian World" and even describes it as "powerful," but he didn't think it was a good mythology *for England.* Though it is now commonly associated with England, the Arthurian legend actually grew up on the other side of the English Channel. Tolkien writes that it is "imperfectly naturalized, associated with the soil of Britain but not with English," and he also describes the elements of Faërie as "too lavish and fantastical, incoherent and repetitive" (144). (In a later chapter we will turn to Arthurian legend and explore how, despite Tolkien's distaste for it, it provides important imaginative source material for many modern fantasy writers, including Tolkien.)

Himself one of the greatest myth makers of the twentieth century—and arguably of all time—J. R. R. Tolkien set out to fill that gap and provide through his Middle-earth *Legendarium* a mythology and body of legend for England. In a famous letter to his publisher Milton Waldman, Tolkien wrote:

> Do not laugh! But once upon a time (my crest has long since fallen) I had a mind to make a body of more or less connected legend, ranging from the large and cosmogonic, to the level of romantic fairy-story—the larger founded on the lesser in contact with the earth, the lesser drawing splendour from the vast backclothes—which I could dedicate simply: to England; to my country . . . I would draw some of the great tales in fullness, and leave many only placed in the scheme, and sketched. The cycles should be linked to a majestic whole, and yet leave scope for other minds and hands, wielding paint and music and drama. Absurd. (*Letters,* 144–45)

Though not intended as a definition of myth or Faërie, this personal letter contains many insights into what myth is. The first observation is that Tolkien associates myth, legend, and fairy tale as part of a continuous whole, which he calls the Literature of Faërie. He makes a similar connection between mythology and legend in the opening paragraph of the foreword to the second edition of *The Lord of the Rings:* "I wished first to complete and set in order the mythology and legends of the Elder Days, which had then been taking shape for some years." There he even ties myth and legend with history. All the components, from the cosmogonic and cosmological—what we might traditionally think of as the mythic—down to the romantic fairy story, are intricately linked and mutually dependent.

This brings us closer—though not to a definition of myth, fantasy, or fairy tale—at least to a picture of how they relate to one another. We should see Faërie as a broad spectrum, or continuum, with myth on one side, and romantic fairy tale on the other, and heroic romance (including Arthurian legend and nearly all of modern fantasy) falling someplace in the middle. Pictorially the spectrum looks something like this, with Faërie encompassing it all:

The Literature of Faërie

Myth	Fantasy & Heroic Romance	Fairy Tale

The continuum can be seen as one of scope. There is a range of geographic scope from global to the local, and a range of historical scope from eons to perhaps a few days. There is also a range in the scope of significance, in the scope of character types, and in the scope of meaning.

Myth, for example, often spans a broad geographic scope, encompassing whole worlds and even spanning different worlds (whence Tolkien's "cosmogony"), bringing us even into the land of Faërie. At the other end, fairy tale usually has a very narrow geographic scope of a single village or wood. Fantasy falls in the middle, broader than a single village, perhaps involving whole realms, but not extending to the heavens. Another way to look at this is to note that the realm of myth is celestial, the realm of fantasy and heroic romance is an earthly kingdom (it doesn't matter which one), and the realm of fairy story is the local village, the cottage in the woods, or the forest out the back door. Likewise, there is a range of historical scope. Myth is timeless. To the extent that it is within time, it may span centuries. Most fairy tales, by contrast, take place in the matter of a few days.[3] Works of fantasy and heroic romance typically span several months or even a few years.

There is also a broad range from myth to fairy tale in the scope of character type as well as in what might be called "significance." In the fairy tale, the result of the events largely affects the lives of one or at most a handful of characters. Cinderella is freed from the domination of her evil stepmother, while little else is said about the consequences of this event for the rest of the world. Hansel and Gretel find their way home, but as far as we know, nobody but their wood-cutter father ever even knows about it; for some readers, it might be nice to know that the witch is dead, and perhaps lots of other children might be spared a terrible fate, but the story does not explicitly deal with these broader consequences. A frog-prince is rescued by enchantment and marries the princess; that a whole kingdom happens to be affected by gaining a good-hearted king is superfluous detail, not central to the story. In heroic romance, by contrast, whole kingdoms are affected, and often a large cast of characters are involved. And the characters are all aware that whole kingdoms will be affected by their actions, and they are often motivated by that realization. The medieval Spanish poem *El cantar de mío Cid* transforms the story of El Cid Campeador into a tale of national significance, connecting El

---

3. Certainly a number of years may pass between events in many fairy tales—"Sleeping Beauty," for example. However, these years are not described. The castle (and its princess) may be under a spell of sleep for decades or even centuries, but the actual narrative events of the fairy tale take place in the few days before the castle falls under the spell or the few days or even hours during which the castle is freed.

Cid's embodiment of religious ideals and heroic virtues to the fate of a whole nation.

Then we come to myth. The events of myth are seen not only to affect the rule of a particular realm, but to dramatically affect the whole history of the world. When Orestes avenges Agamemnon and is prosecuted by the Erinyes, Athena's wise judgment becomes a universal principle of fairness in all human law. In the end, we are more concerned with the principle arising from Orestes' case than with Orestes or Athena.

Likewise, whereas the characters of myth are the gods, and romance and fantasy give us heroes, the fairy story gives us the simpleton, the village wood-cutter, and the tailor. This is often reflected in the narrative voice. From whom does the story come? The gods themselves? The elves and other mighty heroes? Or a Hobbit? In discussing the mythic "power" of Tolkien's *The Silmarillion*, for example, Peter Kreeft writes: "The sense of height comes also from Tolkien's device of suspending the origin of the story between the human and the divine." He goes on to add:

> *The Silmarillion*, though "about" Elves, is haunted by the Valar, who are the gods. . . . They are more than natural forces (thunder), more than concrete individual superhuman persons (Thor), and more than feelings, images or concepts within our thought, dreams, or imagination (awesome power), but they are the source and unity of all three.[4]

By the same token, the *meaning* of myth is often much broader than that of fairy story. The best myths reward endless rereading and can be understood at many levels. The simplest of fairy stories, by contrast, may provide endless enjoyment at each retelling, and yet their meaning is much more readily grasped or intuited—imagined, at least, even if not put into the form of a moral.

Of course the borders between fairy tale and legend, between heroic romance and myth are not sharp lines. There is, as we said, a continuum, a scope, a range. If myth is primarily concerned with the celestial and fairy tale with the mundane, heaven is nonetheless dimly present in the fairy tale, just as earth lurks in the consequences of mythic tales. As Tolkien points out, all the pieces are "more or less connected" and interdependent, "founded on" or "drawing from" one another. If myth and heroic legend *are* two distinct genres, the border is blurred and there is no clear

4. Peter Kreeft, "Afterword: The Wonder of the Silmarillion," from *Shadows of Imagination: the Fantasies of C. S. Lewis, J. R. R. Tolkien, and Charles Williams*, ed., Mark R. Hillegas (Carbondale: Southern Illinois University Press, 1979), 161–78.

line where one stops and the other begins. Tolkien illustrated this broad spectrum with his own body of Middle-earth work, which he referred to as his *Legendarium*. At the one end is *The Silmarillion*, the "large and cosmogonic," and at the other end the romantic fairy tale known as *The Hobbit*, with *The Lord of the Rings* falling in between. Even *The Hobbit* changes course as the book progresses, beginning toward the fairy tale side of the spectrum and moving gently but distinctly toward heroic legend,[5] while *The Silmarillion* moves in the other direction, beginning in "The Ainulindalë" and "The Valaquenta" on the far left as very high myth, relating the actions of the gods, and later moving (in the tales of "Beren and Lúthien" or "Túrin Turambar," for example) toward legend and heroic romance, giving us tales of heroes.

Likewise, Faërie involves both "great tales"—that is, tales told in fullness such as *The Lord of the Rings*—and other tales "only placed in the scheme, and sketched," as is the tale of Nimrodel and Amroth told by Legolas in *The Fellowship of the Ring,* or the even sketchier reference made by Aragorn to Queen Berúthiel's cats. A closely related observation is that myth is not static: where one creative mind leaves off, other minds and hands pick up. Thus myth, which at one level is fundamentally oral and literary, is always taking new forms and even becomes connected to other forms of creative art: painting, music, and drama. W. H. Auden suggests something like this in his introduction to the *Tales of Grimm and Andersen,* where he points out that one of the best elements of fairy tale and myth is that they tend to improve with improvisational retelling, and that it is usually better to tell them from memory than to read them from a book (Auden-1, xiii–xxi). This reminds us that they are vital and alive, and part of our moral imagination, not merely preserved specimens of tales captured in a book.

C. S. Lewis even suggests that myth does not exist in words at all—that is, it doesn't exist in one particular telling.

> Myth does not essentially exist in *words* at all. We all agree that the story of Balder is a great myth, a thing of inexhaustible value. But of whose version—whose *words*—are we thinking when we say this?
>
> For my own part, the answer is that I am not thinking of any one's words. No poet, as far as I know or can remember, has told this story supremely well. I am not thinking of any particular version of it. If the story is anywhere embodied in words, that is almost an accident. What

5. This progression has been traced in Dickerson, 166–74.

really delights and nourishes me is a particular pattern of events, which would equally delight and nourish if it had reached me by some medium which involved no words at all. (*Preface,* xxvi–xxvii)

Even Tolkien's own telling of the important tales of his *Legendarium* changed over the years (often significantly), so that his son and literary executor Christopher, when he sought to publish *The Silmarillion,* had no clear authoritative or definitive versions of various tales and had to choose from several extant versions.

In short, we see that myth (and more broadly Faërie) is expansive. There is a majestic whole, but there are also particulars. There are cycles—repeated themes and threads of stories—but the particulars change and alter from one turn to the next.

Myth and Truth

If we are not yet much closer to a succinct and satisfying definition of myth, at least we may have moved further from unsatisfying definitions. The most unsatisfying definition of (or association with) myth is "falsehood." Myths may be true. Indeed, any myth that has survived through centuries almost certainly contains truth. Or, put another way, something that is *true* and yet fits the picture we have begun to paint of myth—we can't yet call it a "definition"—ought still to be called a "myth." To call something "myth" should not in any way diminish its importance or verity. The same can be said of "fairy story."

For many Christians and other religious believers, this is a particularly troublesome aspect of our attempt to define and understand myth. Part of the trouble comes primarily in response to theologians such as Rudolf Bultmann who have sought to *demythologize* Christianity and the Bible, by which they mean separate the mythic and historic elements of the scriptures from their central message, or *kerygma,* in order to present it in what they perceive to be a more true form. This may be a noble aim, but it implies that anything extraordinary or "mythological" in the scriptures cannot be taken altogether seriously. In *Jesus Christ and Mythology,* Bultmann writes:

This [New Testament] conception of the world we call mythological because it is different from the conception of the world which has been formed and developed by science since its inception in ancient Greece and which has been accepted by all modern men. . . . Modern science does not believe that the course of nature can be interrupted or, so to speak, perforated, by supernatural powers. . . .

Then the question inevitably arises: is it possible that Jesus' preaching of the Kingdom of God still has any importance for modern men and the preaching of the New Testament as a whole is still important for modern men? . . . His person is viewed in the light of mythology when he is said to have been begotten of the Holy Spirit and born of a virgin, and this becomes clearer still in Hellenistic Christian communities where he is understood to be the Son of God in a metaphysical sense, a great, pre-existent Heavenly being who became man for the sake of our redemption and took on himself suffering, even the suffering of the cross. It is evident that such conceptions are mythological, for they were widespread in the mythologies of Jews and Gentiles and then were transferred to the historical person of Jesus. Particularly the conception of the pre-existent Son of God who descended in human guise into the world to redeem mankind is part of the Gnostic doctrine of redemption, and nobody hesitates to call this doctrine mythological. This raises in acute form the question: what is the importance of the preaching of Jesus and of the preaching of the New Testament as a whole for modern man?

For modern man the mythological conception of the world, the conceptions of eschatology, of redeemer and redemption, are over and done with. Is it possible to expect that we shall make a sacrifice of understanding, *sacrificium intellectus*, in order to accept what we cannot sincerely consider true merely because such conceptions are suggested by the Bible? (Bultmann, 11–21).

When Bultmann writes, above, "It is evident that such conceptions are mythological," what he is implying is that *such conceptions are therefore untrue.* Thus, he contrasts mythologies with history. That the myth was "transferred to the historical person" means that mythological elements—which would include, according to Bultmann, the virgin birth and Christ's divine nature as preexistent God—are historically false and did not exist in the real, or *true*, person. It is as though Bultmann were ashamed of the celestial and able to countenance only the far less embarrassing mundane elements in the scriptures. If there is any doubt that this is what Bultmann means, one need only look a little further where he writes "the mythological conception" is "over and done with." We can throw them away. Unknowledgeable and easily deceived ancient men might fall for myths, Bultmann suggests, but the "modern man" knows them for what they are and rejects them; "science" and not myth is what is "accepted by all modern men." He then writes even more plainly: "we cannot sincerely consider" the conceptions as "true." In doing so, he raises doubts that anything mythological can still be "important for modern men."

Now there are (at least) two common responses to Bultmann's view of myth.[6] One is to agree with him that certain biblical conceptions are mythological and therefore, by association with myth, untrue. In this view, modern men should reject mythological biblical conceptions. Presumably *this* is the response Bultmann was hoping for. Another (seemingly but not really) opposite approach is to cling to belief in the fundamental truth of the biblical conceptions and therefore to *deny that they are mythological.* This latter approach strongly denies Bultmann's goal of removing the miraculous from our historical understanding of the gospel and affirms instead that nature *can* be perforated by supernatural powers. This may *seem* like an orthodox Christian response. However, the problem with this second approach is that while denying Bultmann's conclusion, it nonetheless accepts his notion that the mythological is false and somehow contrary to the truly historical. Thus, Christians who take this latter course react very negatively to the connection of biblical narrative with myth.

We take, instead, a third approach, which follows from a different understanding of what myth is, namely, that myths might be fundamentally true and yet still be "mythological." Myth and history are not at odds, nor are myth and truth. To understand this approach, it is helpful to know the etymology of *myth.* The word *myth* comes from the Greek word *muthos. Muthos* originally meant "word" or "speech" and was a near synonym for *logos*—a word later used in the Gospel of John to describe Christ: "In the beginning was the Word (*logos*), and the Word (*logos*) was with God, and the Word (*logos*) was God" (John 1:1). Eventually, both words came to mean "an account" or "a story," or, more particularly, an account of what was true. The verb *muthologeuo,* from which we get our word *mythologize,* meant simply "to relate word-for-word," that is, to give an accurate or verbatim account of an event or a speech. The distinction that eventually arose between the words was that *muthos* came to mean an account *through story,* while *logos* came to mean an account *through reason or proposition.* Though in earlier classical Greek the words *logos* and *muthos* were practically interchangeable, in later classical Greek (for instance, in Plato) *muthos* came to take on a meaning like "fictionalized account." It is nevertheless worth mentioning that Plato, noted as the father of philosophy and of logic in the West, wrote numerous *muthoi*

---

6. We will return to a discussion of the Bible as myth in chapter 2.

as key parts of his philosophical dialogues. In other words, even when *muthos* came to mean a *fictionalized* account, it was still a way of communicating something true—such as a philosophical idea.

Owen Barfield, and later J. R. R. Tolkien (largely influenced by Barfield), believed that myth—meaning here simply a *cosmology* or *a way of understanding the world*—actually came before language. That is, rather than language coming first and providing words so that myths could be "written," language itself grew *out of* our mythological understanding. Verlyn Flieger summarizes Barfield's beliefs about myth:

> Barfield suggests that myth, language, and man's perception of this world are inseparable. Words are expressed myth, the embodiment of mythic concepts and a mythic world view. The word *myth,* in this context, must be taken to mean that which describes man's perception of his relationship to the natural and supernatural world. Barfield's theory postulates that language, in its beginnings, made no distinction between the literal and the metaphoric meaning of a word, as it does today.[7]

This agrees with and articulates more clearly Lewis's ideas that myths exist apart from words. Lewis also wrote, "In myth the imagined events are the body and something inexpressible is the soul: the words, or mime, or film, or pictorial series are not even clothes—they are not much more than a telephone" (*Preface,* xvii–xviii). More important to our present discussion, it also presents myth as a *vehicle* for truth even more powerful than are language and propositional speech—indeed, even as an *embodiment* of truth.

Following this approach, one might agree with Bultmann's assessment that the understanding of Christ as "a great, pre-existent Heavenly being" is "mythological" and yet still accept that understanding as true.[8] Accepting its mythological stature does not deny its verity. Returning once more to "On Fairy-Stories," Tolkien expresses this understanding of myth and Faërie very clearly, especially with respect to the Gospels:

7. Verlyn Flieger, *Splintered Light: Logos and Language in Tolkien's World* (Grand Rapids: Eerdmans, 1983).

8. This is a hypothetical agreement. We are not here claiming to agree with Bultmann's overall assessment. In particular, Bultmann writes: "Modern science does not believe that the course of nature can be interrupted or, so to speak, perforated, by supernatural powers." This notion is not in fact scientific, but is based on Hume's skepticism, and is essentially a faith-based position. Twentieth-century philosophers of science (for instance Feyerabend and Peirce) have shown that science in this way is essentially a religion. Likewise, C. S. Lewis has exploded this notion in his monograph on *Miracles.* However one might fully accept "myth" as an appropriate description of the Bible without in any way diminishing its value or its overall validity or truth.

The Gospels contain a fairy-story, or a story of a larger kind which embraces all the essence of fairy-stories. They contain many marvels—peculiarly artistic, beautiful, and moving: "mythical" in their perfect, self-contained significance; and among the marvels is the greatest and most complete conceivable eucatastrophe [consolation]. But this [Gospel] story has entered History and the primary world; the desire and aspiration of sub-creation has been raised to the fulfilment of Creation. The Birth of Christ is the eucatastrophe of Man's history. The Resurrection is the eucatastrophe of the story of the Incarnation. This story begins and ends in joy. It has pre-eminently the "inner consistency of reality." There is no tale ever told that men would rather find was true, and none which so many skeptical men have accepted as true on its own merits . . .

The Christian joy, the *Gloria,* is of the same kind; but it is pre-eminently . . . high and joyous. But this story is supreme; and it is true; Art has been verified. God is the Lord, of angels, and of men—and of elves. Legend and History have met and fused. (88–89)

What Tolkien is describing is the true myth, or the true fairy story. (Again, myth, legend, and fairy story are all wound into the broader category of Faërie in Tolkien's description.) The Gospel story has the characteristics of myth: it deals with issues of great (or mythical) significance and gives a basis for understanding the world. And it has the characteristics that Tolkien associates with fairy stories: it has "marvels," as one would expect in the Perilous Realm or near to its borders. As with myth, it is "self-contained." As with fairy stories, it contains a eucatastrophe,[9] or "good catastrophe": a happy ending, a sudden joyous turn of events, a consolation.

Yet Tolkien also claims that the story is fundamentally true, not merely in a mythical or metaphoric sense, but even in a very narrow historical sense as well. The Gospels have "entered History and the primary world," he claims, distinguishing this particular fairy story from those that take place in secondary (fictional, subcreated) worlds of literary imagination (and which may also be true, though in a different way). Put another way, he associates the story with our *primary* reality and adds that many skeptical men have believed its historical truth based only on its merits. If we miss these clues, Tolkien is more blunt: "But this story is supreme; and it is true." It is also a myth and a fairy story!

9. Tolkien coined this word from the Greek roots *eu,* meaning good; *kata,* meaning total; and *strophe,* meaning a turn or turn of events.

It is interesting to note, however, that when Tolkien speaks of the Gospels *entering into* history, he is implying that the Gospels in some way exist apart from, or prior to, their historical incarnation. He is suggesting that the Gospel story is a true part of God's eternal being and character, and thus its *entry* into our "History and the primary world" is a revelation of something *already* true about God—mythically true, we might say. The truth of myth, like the truth of the Gospels, does not depend on history any more than it depends on human language. Their truth stands beyond history, enters history, informs history. Human history and human language testify to the truth of myth; they do not contain it. Thus, historical truth is not the only type of truth that may be found in fairy story. The fairy story of the Gospels not only gives us a historical truth about a particular character in a period of history approximately two millennia ago, it also gives us truth about the nature of God independent of those historical events.

If we follow this idea, then we see that fairy tale, like so-called "realistic fiction," may also describe characters and events that are fictional (they do not and did not exist in the history of our primary world) and yet convey profound truth about things like human nature, divine nature, love, or the absolute corrupting power of a Ring whose sole purpose is to enable one to dominate other wills. The fact that such a ring or similar rings have appeared in numerous other earlier myths does not diminish the truth of the particular ring in Tolkien's myth, any more than the appearance of certain biblical themes or ideas in other earlier myths would diminish their truth when they appear in the biblical myth.

Another great modern writer of myth, legend, and fairy story, Walter Wangerin Jr., has made a strong connection between myth and this other type of truth. In his book *The Orphean Passages,* he expresses in slightly different words something of what we think Tolkien is saying in his essay:

> In order to comprehend the experience one is living in, he must, by imagination and by intellect, be lifted out of it. He must be given to see it whole; but since he can never wholly gaze upon his own life while he lives it, he gazes upon the life that, in symbol, comprehends his own. Art presents such lives, such symbols. Myth especially—persisting as a mother of truth through countless generations and for many disparate cultures, coming therefore with the approval not of a single people but of *people*—myth presents, myth *is,* such a symbol, shorn and unadorned, refined and true. And when the one who gazes upon that myth suddenly, in dreadful recognition, cries out,

"There I am! That is me!" then the marvelous translation has occurred: he is lifted out of himself to see himself wholly. (Wangerin, 14–15)

Wangerin not only affirms the possibility of truth in myth but refers to myth as "the mother of truth." He is suggesting the existence of an objective truth that is independent of any time, place, or culture. That is, truth is neither temporally, spatially, nor socially relativistic. It therefore makes sense to *present* truth in a context that transcends specific cultures and reaches instead "through *countless* generations" and "many *disparate* cultures" (emphasis ours). Wangerin's belief, and one shared by the authors of this book, is that myth is a uniquely powerful vehicle for this, "shorn and unadorned, refined and true." When we see the truth in myth or fairy stories, especially when we see the truth *about ourselves,* it is with "dreadful recognition."

There are two ironies of the mythic mode that Wangerin brings out for us here. It moves beyond one *single people*—that is, one culture or one time—to reach *people* in general, and yet in doing so it has the capacity simultaneously to move individual persons even more powerfully. That is, its specific power comes from its very generality.[10] Myth is how we comprehend our own experience. We gaze at myth . . . and see ourselves. And yet at the same time the power of its *generality* comes not from vagueness, but rather from the *concreteness* of its symbols—symbols that are freed from the limiting association with one single people, one single time, one single place. Tom Howard writes in *An Antique Drum:* "As the imagination is a synthetic faculty in the first place, it is, secondly, an image-making faculty; that is, its tendency is from the abstract toward the concrete." He goes on a few pages later to add, "For the effort to clarify and intensify by finding an image is at work on all levels of communication" (Howard, 35, 37).

C. S. Lewis, yet another great writer of fantasy and fairy story, connects myth and fantasy together as members of the broader "Mode" (or category) of Faërie, and he speaks of the power of this Mode that is at work both in generality and concreteness, and in generality found in concreteness. In his essay "Sometimes Fairy Stories May Say Best What's to Be Said," he writes:

10. This doesn't mean that one particular written version of a myth will be understood the same by all people in all times and places. Margaret Mead correctly pointed this out in her work on mythology. But the best of myths—one might say myths at their most mythic—are universal and capable of being translated to other cultures, because what matters most in them is not merely the setting. As Auden says, "In the folk tale, as in the Greek epic and tragedy, situation and character are hardly separable; a man reveals what he is in what he does, or what happens to him is a revelation of what he is" (Auden-1, xx).

The Fantastic and Mythic is a Mode available at all ages for some readers; for others, at none. At all ages, if it is well used by the author and meets the right reader, it has the same power: to generalize while remaining concrete, to present in palpable form not concepts or even experiences but whole classes of experience, and to throw off irrelevancies. But at its best it can do more; it can give us experiences we have never had and thus, instead of "commenting on life," can add to it. (38)

Lewis makes several keen observations here. First, he makes it clear (as Tolkien has also done) that there is nothing about fairy tales that should especially associate them with children or the nursery. It is a powerful form of literature for *all* ages. He then suggests an approach to the intellectual or critical understanding of myth: we start with the concrete—the palpable, the details and particulars of the various myths and fairy tales—and then look from there to the generalizations and classes of experience, seeing them more clearly because we are not distracted by irrelevances. And in agreeing with Tolkien and Wangerin and others about the power of myth and fantasy to give an account of the world, and a glimpse of ourselves, Lewis says something even stronger: that they not only reveal truth about our experience, but actually add to our experience.

In his introduction to the fairy tales of George MacDonald, Lewis makes the same point again. He writes that the *making* of myth

may even be one of the greatest arts, for it produces works which give us (at the first meeting) as much delight and (on prolonged acquaintance) as much wisdom and strength as the works of the greatest poets. . . . It goes beyond the expression of things we have already felt. It arouses in us sensations we have never had before, never anticipated having, as though we had broken out of our normal mode of consciousness and "possessed joys not promised to our birth." It gets under our skin, hits us at a level deeper than our thoughts or even our passions, troubles oldest certainties till all questions are reopened, and in general shocks us more fully awake than we are for most of our lives. (*Preface,* xxviii)

Here Lewis uses the word *myth,* but the context is a discussion of fairy tales. We may take what he is saying to be true of the whole literature of Faërie, from myth to fantasy to fairy tale. And in the last sentences of each of these quotes, Lewis suggests both why we (the authors of this book) read myth, fantasy, and fairy, and why we wrote this book.

2

STORIES AT THE
BOUNDARIES

*Faërie is a perilous land, and in it are pitfalls for the unwary
and dungeons for the overbold.*

J. R. R. Tolkien, "On Fairy-Stories"

We are now, perhaps, a little closer to defining myth—or at least to providing a meaning for the term as we use it in the book. One last comment is necessary before trying our hand. Throughout history, various religions and worldviews have often distinguished between the physical/material world and the spiritual: between the seen and the unseen, or the natural and the supernatural. Of course, not everybody believes in both of these worlds. Materialists, on the one hand, deny the existence (or at least the relevance) of the spiritual world, claiming that the material (i.e., physical) reality is the *only* reality. On the other hand, there are some—Gnostics and some Platonists, for example—who deny the relevance of the material world, claiming that either some spiritual world or the world of thought and idea is all that matters. Whatever view one holds, however, both the material and spiritual realms, the natural and supernatural, have been subjects of literature, art, meditation, and philosophic inquiry for as long as humans have been putting thoughts

39

One can not deny man has a
spiritual nature and a longing for life after death

to words. Even if one or the other is just an illusion, it has been a convincing illusion.

And then there is the human, the spiritual animal: a creature who seems to be at once part of both worlds. "A little lower than the angels," as the psalmist puts it (Ps. 8:5 KJV). Or, in Aristotelian terms, a "rational animal"—one endowed with the reason of the gods, but the mortality and temporality of the animals. Throughout history, our literature has attested to our spiritual restlessness, and our sense of being caught between two worlds. "My heart is restless till it finds its rest in Thee, O God," says Augustine. "To be or not to be," asks Hamlet. "There is only one truly serious philosophical problem, and that is whether or not to commit suicide," says Camus.

What is this restlessness, this mystery of our being in the world, and what are we to do with it? In no place is that more present than in our approach to death and our sense that death is somehow *un*natural. Ernest Becker writes:

> Man is literally split in two; he has an awareness of his own splendid uniqueness in that he sticks out of nature with a towering majesty, and yet he goes back into the ground a few feet in order to blindly and dumbly rot and disappear forever. It is a terrifying dilemma to be in and to have to live with.[1]

Dick Keyes writes: "Death is God's indelible and inescapable stamp of 'Failure' on man's attempt at Godhood." He goes on to explain:

> Death is a problem only because "[God] has put eternity into man's mind" (Eccl. 3:11). Death would not be so outrageous were it not for all the human expectations that it negates. Man has illusions of being God, his mind can span millions of years, and yet he will become dust. (Keyes, 40–41)

These are only a few examples of this awareness of some spiritual split in the world. Others abound. As Emmylou Harris sings, "If there's no Heaven, what is this hunger for?"[2] Of course, death is completely *natural* if by *natural* we mean "having to do with nature." All living things *naturally* die, and if the materialists are right, then nature is all there is and resistance is futile. But if the human is an eternal being, then death

---

1. Ernest Becker, *The Denial of Death* (Free Press, New York, 1973), 26, quoted in Keyes, 26.
2. "The Pearl," on *Red Dirt Girl* (2000). Song published by Poodlebone Music, administered by Almo Irving.

is *un*natural in the sense that it is at odds with our *nature*—that is, our human eternal nature. Philosopher Peter Kreeft writes:

> Death is the most natural thing in the world; why do we find it unnatural? ... We complain about death and time. ... There is never enough time. Time makes being into non-being. Time is a river that takes away everything it brings: nations, civilizations, art, science, culture, plants, animals, our own bodies, the very stars—nothing stands outside this cosmic stream rushing headlong into the sea of death. Or does it? Something in us seems to stand outside it, for something in us protests this "nature" and asks: Is that all there is? We find this natural situation "vanity": empty, frustrating, wretched, unhappy. Our nature contradicts nature. (Kreeft, 212–13)

Put another way, if resistance is futile, then why is the impulse to resist so strong? Some might say that this is simply an evolutionary advantage given us by nature to ensure the proliferation of our genes, but this invites the big question: "Why on earth should nature care about that?" If nature wants us to live now, why then do we also have a hunger for life after death? After all, belief in heaven might make us nonchalant about our life on earth (and therefore less fit to live here), as Nietzsche complains. But we do have the hunger, and it is hard to deny expressions of it in our culture. Kreeft argues that man's spiritual nature is evident in a longing for heaven universal to every member of our race. It is not merely an escapist longing, evident in times of suffering, but rather a longing that can be felt "also in the middle of our truest earthly sweetness: hearing a symphony, seeing a sunset, complete sexual love. It is the highest life that sets us longing for something more than this life" (Kreeft, 58).

In Tolkien's Middle-earth *Legendarium*, it is a fundamental tenet that members of our race (the race of Men), as well as Elves, are beings of both flesh and spirit. In an essay in *Morgoth's Ring: The Later Silmarillion* (an essay written as a commentary on the "Athrabeth Finrod Ah Andreth"), he writes: "There are on Earth 'incarnate' creatures, Elves and Men: these are made of a union of hröa and fëa (roughly but not exactly equivalent to 'body' and 'soul,' a somewhat Aristotelian or Thomist view)" (*MR*, 330).[3]

---

3. This is the second of seven basic tenets. In introducing this, Tolkien writes: "With regard to King Finrod, it must be understood that he starts with certain basic beliefs, which he would have said were derived from one or more of these sources: his created nature; angelic instruction; thought; and experience."

"And this composition of soul and body," Plato writes in the *Phaedrus*, "is called a living and mortal creature."[4]

Connecting Tolkien's basic belief in humankind's spiritual nature to the thoughts of Keyes and Becker, it is not surprising that death was also a central theme in much of Tolkien's writing—he once wrote that mortality was the central theme of *The Lord of the Rings*—or that he saw death as the most important theme in the best fairy tales of the great nineteenth-century fairy-tale writer George MacDonald.[5] In any case, even the materialist who denies the reality of the spiritual world must explain away humanity's seeming—and in the materialist view, misdirected—sense of spirituality.

Three Faces of Myth and Faërie

So how does myth view the natural and the supernatural? And what about people, who seem to fall in the uneasy category in between, creatures both physical and spiritual? We return again to Tolkien's essay, and a brief observation he makes about fairy stories:

> Even fairy-stories as a whole have three faces: the Mystical toward the Supernatural; the Magical toward Nature; and the Mirror of scorn and pity toward Man. The essential face of Faërie is the middle one, the Magical. But the degree in which the others appear (if at all) is variable, and may be decided by the individual story-teller. (*Essay,* 28)

The first thing to notice again is how broad the category of Faërie is. There is considerable room for variation from individual storyteller to storyteller, and Tolkien makes reference to "fairy-stories as a whole" to take account of that. Even so, there are three essential "faces" that are (in Tolkien's view) common to all true fairy stories, and which describe the way that the three elements of reality—the natural, the supernatural, and man—ought to be presented, each with a different face.

The first face is the mystical toward the supernatural. Though Tolkien does not explain this here, we can guess what he means from hints here and in his other writings. There is a supernatural world: a world of angels and demons, and in Tolkien's view a God over all: Eru Ilúvatar, to

---

4. Plato, *Phaedrus,* 246c. Jowett translation.
5. Tolkien writes in "On Fairy-Stories": "Death is the theme that most inspired George MacDonald" (*Essay,* 62).

use his Elvish name. Speaking of this supernatural world, Gandalf says of the Elf warrior Glorfindel, "Those who have dwelt in the Blessed Realm live at once in both worlds, and against both the Seen and the Unseen they have great power" (II/i, 235). Fairy tale does not deny the supernatural but rather in some way depends on its existence. However, the supernatural remains in the background, Tolkien tells us; it must be viewed with some sense of mystery and awe. (Thus, in *The Lord of the Rings,* comments like Gandalf's above are rare.) In other words, fairy tale is not a place to deny the supernatural, but neither is it a place for systematic theology or philosophy of religion. Fairy tales do not deal in mere propositional truth or morals, as fables and sermons so often do, and we should not look to them for that.

This is not to say that myth and fairy story cannot contain religious truth. Earlier in the essay Tolkien writes, "Something really 'higher' is occasionally glimpsed in mythology: Divinity, the right to power (as distinct from its possession), the due of worship; in fact 'religion'" (51). Or as he writes in another letter, fairy stories "*must* contain elements of moral and religious truth (or error)" (emphasis ours). Tolkien himself was a devout Catholic Christian, and he saw his Middle-earth *Legendarium* as being fundamentally Christian.[6] However, the religious elements should not be "in the known form of the primarily 'real' world" (*Letters,* 144). (And that is another of Tolkien's criticisms of the Arthurian world. "It is involved in, and explicitly contains the Christian religion" [*Letters,* 144]).

The second face is the Magical toward Nature. This is the essential face, and the face that is most important in our definitions of myth and fantasy, as well as Tolkien's own understanding of fairy story. Nature is magical. Trees can live and move and speak and, perhaps, get angry and defend themselves; flowers are inhabited by fairies; a frog may contain an enchanted prince (or the frog itself may be enough enchantment without the prince); mountains can cast stones upon unwary travelers; and people can learn the ancient speech of animals and communicate with them. The fairy story does not deny the validity of science, but it denies that

---

6. In a personal letter discussing various influences on *The Lord of the Rings,* Tolkien described what he considered the most important influence: "I am a Christian (which can be deduced from my stories), and in fact a Roman Catholic" (*Letters,* 288). In another personal letter, he notes: "The Lord of the Rings is of course a fundamentally religious and Catholic work, unconsciously at first, but consciously in the revision" (*Letters,* 172). The specifics of that Christian influence have been the main focus of several books, including B. Birzer's *J. R. R. Tolkien's Sanctifying Myth* and R. Woods's *The Gospel according to Tolkien: Visions of the Kingdom in Middle-Earth.* It has also been pointed out in numerous other books, including T. A. Shippey's *J. R. R. Tolkien: Author of the Century* and M. Dickerson's *Following Gandalf: Epic Battles and Moral Victory in* The Lord of the Rings.

empirical science is the *only* way to understand nature. More important, myth and fairy stories, in giving us a glimpse of the forests and lawns of Faërie, may also give us a new appreciation for the beauty and magic of the tree and blade of grass in our front yard. As Tolkien writes, "It was in fairy-stories that I first divined the potency of the words, and the wonder of the things, such as stone, and wood, and iron; tree and grass; house and fire; bread and wine" (*Essay*, 78).

A related comment should be made at this point about the distinctions between fantasy and science fiction, earlier called *scientifiction* and now just *sci-fi*, for short. In the publishing world today, fantasy and sci-fi often go hand in hand. Walk into most bookstores, and you will find a single section devoted to both. This is, in many ways, an odd marriage; despite some superficial similarities, sci-fi and fantasy are substantially dissimilar—indeed, almost polar opposites. Science fiction often asks how things might be in the future of our world, or perhaps in the present of our universe but in some yet unexplored place (deep undersea, on Mars, in a distant corner of a distant galaxy). In the former case, sci-fi generally assumes a naturalistic process at work in history and astronomy, and extrapolates through time from present conditions to future conditions. Sci-fi set elsewhere in the universe has similar principles, but extrapolates through space (rather than time) from what is known (scientifically) here on earth. Thus, most sci-fi is predictive or speculative. Classic examples include George Orwell's *1984*, Jules Verne's *20,000 Leagues under the Sea*, Arthur C. Clarke's *2001: A Space Odyssey*, William Gibson's *Neuromancer*, Isaac Asimov's *I, Robot* stories, and Philip K. Dick's *Do Androids Dream of Electric Sheep?* Fantasy, by contrast, doesn't ask how things will be in this universe in the future, or in some unexplored reaches of the present, but asks instead how things *might* be in some *other* possible world, where creatures are not bound by science. Or in some rare instances it explores how things might *have been* in our own universe if it were inhabited more visibly by beings not governed by the laws of physics as we know them.

In fact, the differences between sci-fi and fantasy go even deeper and relate directly to the first two faces of myth. As the very name suggests, science fiction is based on science—or, more accurately, on the assumption that *everything is explainable by science*—and science works, practically speaking, on naturalistic assumptions.[7] Sci-fi may contain strange

7. We are speaking somewhat loosely here in order not to descend into the complexities of modern philosophy of science. It might be better to say that scientists rely on materialist (or naturalistic) assumptions in constructing their experiments, like the uniformity of natural causes in a closed system, an unspoken premise of the scientific method. Scientists themselves need not be materialists, and many are

phenomena and fantastic devices, but the phenomena and devices are ultimately explainable by science and naturalistic causes. Even if the author doesn't actually present such explanation, it is assumed to exist. Fantasy and fairy tale, by contrast, allow for and even depend upon the supernatural—that is, upon enchantment and magic and powers that are not limited by any material laws or enslaved to naturalistic cause and effect. We see this in both the mystical face toward the supernatural, and the magical face toward nature.

The devices of sci-fi and fantasy may look similar. For example, in both cases a man may be transformed into a frog. In the former, however, the explanation is scientific: some technology is able to rearrange the genetic structure of the body, while leaving some portion of the brain's memory intact. In the latter case, it was a witch who enchanted a prince (or princess), and there is no scientific explanation. Or consider various works of fantasy, such as Madeleine L'Engle's *A Wrinkle in Time* or Patricia McKillip's *Riddle-Master of Hed* trilogy, in which various characters learn to move instantly across space by magically casting their minds ahead of their bodies and then simply stepping into that new space. A similar result is sometimes accomplished in sci-fi, in the *Star Trek* mythology, for example, in which a person (or object) is "beamed" through space by some feat of modern science and engineering. Despite a similarity in results, the means and underlying assumptions are very different in science fiction than in fantasy.

There are three other related differences that one can often—though not always—note between sci-fi and fantasy. These are generalizations, and not rules or definitions, meaning that there are notable exceptions. Nonetheless, they are easy to see. First, sci-fi tends to be marked by a progressivist's optimism about the power of scientific knowledge to improve the lot of humanity. Some of the most famous early works of science fiction are utopian dreams, for example, Edward Bellamy's *Looking Backward*, and some of the writings of H. G. Wells and Jules Verne.

---

not. However, their scientific *experiments* deal with observed effects in the natural world in an attempt to discover natural laws. Of course, both this reliance and the assumption that one *can* discover real natural laws indicate a realism that cannot itself be explained by these naturalistic assumptions. That is, many of the underlying assumptions or presuppositions upon which the scientific method is based, such as the assumption of a consistent ordered universe in which experiments are repeatable and "laws" don't change arbitrarily, are themselves not scientific assumptions but metaphysical assumptions necessary to begin science. Many of history's most famous scientists (e.g., Roger Bacon, Newton, Copernicus, and even—as Charles Hummel points out in his book *The Galileo Connection*—Galileo) were professed theists whose explorations of naturalistic phenomena in the natural world were motivated by theistic assumptions about the nature of the universe.

Those who hold to this progressivist's optimism will tend to prefer science fiction. Those (like the authors of this book) who prefer fantasy to science fiction defend their preference, noting that honest contemplation of the previous century leads one to wonder whether science has improved our lives or just made us better at killing one another. A second trend is that the plot and its resolution in sci-fi usually hinge on *technology*. This means that the determining force in resolving conflicts (or winning battles) is not necessarily fate or virtue, but who has the most powerful technological devices. In this regard, *Star Wars,* for all of its external sci-fi trappings, functions in places more as myth. "The Force" in the first three *Star Wars* movies (episodes 4, 5, and 6) belongs to the genre of fantasy (and those who use the Force need to hold a mystic faith in it), whereas in the subsequent movies (episodes 1, 2, and 3), it has been converted into a material cause best explained by science and measurable by technology. By contrast, a few parts of the *Harry Potter* sequence—which by and large is fantasy—actually function more like sci-fi: the fastest Quidditch players are not the ones with the most powerful magic, but the ones who have the latest brooms, that is, the greatest technology.

A final difference is that fantasy has a more complex view of causation than does most sci-fi. This goes beyond the already observed distinction that everything in sci-fi is explainable by science, and gets at the notion of *purpose*. Fantasy's view of cause is one that corresponds more to Aristotle's view of there being four causes (formal, material, efficient, and final) for everything, over against the Enlightenment and Newtonian view of there being only two causes for every event, the material and the efficient (i.e., matter and energy). The formal cause is the idea of the thing; the final cause is its purpose. Modern science was made possible in part by severing considerations of final and formal causes from empirical research. This has been a productive strategy for science, but it means that science (and subsequently, sci-fi) finds it difficult to consider purpose and meaning. But fantasy and myth are always charged with both purpose and meaning. In sci-fi, discussions of sin and virtue, of grand purpose and meaning, and of fate and free will are usually a little out of place (though some sci-fi authors do engage in these discussions). Sci-fi tends to settle these questions by bowing to materialism and by dismissing unscientific answers as mystical and therefore untrue or unimportant. (Again, we are oversimplifying for the sake of brevity, and there are counter-examples.) The crucial element in sci-fi is the natural (matter, energy, and technology); the crucial element in fantasy is the interaction of the natural with the supernatural. Thus, despite a few exceptions, we see that the fantasy genre (as distinct from science fiction) relies heavily upon what is rightly called supernatural.

If we accept this distinction, then we see that even something like C. S. Lewis's "space trilogy" rightly belongs in the category of fantasy, and not science fiction, on the grounds that the trilogy is strongly dependent on the presence of the supernatural. At this point, those who have always considered these three books to be science fiction will conclude that our distinction must therefore be lacking (since it fails in its categorization of these books). To defend this categorization, we must therefore appeal to something apart from our distinction and argue on other grounds that the trilogy really is fantasy. Though *Out of the Silent Planet* and *Perelandra* both involve space travel—a common aspect of much science fiction—the means of propulsion through space in the first book is considered by the author to be irrelevant and uninteresting to the story. Then, once the hero lands on Mars, all technology disappears. As to the second of these books, we need note only that the space travel is accomplished by the hero being placed into a casket and getting pushed to the distant planet of Venus by angelic beings. As Lewis himself wrote, "I took a hero once to Mars in a space-ship, but when I knew better I had angels convey him to Venus" (*OnSF*, 68). The third book of the series, *That Hideous Strength*, despite a lack of space travel, is actually the closest to predictive science fiction. (Those working in academia might find Lewis's predictions uncannily accurate.) Here, however, the "battle" is ultimately won by a combination of the druidic powers of Merlin returned to twentieth-century England (an example of the magical face toward nature), and by the supernatural intervention of the angelic powers introduced in books 1 and 2 (an example of the mystical face toward the supernatural).

If this intuitive argument does not convince the reader of our categorization, we appeal to comments by Lewis himself. In an essay, "On Science Fiction," delivered to the Cambridge University English Club in 1955, Lewis includes fantasy under the general heading of science fiction. He goes on, however, to describe fantasy as a distinct subspecies, very different from all other subspecies of speculative science fiction, and the only subspecies to which he was drawn. He describes the subspecies of fantasy as having "an imaginative impulse as old as the human race." The main identifying feature of this genre is that it brings us to strange worlds. Rather than stories about space-travel, it has "stories about gods, ghosts, ghouls, demons, fairies, monsters, etc." He explains that "pseudo-scientific apparatus" is acceptable in such a story, but he is "inclined to think that frankly supernatural methods are best." In short, what Lewis is really describing in his essay is not fantasy as a subspecies of science fiction—though he uses that phrase, he goes on to explain that fantasy is far too different from all other subspecies—but rather fantasy and science fiction as both distinct subspecies of the category referred to earlier by Tom Shippey as the *Literature of the Fantastic.* (Tom Shippey also includes in that category horror stories.) And from Lewis's own descriptions of these categories, we see that his space trilogy belongs with fantasy rather than with speculative science fiction. But in case we fail to make the connection, he then goes on in the essay to explicitly place his own space trilogy in this subspecies called fantasy (*OnSF,* 67)! And on the title page of *That Hideous Strength,* he describes it as a "modern fairy-tale for grown-ups."

Returning now to Tolkien's three faces, this brings us to the third and final face: the mirror of scorn and pity toward man. Here we come back to the strange place man has as a spiritual animal: a creature of both body and soul, flesh and spirit. It's difficult to deny that we've made a mess of the world and a mess of our lives. Glance at the front page of any newspaper. Look at the crime, poverty, and hatred in the city streets, the history books, the neighborhood schools. Look at the corruption in the halls of political and financial power. As a race, we are worthy of scorn. If our praise of good actions and our blame of moral failures mean anything at all, then we are more than mere biological machines. Praise and blame seem to point to a real moral nature in humans, and to a real moral standard in the world. The way we treat one another and our world is not without consequences. We have earned our own scorn.

But we also feel pity: pity not in the condescending sense, as merely another word for scorn, but pity in the sense of sorrow and the desire to see restoration: pity that is much closer to mercy. It was, as Gandalf tells Frodo, pity that stayed Bilbo's hand and kept him from killing Gollum when betrayed at the end of the riddle game. Gandalf does not deny that Gollum deserved death, but in addition to the good of justice he speaks of another good embodied in Bilbo's pity. "The pity of Bilbo may rule the fate of many," Gandalf says (I/ii). This kind of pity is meaningless if it does not first recognize that scorn is also deserved, but it moves past scorn. We pity as well as scorn ourselves. We pity ourselves as a race. We also pity ourselves and each other as individuals. We feel regret and remorse for our own actions, and at the moments of greatest awareness of our common humanity, we feel sympathy for the perpetrators as well as the victims. Even at the worst of evils, we hope for redemption—even while we hope for justice. We want Gollum to become Sméagol again.

Frodo especially must hope for Gollum's redemption, because he sees in himself the capacity to become what Gollum has become. And so it is with all of us. If we see in others a cause for scorn, then we must see it in ourselves as well. Don't remove the speck of dust from the eye of another, Jesus teaches, until you've removed the log from your own. And the flip side of the coin is this: if you want to be shown pity, then show pity to others. Thus it is that Tolkien, most importantly of all, speaks of this third face as a mirror: it shows us ourselves.

All of this brings us back to Walter Wangerin Jr.'s comment about the power of myth: "When the one who gazes upon that myth suddenly, in dreadful recognition, cries out, 'There I am! That is me!' then the marvelous translation has occurred: he is lifted out of himself to see himself wholly." Myth, at its best, is both a distant view into the whole and a close mirror of the personal.

Defining Myth and Fantasy?

What we presented in the previous section provides a good working definition of the literature of Faërie as a whole.

The literature of Faërie is any literature that presents these three faces: "the mystical toward the supernatural, the magical toward nature, and the mirror of scorn and pity toward man."

Within that broad class, we can think of its subspecies—myth, heroic fantasy, and fairy tale—in terms of the continuum discussed in the previous chapter.

This is, of course, only one way of defining our terms. In fact, Tolkien himself was reluctant to define fairy stories, and we are equally hesitant to think that any one description does justice to the whole. Nonetheless, providing some boundaries or limits on what is meant is necessary if anything at all is to be said. Discussing some important mythologies and then exploring their relationship with modern fantasy is yet another approach that works in some sense through story rather than through propositional definition (an approach very apt for the discussion of a genre of literature that itself works through Story and not through proposition). We will take this approach in later chapters.

Yet another approach comes from our understanding of the realm of Faërie itself, and especially from understanding its borders with our world.

The literature of Faërie is that literature that takes place in the Perilous Realm of Faërie—or, more specifically, near to its borders.

We might say that the subgenre of myth is that set of stories that takes place in Faërie but near to the borders of our world, while the subgenre of fairy stories is that set of stories that take place in our world but near to the borders of Faërie. In either case, it is the boundary of the Perilous Realm that is important. The literature of Faërie takes place where the two worlds meet: Asgard and Middengard, Olympus and Piraeus, the supernatural and the natural, the celestial and the mundane, Valinor and the Shire, the sacred and the profane, Faërie and Wotten Major.

If we consider our discussion of man earlier in the chapter, then understanding Faërie in this way also argues why it is such an important category of literature. If man is indeed the spiritual animal, the creature who lives at once both in the world of the seen and the unseen, then those stories that take place in both worlds—that is, on the borders of Faërie—will be far more relevant than stories that take place entirely in one world to the exclusion of the other. Explaining something of what drew him to Charles Williams's fantastic novels, T. S. Eliot writes, "For him there was no frontier between the material and the spiritual world. . . . To him the supernatural was perfectly natural, and the natural was also supernatural" (Eliot, xiii–xiv). In other words, Charles Williams (or at least his novels) seemed to live right on that boundary.

Seeing this about Faërie, and about myth and fairy tale as two ends of the spectrum, we can turn specifically to modern fantasy. Again, as we did with myth in the previous chapter, we begin with etymology. *Fantasy* is also from a Greek word, *phantasia,* meaning "representation" or "appearance." It comes to English as a technical philosophical word in Aristotle and Augustine, then in later Latin writers. Its technical use was usually epistemological or psychological, to distinguish between objects as they exist in the world and their *representation* in our minds or understanding. There is a tree in my backyard, and I know it well. In my mind, then, there is a *phantasia* of the tree that corresponds closely to the tree.

This is striking. In both cases, the words *myth* (or *muthos*) and *fantasy* (or *phantasia*) originally meant *accurate representations or accounts of real things.* In time, they came to mean, at least in common usage, inaccurate, fictional, or false accounts of things. How did this happen? Plato needed to distinguish between those accounts of nature that effectively prevented people from seeking truth and those that fostered further inquiry. He called the former *muthoi.* Even though he himself wrote other *muthoi,* the name stuck.[8] In the case of *phantasia,* the shift occurred closer to our time. In the modern era, skepticism about whether and how closely our mental concepts corresponded to the world, combined with the growth of modern science and logic, led to the use of *phantasia* and its derivatives in a disparaging manner, such as: "If we cannot know that our ordinary knowledge of the world is accurate, then what we know is mere fantasy." In both cases, it was in the modern era that these words began to lose the ring of truth, perhaps due to an impoverished sense of the worth of stories, or an inflated sense of the ability of modern science to help us know the world accurately, or both.

Does science help us know the world better? Certainly, in some ways, it does. But in other ways, it does not. Some have argued that our imaginations are the most important tools we have for understanding the world. Thomas Howard writes:

> Imagination is, in a word, the faculty by which we organize the content of our experience into some form, and thus apprehend it as significant. Put another way, it is what makes us refuse to accept experience as mere random clutter, and makes us try without ceasing to shape that experience so that we can manage it. (Howard, 25)

Imagination allows us to deal with images, to make connections, and ultimately to shape our experience by finding meaning. As such, imagination does what science cannot. Howard explains earlier:

> This mind saw things as images because it saw correspondences running in all directions among things. That is, the world was not a random tumble of things all appearing separately, jostling one another and struggling helter-skelter for a place in the sun. On the contrary, one thing signaled another. One thing was a case in point of another. . . . [But] the laboratory has no equipment for chasing and tracing these orbiting and glorious correspondences in which the lion and the king appear as images; that is, as *serious* suggestions of something real. (Howard, 14–18)

8. But compare this with what Plato has his Socrates say at *Gorgias* 523a1–2: "it will seem a *muthos* to you, but it is a *logos* to me." For Plato there are *muthoi* that are really the *truest logoi* that can be given.

Imagination is also the fundamental faculty that makes fantasy possible. When the imagination is lost, so is our ability to appreciate fantasy. But imagination is like a muscle that must be exercised or it will atrophy. And it is equally true that fantasy is the thing that most feeds the imagination. Fantasy thus goes hand in hand with imagination that enables us to apprehend our experience as significance—to shape our experience so that we can manage it.

For this reason, Tolkien and others have sought to reclaim the term *fantasy* to mean something more like the meaning of its Greek ancestor. Though Tolkien was rightly hesitant to give any single-sentence definition of fairy story, he did write that *fantasy* was not something to be embarrassed about in literature, but rather was one of the four most important values of fairy story (along with *recovery, escape,* and *consolation*): "Fantasy, the making or glimpsing of Other-worlds, was the heart of the desire of Faërie" (*Essay*, 64). A little later he explains some of his ideas in more detail, applying the word *Fantasy* to describe them:

> For my present purposes I require a word which shall embrace both the Sub-creative Art in itself and a quality of strangeness and wonder in the Expression, derived from the image: a quality essential to fairy-story. I propose . . . to use Fantasy for this purpose: in a sense, that is, which combines with its older and higher use as an equivalent of Imagination the derived notions of "unreality" (that is, of unlikeness to the Primary World), of freedom from the domination of observed "fact," in short of the fantastic. I am thus not only aware but glad of the etymological and semantic connexions of *fantasy* with *fantastic:* with images of things that are not only "not actually present," but which are indeed not to be found in our primary world at all, or are generally believed not to be found there. (69–70)

This notion of *sub*creation, or subcreative art, was important to Tolkien. He uses the phrase often to distinguish between creation *ex nihilo*, from nothing, which only God can do, and what we do. Human artistic endeavor is similar to what God does, but different. Though we cannot give to our creations new material reality, we can create new worlds in story.

Based on these ideas, it is tempting to describe fantasy literature as simply "the literature of the fantastic," but this definition would be too broad rather than too narrow and might also lean too much on very subjective views of just what is fantastic. As noted, much of science fiction literature can be thought of as literature of the fantastic, and yet it differs greatly from fantasy. Instead, we would describe it as follows:

> Fantasy is imaginative literature that gives glimpses of subcreative otherworlds, literature free from the domination of observed fact, providing instead images of things not found in our primary universe.

This, not surprisingly, gets us back to the idea of the borders of the realm, for the literature described here is the sort of literature we would expect at the borders: when Men venture to cross the borders and journey into the Perilous Realm, or when the inhabitants of that realm make themselves known in ours.

Fantastic literature is like a periscope. Periscopes bend our vision to allow us to see above and out of our world to help us understand our world better. Except fantasy literature does not bend our vision; at its best, it straightens our vision by showing us what is really there though often unseen. Fantasy encourages escape into realms of possibility; possibility engenders hope. Fantasy, then, is essentially hopeful literature. But the hope is real, and for hope to be real, there must be real danger as well. So fantasy is perilous, or contains a story of real peril. Myth, a subset of the fantastic, is that part of Faërie that pertains to cosmogony.

Spells and The Spell: Enchantment and Fantasy

Whether you find our particular definitions of Faërie and fantasy satisfactory or not, the literary genre of fantasy has blossomed in the twentieth century and continues to flourish into the twenty-first. What does it mean that fantasy is a literary mode of the twentieth century, as Shippey stated? It is not a new form of literature. As we will explore later in the book, it has roots in ancient epic, northern saga, and medieval romance. Yet it has taken new directions in the past fifty years (and draws a very large reading audience). Look no further for evidence than the works of J. R. R. Tolkien or J. K. Rowling—and the spin-off movies. Yet the fantasy genre also has its share of detractors, many of whom come from evangelical communities. The *Harry Potter* stories, for example, have caused uproar in some evangelical Christian churches.

In some sense, this ought to be surprising. Fantasy literature should have an ally in Christianity, in that both affirm the existence of the supernatural and of moral freedom, both affirm the importance of our choices, both encourage escape from materialist determinism, and both find a materialist worldview to be insufficient. Part of the issue is what, exactly, is meant by "supernatural." For some writers—C. S. Lewis and J. R. R. Tolkien would be included here—*supernatural* may explicitly mean something divine or angelic. For many, however, it relates more vaguely to magic and enchantment. Wizards are common figures in fantasy literature, as are witches in fairy tales. Dragons appear, too, and when they do we must beware of their spells. There are magic rings, used for both good and evil, and magic cloaks and staffs. And with all this enchantment floating around, it is not surprising if the reader becomes the victim (or beneficiary) of the enchantment. Tolkien writes:

> Faërie contains many things besides elves and fays, and besides dwarfs, witches, trolls, giants, or dragons: it holds the seas, the sun, the moon, the sky; and the earth, and all things that are in it: tree and bird, water and stone, wine and bread, and ourselves, mortal men, when we are enchanted. (*Essay*, 38)

This is why Tolkien warns travelers who would enter into Faërie. It is not called the Perilous Realm for nothing. "In it are pitfalls for the unwary and dungeons for the overbold" (*Essay*, 33). Dante similarly warns his readers and himself when he advances into the Inferno and reads what is written at its gate: "Abandon all hope, ye who enter here." The fantastic journey is perilous, not merely whimsical. Of course, the same should be said about the sacrament of Holy Communion. The apostle Paul warns his readers not to take it lightly (1 Cor. 11:27–29). It is not accidental that Tolkien connects these two, speaking of the sacramental bread and wine as enchanted elements whose meaning Faërie can help us more clearly see.

If enchantment is a perilous thing, it is also a troublesome thing, especially for some religious readers. We have read book reviews in Christian publications that have strongly advised against reading certain books simply because they include magic. We have known of classrooms in public elementary schools where teachers, at the demands of parents, had to excuse certain children from reading aloud from books involving magic. Should fantasy literature be rejected simply because of its use of magic or enchantment? Is the correlation between fairy tale and enchantment merely an accident?

Let us briefly consider that second question in a different light. What comes to mind when you think of a *spell*? For most people, it has the connotation of magic or enchantment. A spell is what a wicked fairy-tale witch casts over a beautiful young princess so that she will sleep an enchanted sleep. The *World English Dictionary* defines a spell as: "a word or series of words believed to have magical power, spoken to invoke the magic."[9] For those in a Christian tradition, therefore, a spell is thus likely to be viewed as a thing of evil; the idea of casting spells will certainly raise all sorts of questions and concerns about the occult or modern-day witchcraft.

In Old English, however, the word *spell* had a somewhat different meaning. Originally the word *spell* meant "story." Hence, *gód spell* is "good story"—the close translation to Old English of the Greek *euangelion,* or "good message." Thus, when Christians came to England, they called the *euangelion* the *gód spell,* which later become the *gospel:* the good story.

So how did the word change meanings? How did a *story* become *magic*? The change is not so dramatic as it might at first appear. After all, a good story (or Old English *spell*) really does cast a spell (in the more modern use of that word). The best sort of story enchants the listener or reader; while he or she is hearing the tale—listening to the "series of words" used to tell the tale—the characters seem real for a time. Indeed, the mark of a successful writer is the ability to make characters so real to us that we care about them. On the other side, if when reading a book (or watching a film) it ceases to seem real to us (we cease to be able to believe that what is taking place could be "true" within the context of the story), then that book (or film) has failed. When the reader finds herself or himself on the outside of the story looking in, with only critical faculty and no engagement in the story, then the story ceases to function as Story in the fullest of its power.

This principle can be taken a step further. With the best of stories, we are compelled by the truth that dwells in them, and while the story dwells in us, that truth dwells in us, too. An illustration might help explain this. The Brothers Grimm's "The Hare and the Hedgehog" begins like this: "This story, my dear young folks, seems to be false, but it really is true, for my grandfather, from whom I have it, used always, when relating it, to say, 'It must be true, my son, or else no one could tell it to you.'"[10] In one sense this is false: anyone can tell a lie. But that is not what the storyteller means. What he means is that when you listen to this story

9. Encarta® World English Dictionary © 1999 Microsoft Corporation. All rights reserved. Developed for Microsoft by Bloomsbury Publishing Plc.

10. Jacob and Wilhelm Grimm, *German Fairy Tales.* Helmut Brackert and Volkmar Sander, eds. (New York: Continuum, 1985), 252.

(preferably read aloud—it's better that way), you will hear the truth of it. The story is about a hedgehog that outwits a hare in a running race. That part seems false. But the story is decidedly true in another way, and when you hear it, you will see what we mean. You will be so enchanted by the truth of the story that you will forget that hares and hedgehogs do not drink brandy, wager coins, or enter running races. True stories are enchanting in that way, and the best enchantments enchant by means of the truth. And thus in modern English *spell* eventually came to mean no longer "story" but "enchantment." In some sense, then, the connection between the gospel (*gód spell*) and *enchantment* is more than accidental. As author Tom Shippey wrote, "Gospel means Christian message; means good story; means powerful enchantment" (Shippey, 260).

Though all good stories should still be able to cast a certain spell, in fairy stories especially—and more broadly in the genres of literature known as fantasy and myth—enchantment is both a goal and a tool. And it is a tool that is used to powerful effect. "He who would enter into the Kingdom of Faërie," Tolkien writes, "should have the heart of a little child." In choosing this language, Tolkien is making a clear connection to the gospel and to Jesus teaching about the kingdom of heaven. He continues, "For that possession is necessary to all high adventure, into kingdoms both less and far greater than Faërie" (*Essay,* 66). *Gospel means Christian message; means good story; means powerful enchantment.* It is precisely the enchantment—the fantasy—that enables or empowers this effect. C. S. Lewis writes:

> If good novels are comments on life, good stories of this sort [myth and fantasy] (which are very much rarer) are actual additions to life; they enlarge our conception of the range of possible experience. Hence the difficulty of discussing them at all with those who refuse to be taken out of what they call "real life." (*OnSF,* 70)

It is ironic, then, that some of the strongest opposition to literature of enchantment would come from the evangelical (or good-news-telling) community. J. R. R. Tolkien says of this enchanting strangeness of fantasy literature: "Fantasy (in this sense) is, I think, not a lower but a higher form of Art, indeed the most nearly pure form, and so (when achieved) the most potent)" (*Essay,* 69). There's truth and beauty all over the place. The world is rife with it. Or, to use Ransom's words from C. S. Lewis's *That Hideous Strength,* explaining the Arthurian magic come to life in England, "This haunting is no peculiarity of ours. Every people has its own haunter. There's no special privilege for England—no nonsense about a chosen nation. We speak about Logres because it is *our* haunting, the one we know about" (*Hideous,* 370). To paraphrase Justin Martyr, all truth is God's truth, wherever it's found, so don't be surprised to find it side by side with enchantments.

Chasing Down Allegories?

If one mistake in approaching fantasy is to reject it altogether because of the presence of enchantment, and another is to reject it as untrue and devoid of meaning, and yet another error is to try too hard to force an allegorical meaning onto a particular work of fantasy. All three of these mistakes have been committed by well-meaning readers. Certainly some works of fantasy lend themselves more to allegorical interpretation than do others. C. S. Lewis's *The Lion, the Witch, and the Wardrobe* is difficult to read without some of the imagery being understood allegorically, as is Tolkien's short story "Leaf by Niggle." *The Hobbit* and *The Lord of the Rings,* by contrast, defy any attempt at allegorical interpretation. So why should the reader beware of forcing allegorical interpretations of fantastic literature or of explaining those works that do support allegorical understanding solely by the obvious allegorical interpretation?

The first reason is simply that once the process begins, it is far too tempting to carry it to extremes. That is, once we begin to see (or think we see) allegories in works like *The Lion, the Witch, and the Wardrobe*—Aslan, the son of the Emperor-over-the-Sea, is a stand-in for Jesus, while the Emperor himself is God the Father—we then insist on interpreting in this fashion *everything* in Lewis's *Chronicles of Narnia* (and in every other fantasy book we read). Numerous critics have insisted on allegorical interpretations of *The Lord of the Rings,* for example, even though Tolkien repudiated such suggestions,[11] and the interpretations themselves fail to stand up to close scrutiny. Nonetheless, the temptation to see allegory, much like the temptation to use the Ring, is too powerful for many to resist.

---

11. "As for any inner meaning or 'message,'" Tolkien writes in the foreword to the second edition, "it has in the intention of the author none. It is neither allegorical nor topical." He goes on to specifically deny any allegory between his legendary war and World War II. "The real war does not resemble the legendary war in its process or its conclusion. If it had inspired or directed the development of the legend, then certainly the Ring would have been seized and used against Sauron; he would not have been annihilated but enslaved, and Barad-dûr would not have been destroyed but occupied" (*Foreword*).

Indeed, Tolkien is well known for his distaste of allegory. In the famous foreword to the second edition (of *The Lord of the Rings*), he writes, "I cordially dislike allegory in all its manifestations, and always have done so since I grew old and wary enough to detect its presence." He saw a danger not only in critics and readers *searching for* nonexistent allegory, but also in writers *putting in* too much allegory. For this reason he did not approve of some of the work of his friend C. S. Lewis. Although he himself wrote a small number of pieces that are undeniably allegorical, in his own Middle-earth *Legendarium* he worked hard to remove any explicit representation of religion in the form known in our primary world. In an earlier book, Dickerson summarized why Tolkien would have avoided allegory in *The Lord of the Rings*, saying that strict allegorical symbolism, especially religious imagery,

> would interfere with the deeper and more profound Christian themes by trivializing them; not to mention that it likely also would cost Tolkien numerous readers who do not share his Christian faith! When readers suspect allegory, they either quit reading (as Tolkien likely would have done) or start chasing exact parallels—*this* equals *this,* and *that* equals *that*—and proceed as if the story can be reduced to mathematical equations rather than appreciating what is actually there. By contrast, the fabric of reality is far more complex, far richer and more wonderful than a formulaic representation of one idea by one narrative symbol. (Dickerson, 218)

Brad Birzer is somewhat more blunt and succinct in his critique of allegorical writing: "A true artist taps into the truths of God's Creation. He does not take blatant truths and make them more blatant."[12]

This relates to a second reason not to spend too much time focusing on allegorical interpretation even when a work does lend itself to such an approach. Reducing a rich narrative to its (real or imagined) allegorical value is much like reducing a person to a mere label. Labeling a person ("conservative," "liberal," "bigot," "intellectual," "environmentalist," "fundamentalist," etc.) exposes us to the temptation of thinking we know everything there is to know about the person and that we are free from listening to them and engaging their ideas. Such "freedom" becomes slavery to a particularly narrow way of seeing the world (and literature). Likewise, once we find the allegorical, we feel that we have done our jobs as readers and needn't think any more. "Aslan is Christ," we say, much

---

12. Brad Birzer, "Stephen Lawhead and the Conundrum of Celtic Catholicism," *Saint Austin Review* (forthcoming, 2006).

as we'd say 1 + 1 = 2, and we cease to wrestle with what Lewis might be showing through Aslan's complex character. Thus, when a reader focuses on the allegory, rather than on the story itself or on the complexities that might be found in the imagery, the reader ceases to learn. Thomas Howard, in his book *The Achievement of C. S. Lewis*, explains this well.

> If we were to claim that there is a significant correspondence between Narnia and the real world, then we have opened up the troublesome topic of allegory, and everyone is off chasing parallels. Aslan equals Christ; the White Witch equals Lilith; Peter equals Saint Peter, and so forth ...
>
> But the connection between what we find in Narnia and anything in our own story is closer to analogy, where we say, not "Aslan equals Christ," but rather "As Christ is to this story, so, in a measure, is Aslan to that one." It is at least partly the difference between *symbols* and *cases in point*, which we run into every day. You may see a boy offer to carry a grocery bag for a woman. He is not a symbol of Christ (carrying someone else's burden): rather, he appears in this little act as a case in point of the same thing which was also at work in Christ's act, namely Charity, which always "substitutes" itself for the good of someone else. . . .
>
> Thus we make a mistake if we try to chase symbols up and down the landscape of Narnia, or if we try to pin down allegories. It is much better to read these tales for what they are, namely, fairy tales.[13]

Thus insightful scholars like Howard suggest that even with works like Lewis's, we do a disservice to both the author and ourselves if we limit our understanding to mere allegory.

There is a third reason why we shouldn't force fantastic literature to speak allegorically: it is not intended to do so. Fantasies are stories, not preachers. Of course, fantasies and fairy stories *may* contain occasional allegories, or may seek to express a single propositional truth. We see this in Hans Christian Andersen, who crafted his stories to illustrate moral truisms; "The Ugly Duckling," for example, can be seen as an allegory of human potential. Much of what George MacDonald and C. S. Lewis wrote also contains figures and tropes that are plainly allegorical. Despite his dislike of allegory, one may even find passages in Tolkien that lend themselves to allegorical interpretation. But in fantastic literature, the allegories, if they are there, always serve the story, and not the other way around. Their presence in the story is only part of the story's richness.

13. Thomas Howard, *The Achievement of C. S. Lewis* (Wheaton, IL: Shaw, 1980), 26–27. This book has been reprinted under the title *C. S. Lewis, Man of Letters: A Reading of His Fiction* (Eugene, OR: Wipf & Stock, 2004).

In fact, if the interpretation of any given story is exhausted with an allegorical interpretation, it's most likely not good literature.

T. S. Eliot, in contrasting Charles Williams's novels with more allegorical works (such as those of G. K. Chesterton), explains the strength of fantasy literature.

> Chesterton's *The Man Who Was Thursday* is an allegory; it has a meaning which is meant to be discovered at the end; while we can enjoy it in reading, simply because of the swiftly moving plot and the periodic surprises, it is intended to convey a definite moral and religious point expressible in intellectual terms. It gives you *ideas,* rather than *feelings,* of another world. Williams has no such "palpable design" upon his reader. His aim is to make you partake of a kind of experience that he has had, rather than to make you accept some dogmatic belief. . . . Williams is telling us about a world of experience known to him: he does not merely persuade us to believe in something, he communicates this experience that he has had. (Eliot, xiv–xv)

Fans of Chesterton may argue that Eliot has misread Chesterton, and that *The Man Who Was Thursday* should not be read as an allegory, or that its meaning transcends any one limited allegorical interpretation. In making that argument, however, they are agreeing with the underlying premise: the best works of fantasy communicate something beyond a single "definite moral," dogmatic belief, or "religious point expressible in intellectual terms," and get instead at some experience—a whole "world of experience," even—that must be understood via story and imagination. What is the revelation that occurs in Flannery O'Connor's fantastic story "Revelation"? If any single answer to that question is inadequate to capture the entire story, you know that it, like the tales of Charles Williams, is still a great story.

We can see this in a different light by pointing out that the intent to teach something is essential to allegories, as it is to parables and fables. These genres are inherently didactic. This explains why the audiences of Jesus's parables were often left seething in anger after certain of his parables; they understood the point, and they also understood that it was directed at them. Regarding his book *Conversations with Jesus,* Harold Fickett has described a parable as a story that can get you killed. He says this in praise of the power of parables. Parables can be very valuable, and a good parable-maker and -teller can be a wonderful teacher. But fairy tales are not parables and are not intended to be. Good fantastic literature is never didactic. The intent to teach is not essential to works of the genre. None of this is to say that fantasy literature does not teach, or that the reader does not learn, only that teaching is not its fundamental aim. To force it to act as an allegorical moral is to impoverish it. Indeed, among those forms of literature that are essentially didactic, the closer the story comes to fairy tale, the better it is. Part of what makes Jesus's parables so rich is that they are *not* exhausted by a single reading but often function as illustrations of the gospel on many levels. They are good stories, and they are full of meaning. Tolkien writes that "the more 'life' a story has the more readily will it be susceptible of allegorical interpretations: while the better a deliberate allegory is made the more nearly will it be acceptable just as a story" (*Letters*, 145). Is the parable of the prodigal son a story about the younger brother, the older brother, or the father? Even Aesop's fables and Charles Perrault's fairy tales, which end with a single moral that purports to translate the story into a principle of moral or ethical conduct, are richer than the allegorical principle, since they function as good stories that can stand alone without the interpretation.

Again it is Tolkien, continuing in the foreword to the second edition, who, by contrasting allegory with myth,[14] probably summarizes best the trouble with writing fantasy literature allegorically:

> I much prefer history, true or feigned, with its varied applicability to the thought and experience of readers. I think that many confuse "applicability" with "allegory"; but the one resides in the freedom of the reader, and the other in the purposed domination of the author. (*Foreword*)

Mapping Our Territory (and Its Perils)

If we don't understand fantasy by means of allegory, how *do* we understand it? Part of the answer to this question has been scattered throughout the first two chapters—and more of the answer will be found through the remainder of the book. Still, it is worth ending this chapter with a few summary thoughts.

The simplest answer—one that does not necessitate a book such as this one—has been suggested in the first two chapters as we have sought to define myth and fantasy and fairy story. The answer follows from

14. In the quote below, Tolkien explicitly contrasts allegory with "history, true or feigned." However, the context of this comment is a discussion of fantasy literature, and elsewhere Tolkien explicitly associates myth with his heroic legend on the border of history.

the comments of Walter Wangerin: at one level we don't have to *seek* to understand it at all. We simply gaze upon the myth and allow the "dreadful recognition" to happen when it happens. We don't do anything to the myth, but let the myth do its work on us; we allow it "to lift us out of our experience." In such a way, it will by its being be a "mother of truth through countless generations and for many disparate cultures." We let it get under our skin, as Lewis says. We don't hit the myth or fairy tale; the myth or fairy tale hits us ("at a level deeper than our thoughts or even our passions"). It is doing the work, not us. We are simply the objects of that work, as it "troubles oldest certainties till all questions are reopened, and in general shocks us more fully awake than we are for most of our lives." For this to happen, we must read myth, fantasy, and fairy tale. It is not enough merely to read a myth or fairy tale once. We must read them over and over. We must be steeped in them. As W. H. Auden writes about the Grimms' fairy tales: "So let everyone read these stories till they know them backwards and tell them to their children with embellishments" (Auden-2). In doing so, we let the tales train our imagination—a process that needs no conscious guidance. Again, Auden points out what happens to the one who reads fairy tales:

> From the properties (the castle on the mountain, the cottage in the wood, the helpful beasts, the guardian dragons, the cave, the fountain, the trysting lane, etc.), he will acquire the basic symbols to which he can add railway trains, baths, wrist-watches and what-have-you from his own experience, and so build up a web of associations which are the only means by which his inner and outer life, his past and his present, can be related to, and mentally enrich, each other. (Auden-2)

Myth and fairy tale provide the symbols that enable our imaginations to make sense of the world, and to see it as meaningful. And as we let the world of Faërie enrich our imagination, we also let it train our morals, teaching us that there are, in fact, taboos, and woe to the one who lightly breaks them.

But what of a more conscious approach? Though we don't want to approach Faërie, including its subgenre modern fantasy, with the same analytical approach we would take with a modernist novel or a Shakespearean play, nonetheless a book such as this has critical approaches to suggest. What approach do we take? One has already been suggested: we look for the generalizations in the concrete. How we do this, as well as other aspects of our answer, will come from understanding the roots of modern fantasy in myth, heroic romance, and fairy tale. The modern fantasy writer, the mythopoet, doesn't invent stories out of whole cloth but relies on traditions of story already present in culture. Tolkien's analogy—which we will explore later—is to a cauldron or pot of soup, out of which the author of fantasy draws his material, and into which is always being added new material. To understand modern fantasy, we must explore the contents of this cauldron (the task of the next four chapters).

With all of this, however, comes a warning—or perhaps it is a promise. Tolkien was not being frivolous when he called Faërie a Perilous Realm. In George MacDonald's *Phantastes,* the protagonist opens up a desk and gets drawn into Faërie. Something similar happens to Tolkien's Smith, when as a child he goes to a great feast in Wootton Major, eats a slice of cake, and comes into possession of a fay-star that gives him entrance into the Perilous Realm. Once you open the desk, or come into possession of the star, or pass through a wardrobe, you may end up wandering, and you will certainly face dangers. The danger is real. As Lewis reminds his readers on more than one occasion, Aslan is not a tame lion. Thus, Tolkien begins his famous essay "On Fairy-Stories" as follows:

> I propose to speak about fairy-stories, though I am aware that this is a rash adventure. Faërie is a perilous land, and in it are pitfalls for the unwary and dungeons for the overbold. And overbold I may be accounted, for though I have been a lover of fairy-stories since I learned to read, and have at times thought about them, I have not studied them professionally. I have been hardly more than a wandering explorer (or trespasser) in the land, full of wonder but not of information. (*Essay,* 9)

We, the authors of this book, make the same confession as Tolkien: we are merely wandering explorers full of wonder—certainly less full of information than he was. We give the same warning as well: the land is perilous. Yet we also offer the invitation to explore the land with us. Smith does so. He explores the land. And after many years of wandering, he finally meets the queen and his heart's desire is granted. He is never the same. Wonder is repaid.

3

BIBLICAL MYTH
AND STORY

Myth is the story of the god made imaginable.
Charles S. Peirce

Baptism or death? This was choice that King Charlemagne gave to the residents of Saxony in the second half of the eighth century. Charlemagne's father, Pepin, had contained but never defeated the pagan Saxons of Saxony, and they had since made repeated incursions into Gaul, looting and burning churches. Believing that this tribe would be better citizens—more peaceable, and easier to rule—if he could baptize them, Charlemagne's plan was not merely to defeat them in battle, but to force them to convert to Christianity. Thus, he offered the conquered Saxons a choice of baptism or death. As history shows, however, such forced conversions are rarely if ever effective. On one day alone, Charlemagne beheaded 4,500 Saxon rebels. And not long after, while Charlemagne was off fighting in Spain, the stubborn Saxons rebelled again.

Eventually, many Saxons did convert to Christianity. It was not the sword that won them, however, but story. What story would have such power? The Gospel story—though not quite in the form it appears in the Bible. In the early ninth century a great poet, one whose name we do not know, "rewrote and reimagined the events and words of the gospel as if they had taken place and been spoken in his own country and time" (Murphy, xiii). This unknown poet sought to get at the heart of the *myth* of the Gospels, apart from their particular setting in first-century Palestine. What resulted was the *Heliand,* a brilliant poem in the Old English language, telling the story of the Gospels using the alliterative mode of Old English verse, and in the heroic style of *Beowulf* and *The Battle of Maldon.* Jerusalem is a hill-fort, the disciples are thanes, and Jesus is both a powerful magician and the greatest of chieftains. The *Heliand* begins thus:

> There were many whose hearts told them that they should begin to tell the secret runes, the word of God, the famous feats that the powerful Christ accomplished in words and in deeds among human beings. There were many of the wise who wanted to praise the teaching of Christ, the holy Word of God, and wanted to write a bright-shining book with their own hands, telling how the sons of men should carry out His commands. Among all these, however, there were only four who had the power of God, help from Heaven, the Holy Spirit, the strength from Christ to do it. They were chosen. They alone were to write down the evangelium in a book, and to write down the commands of God, the holy Heavenly word. No one else among the heroic sons of men was to attempt it, since these four had been picked by the power of God: Matthew and Mark, Luke and John were their names. They were dear to God, worthy of the work. The ruling God had placed the Holy Spirit firmly in those heroes' hearts, together with many a wise word, as well as a devout attitude and a powerful mind, so that they could lift up their holy voices to chant God's spell. There is nothing like it in words anywhere in this world! (*Heliand,* 3–4).

What is remarkable about this is that the poet was able to tell the story of the Gospels—the central, unifying story of the Bible—in a new language, in new form, while maintaining their essential meaning.[1] At twice the length of *Beowulf,* the *Heliand* was also written to be performed not in the church but in the medieval mead hall, where other heroic verses were

---

1. By way of comparison, numerous authors today have sought to do with the Bible and American culture what the *Heliand* poet did in the ninth century with Saxon culture: they have retold (not merely translated) biblical stories for contemporary readers, while seeking to keep the essential mythic elements of the stories. Some notable examples include Eugene Peterson's *The Message* (Colorado Springs: NavPress, 1993), Walter Wangerin's *The Book of God* (Grand Rapids: Zondervan, 1996), Frederick Buechner's *Son of Laughter* (San Francisco: HarperSanFrancisco, 1993), and Harold Fickett's retelling of many of Jesus's parables in his book *Conversations with Jesus: Unexpected Answers to Contemporary Questions* (Colorado Springs: Piñon Press, 1999).

sung. What this shows is that the Bible has immense mythic power and is indeed centrally mythic. The author of the *Heliand* recognized that the Bible is not merely religious creed but "God's spell." That is, it is not in essence a theological or philosophical system, but Story.

This spell—the great biblical Story—embodies ideas that have been key in informing nearly all the myth and fantasy of the West. These ideas include the importance of storytelling to forming and maintaining community; the use of parallel worlds to gain insight into this world; the notion that there is an invisible moral battle in which the visible world participates; the falsity of theistic or material determinism and the concomitant reality of human moral freedom; the importance of speech; the idea that the world is reasonable and so susceptible to inquiry (as opposed to being random or guided by the unpredictable whim of the gods); and the goodness of this created physical world.

Three Ways the Bible Functions as Myth

In the first two chapters, we introduced the notion of *the Bible as myth* and explained what we did and did not mean by that. Any discussion of myth in the Bible is sure to make many readers uncomfortable. Some disagree with us because they don't accept the Bible as mythic at all; they want to accept its truth only in nonmythic ways (historical, propositional, creedal, etc.). Others disagree with us because they do accept the Bible as mythic, and therefore they view it as fundamentally less true. As ought to be clear at this point in the book, our view of the Bible *as myth* elevates rather than diminishes its status *as truth*. However, because of the potential disagreement, as we start to explore further the biblical myth, it might be helpful to start off on common ground, and to say a few things about the Bible that nearly anybody who reads it agrees upon.

The world *bible* comes to English from the Greek *biblia,* the plural of *biblion,* or book. *The Bible* (*ta Biblia* in Greek) originally meant "the books." The neuter plural noun *biblia* in Greek looks like a feminine singular noun in Latin, so from early Christian times, it has been customary to think of the Bible as a singular noun. Yet the Bible is not one but many books. Thirty-nine of these are the Jewish scriptures and are written almost entirely in Hebrew (there are small sections in Aramaic or Chaldee); the other twenty-seven are additional Christian scriptures and are written almost entirely in Greek (with occasional words or phrases in Aramaic).[2] These books are of varying genres of literature, including historical narrative, poetry, apocalypsis, prophecy, Gospels, and epistles. Often several of these genres are mixed together in a single book. They were written over a period of more than a millennium, apparently by several dozen authors, with the latest of them appearing to have been written in the first or second century AD. The collection of books that make up the *one* book called *the* Bible reached its current form, or canon, by the middle of the fourth century AD. The version of the Bible we have is essentially unchanged over the last sixteen centuries.

How does the Bible fit into our discussion of myth and fantasy? First of all, it is the most reproduced and translated book in history. No other book has had more copies printed or read. Some have noted the cultural impact of Tolkien's work by discussing the various film adaptations, especially the phenomenal success of Peter Jackson's recent films. But dozens of films have been based on biblical narrative, including Charlton Heston's *The Ten Commandments,* Mel Gibson's *The Passion of the Christ,* and *The Jesus Film,* which (as of August 2004) had been translated into 863 languages and shown to nearly six billion people worldwide.[3] In short, the Bible is one of the most important and influential books in history.

The stories in the Bible have also had a profound impact on the history of literature around the world. Biblical words, phrases, and stories have insinuated themselves into our language. Harold Fickett writes, "Although people within the Western society share less and less in terms of a common intellectual tradition, speaking of a wayward child as a 'prodigal son' summons a host of instant associations. Newspaper headlines and stories still use the shorthand of the 'Good Samaritan'" (Fickett, 14–15). When we speak of "seeing the writing on the wall," or of someone being the "apple of my eye," or of God (rather than of gods), hell, or paradise, we show the way our image of the world has been shaped by biblical language. One need not believe in a literal hell to have had one's view of the possibilities of afterlife shaped by biblical metaphysics. Our language reflects our cultural heritage, and that heritage is heavily freighted with biblical concepts and overtones, most of which we think of as having little or no religious content.

Because of its great influence on the way we think, some knowledge of the Bible is essential to understanding the roots of fantasy literature.

---

2. Orthodox and Roman Catholic Bibles contain several more books, but these sixty-six are common to all Bibles.

3. http://www.jesusfilm.org/progress/stats.html.

Beyond that, the Bible's many genres have some elements in common that are germane to any discussion of the mythic and the fantastic. According to Christian tradition, what makes the diverse books of the Bible into a coherent whole is their shared concern with God's revelation to the world through the nation of Israel and the person of Jesus of Nazareth. The revelation of God to the world is an instance of what we have been talking about as Faërie: events on the border between the celestial and the mundane.

Having noted what makes the Bible into a coherent whole, we also must note that what makes the biblical stories stand apart from all the other instances we are considering is that the biblical revelation also frequently offers itself as historically true. Nearly all the books of the Bible are explicit in their concern with God (Esther and Song of Songs are exceptions in never mentioning God) and, as such, testify to miraculous or prodigious events *in history*. In other words, the Bible contains mention of historical events whose cause is supernatural. These events are taken both as evidence of the revelation of God and, to varying degrees, as the content of the revelation itself. If the Bible and its advocates had been content with calling it mythic *fiction*, there would be little controversy about the Bible. No one bothers to point out that elements in the stories in *Grimm's Fairy Tales*—talking animals, for instance—seem implausible, because no one claims that those stories are historically true. But the claim the Bible makes about itself, and that many Jews and Christians have made about the Bible, is not only that the stories are unusual, but that most or all of them are also historically true.[4]

This presents an interesting case for us: in the Bible we find plainly mythic elements—stories of the divine that have relevance for the world of humans—to which is also ascribed historical legitimacy. Furthermore, these mythic elements are often closely paralleled by myths found in many or all cultures, like the stories of creation, the flood, and the just man who suffers. Indeed, it may be that the authors of the Bible borrowed from these stories and corrected them. Or it may be that these stories are based

---

4. We say "most or all" because there are stories in the Bible, for instance the parables of Jesus or of the woman from Tekoa in 2 Sam. 14:5ff, about which no claim is made for their historical veracity. As we will see later in the chapter, their potency arises not out of their historical truth but their truth as stories, that is, their mythic truth. Of course, there are also honest disagreements among religious Jews and Christians concerning the degree and nature of the historicity of other stories that have a poetic or fantastic literary flavor, such as the creation stories in Genesis and the entire book of Job. However, the authors of the central story of the Bible, recounted in the Gospels of Matthew, Mark, Luke, and John, plainly intend their story to be taken as literally true, and not merely as allegory. (Cf. the introduction to Luke's Gospel, for instance.)

on historical facts—for instance, that Adam and Noah and Job were real men who lived and acted just as the Bible stories recount—and thus we should expect to read about them in numerous places just as we might expect to read about major news stories in several different papers. But in neither case is the veracity of the stories impugned, and in neither case is the mythic element eliminated. Tolkien saw the two aspects of the Bible—the mythical and the historical—as fundamentally compatible. As we saw earlier, he describes how many skeptical men have accepted the historical truth of the gospel based on its own merits, and in almost the same breath he discusses the gospel as a perfect fairy tale with beautiful mythic elements. One might even say that the mythic underscores the truth of the stories.

Our primary concern in this chapter, however, is with the mythic elements; it is not to enter a debate about the historical reliability of the Bible or to explore claims of the Bible's propositional revelation about God. To explore mythic elements, however, we do need to consider briefly which biblical passages should (or should not) be understood mythically and why. It might be helpful to think of three different ways in which the Bible contains myth. First, there are plainly mythic passages in the Bible: passages that have primarily or only a fantastic or otherworldly character. The dialogue between Satan and God in the book of Job and the apocalyptic visions of Daniel and Ezekiel are examples of this. These passages don't try so much to describe historical events in our world as to give us a sense of the cosmic importance and meaning of worldly events. They picture the world *sub specie aeternitatis*—from the perspective of heaven. Some of the Revelation of John, especially the descriptions of the war in heaven, function similarly.

Other passages are plainly historical and this-worldly. The narrative events of Jesus's birth and youth in Luke's Gospel, or the accounts of Paul's missionary journeys in the Acts of the Apostles, or of David's ascendancy to the throne of Israel in the books of I and II Samuel, are examples of this. These narrative and historical passages are significant because they too are mythic in a second way: they attempt to tell a historical story, but they see the significance of that story as having to do with God, and God's interaction on earth. They see this world as haunted by the heavenly realm; this world and the otherworld are not separated. Even stories like Esther, which never even mention God or propose theological truths, are telling the story of God's chosen people, the Israelites. Thus, every story in the Bible is mythic, inasmuch as it can be located somewhere along the continuum we talked about in the first chapter.

The third way is viewing it as a whole, in which case it appears as the Grand Myth. What appear as loosely connected narratives about individuals become or contain a single cohesive Story of mythic significance, much in the same way that the separate tales of Fëanor, Beren, Turin, Tuor, and others combine in Tolkien's *The Silmarillion* to present a single cohesive mythic picture of Middle-earth. Thus, the answer to our question is that the whole Bible should be taken into account as speaking mythically, but not all parts of it in the same way.

The Bible as a Whole: *Muthos* of Worlds and Wars

We will both introduce and conclude our discussion of the Bible by considering this third way that it functions as myth: not as a collection of unrelated stories but as a cohesive whole. The Bible is no *mere* collection of wondrous stories intended only to delight and amuse; its stories are not *merely* marvelous. The mythic element in them declares them to be of universal significance. They signify; they *mean* something. In the mythic elements, truth is richly apprehended on multiple levels. The stories are appealing and can be understood by the wise and the simple alike, across time and cultures. The mythic is our invitation into the stories, whereby we come to understand God and God's creation, and without which our propositional and creedal knowledge of God makes little sense.

Consider this: only a small portion of the Bible contains propositional information about God. Why is this? Propositions attempt to define God, to capture God in information that we can handle, hold, conceive, wield. And there is a risk that if religion is only theological propositions—a series of affirmations about God—then it becomes an idol. It does not grow; it can only decay. Graven images of God become barriers to knowing God, because they satiate the imagination with thoughts: "God is like this, and that is all." Propositions, if they stand alone, can do the same thing. But from start to finish, the Bible is full of stories. It is one grand narrative composed of hundreds of small narratives. And even within the Story, story-telling characters like Nathan the prophet, the apostle Paul,[5] or especially Jesus appear, telling stories within the Story. The Bible is not so much concerned with defining God as with describing God, and telling a story. The aim of the story is not to capture God but to point

5. Consider in the book of Acts how many times Paul recounts the story of his own conversion.

to God and to invite the reader to engage in the adventure of seeking God. Christians do well to affirm objective theological truth, but rather than then claiming a complete knowledge of that truth, might do better to claim a knowledge of the One who is the truth. Such knowledge is often better gained through story than through propositions. The authors of the great creeds of the church knew this as well. The creeds all run like stories, too, affirming what God has done. As Charles Peirce, the American philosopher, put it, "myth is the story of the god made understandable."[6] This does not mean that God is whatever myths say God is; it means that when we tell the highest myths, the ones about God, we are doing the best we can to comprehend God.

Consider that among the biblical stories, there are certain images that are oft repeated, and we can gather something of their importance from their frequency. Some of the most frequent sets of images are those of heaven, and the contrasts between heaven and earth, and also between heaven and hell. In the case of heaven and hell the imagery is not merely a contrast, but a *war*. The apostle John tells us that there is a war "in heaven" between the servants of heaven and those of hell, but it is also a war that takes place on earth, whose battleground is human history (Rev. 12:7–9; Dan. 10:13–21), and whose participants are humans as well as spiritual beings: angels of heaven and hell (Eph. 6:12–18; 1 Pet. 5:8). Indeed, from the third chapter of Genesis onward, all of earth's history can be (and ought to be) understood in the context of that war: the "enmity" on earth between the offspring of Eve and the offspring of the Serpent (Gen. 3:15). It is important to note that in the Christian understanding, this does not justify a call for *jihad;* the Bible also makes it clear that the war is not against flesh and blood, but against spiritual wickedness. Nonetheless, there is an unmistakable influence of this mythology on fantasy literature; nearly all of modern fantasy literature echoes this battle, giving us a glimpse of some fantastic war between good and evil, where the battlefield is an earthly realm. Heaven, hell, and earth are all important.

Not surprisingly, then, the Bible is replete with mythic language that attempts to relate the concerns of heaven to those of earth. This is no small task, because we lack sufficient words. The Bible is predicated on the view that there is a God and there is a heaven, and that human knowledge of these facts is invaluable. But God and heaven and all their

---

6. *The Charles S. Peirce Papers,* microfilm edition, Harvard University Library, Photographic Service, 1966 (891.lxvii, 1864 December 18).

concomitant theological and moral and metaphysical notions wind up being difficult to grasp. As the German poet Hölderlin wrote, "Near, and [yet] difficult to grasp, is God."[7] In the Western literary tradition, the Bible is a key source of the notion that there are parallel worlds, one a world of power and matter, one a world of action and form.[8] Myth and fantasy in general make significant use of this notion of parallel worlds, especially as it is developed later in the Western tradition. Eventually, the concept of parallel worlds led to the exploration of not one but many possible worlds, including other worlds of power and matter, similar but not identical to our own. These other possible worlds are worlds in which the same general rules apply as in ours. By observing these worlds with the mind's eye, authors and readers are able to bend certain rules of nature in order to consider more closely the *moral* rules that are at play in our world. The Narnia stories of C. S. Lewis and Madeleine L'Engle's series beginning with *A Wrinkle in Time* are two examples, but the list could be expanded to include the interplanetary element of science fiction and most utopian fiction from Thomas More, Jonathan Swift, and Edward Bellamy through Ursula Le Guin and Joan Slonczewski.

Heaven and hell are so different from our experience that they are impossible to understand without some translation. However, this translation cannot happen in the usual way, where the translator can use our experience to teach us a word, pointing to an object like a tree and speaking the name *tree*, or saying the same word in different languages: *tree, Baum, árbol, drzewo.* How can mortals have experience of the affairs of heaven in order that we might learn its language? Heaven and hell are not visible to mortals for God to point to, and we don't know their languages. ("No eye has seen, no ear has heard, no mind has conceived what God has prepared for those who love him."[9]) The concepts must be explained to us in terms we can grasp, with analogies to the world of our experience. This is made possible by having the whole world shot through with meaning. The Bible's creation myth is unique in having the entire cosmos created by a single God who creates by *logos*. Since

7. *"Nah ist / und schwer zu fassen, der Gott."* Friedrich Hölderlin (1770–1843), "Patmos" (1802). Our free translation.

8. We could similarly describe heaven as a world of power, except that for the Western philosophical and theological tradition, power is the possibility of action, and so implies an inertness. The realm of heaven has therefore been conceived as the realm not of power, but of action that awakens, informs, and guides the power in this world.

9. 1 Cor. 2:9 and Isa. 64:4.

logos means both "speech" and "reason," everything spoken into being by God is made according to some reason. Everything in creation becomes a case-in-point of the intentions of heaven. In a sense, the whole world becomes enchanted with "God's spell." The whole of creation is an attempt by heaven to make itself known to earth.[10] The experience of heaven has slowly and gently spoken itself into our world. The stories of the Bible represent the celestial in mythic form. They tell of the universal in the particular terms of our experience.

This is not and cannot be an instant process, any more than learning any new language can be. In the stories of the Bible, it appears that it is only as heaven reveals itself to humanity—as it breaks through to our conscious life—that humans develop such an understanding. Thus, in the beginning of the Bible there is no discussion of heaven and hell, and no mention of Satan; all that matters of heaven is its inhabitant, God. The concepts are then developed slowly in the Bible, as a courtship rather than a violation, using imagery and story from our world. The opening lines of Genesis and of the Gospel according to John indicate that this is what has happened: God spoke and the words took on material being. God's *fiat* became physical being.[11] God's *logos* translated itself from pure reason to a story in time, to history.[12] Of course, the imagery of heaven is only imagery and ultimately falls short. Furthermore, learning the language requires willingness and attention on our part. Nonetheless, for the willing ear, it gives to the inhabitants of earth some glimmer of understanding of the heavenly.

This process perhaps can be seen most clearly in looking at four terms: *God, Satan, heaven,* and *hell.*

God and Satan

God is the main figure of the Bible. Understanding God requires some mental acrobatic skills. God is, in one sense, incomprehensible, but God makes himself comprehensible in the whole of creation. So all created

10. This is an important part of why the authors of the New Testament and subsequent Christian authors have so strenuously opposed the Gnostic notions of an evil creative power and of the sinfulness of matter. If matter is good, then the whole universe can be shot through with positive meaning, and the whole world can be good.

11. As in *fiat lux,* "let there be light." God in Genesis speaks these phrases, and then the things named come into being.

12. In the Gospel of John, Jesus is referred to as the *logos* of God. This parallels the opening verses of the creation story in Genesis.

things can serve as images of God. Christians agree with idolaters and pagans that the eternal is seen in all material things. The danger, according to Christians, is if the tangible thing becomes the final resting place of our affection and worship. These things all help us to understand God. As Thomas Aquinas (1225?–74) argued, God shows himself to humans through a virtual infinity of objects over a virtual infinity of time. Apart from showing the actual infinity of God's mind to the world, this is the only way God can be translated into finite space and time. In the beginning, we are told, God and people shared the same living space: God walked in the Garden of Eden with Adam and Eve, the first humans. Soon, however, Adam and Eve were evicted from Eden for their disobedience, and now we no longer dwell where God is visible. What is plain from the earliest stories, then, is that God is the omnipotent creator, concerned with moral law and justice, severe but merciful (he expelled Adam and Eve from Eden but did not kill them as he had threatened to do), and, significantly, invisible.

One other aspect of God should be mentioned: God speaks. God speaks to himself, as though carrying on an inner dialogue in the opening lines of Genesis, and God speaks to Adam and Eve. This aspect of God has several ramifications for literature. First, God is invisible but to some degree audible. This means that God can show up as a voice, either disembodied (as in a dream or vision) or embodied through a prophet. Second, since God is invisible, no physical representation of God can be made, and any attempt to do so is a punishable offense. However, God can be represented in words. The Jews thus became the first "people of the book." If God is known through words, then the learning of words is essential. This results in universal literacy (for males, anyway) and the development of the technology of frequent reproducing of texts. These in turn become the building blocks of more literature, usually commenting on sacred texts, but slowly branching out from there into other genres. Subtly, this sets the ground for considering *all* literature to have within it something of the inspiration of God. Especially as these texts become adopted by other cultures (notably in medieval Europe), mythic, poetic, and fantastic literatures are all seen as ways of conceiving some aspect of the invisible God. The opening verses of Snorri Sturluson's (1179–1241) *Prose Edda* (which we will talk about in more detail in a later chapter) is an excellent example of this, fusing the elements of all the great myths (of the Jews, the Greeks, the Romans, and the Norse) with the stories of the Bible, as though they all told a coherent and consistent tale about the cosmos and God.

It is worth noting that God in the Bible has not one name but scores of names, each attempting to explain some aspect of God, none completely succeeding. The great name of God in the Bible, by which he reveals himself to Moses, is unpronounceable and untranslatable into English. It is written with the four consonants YHWH, and is usually translated as "the Lord" or, occasionally, "Jehovah," since "Iehovah" is how it might be translated were it written in Latin. It is probably related to the verb *to be*, indicating God's essential relation to Being itself, and the rabbis who translated it into Greek for the Septuagint version of the Bible translated it as *ego eimi*, or "I Am."[13] When John wrote his Gospel, he similarly used over a dozen names for Jesus in his first two chapters, to underscore the divinity of Jesus, and three times he used for him this name *ego eimi*.[14] The New Testament, then, both simplifies and complicates the notion of God. God is simplified by becoming a human, and therefore becoming more comprehensible to us. At the same time, God is complicated by having his being in three persons—if we include, as the New Testament authors do, the Holy Spirit as the third person of the Trinity.

Unlike God, Satan is a minor character. He is important but has very small power. The war between God and Satan—between heaven and hell—is not depicted as a war between two equals. God has all the power and at the right time will simply end the war, banishing the enemy forever. At the height of his development in the Bible, Satan's role is to accuse, slander, and mislead. That is, his strength is in deception more than in any physical force (creative or destructive). Indeed, the very name *Sâtân* means "accuser." Likewise, the New Testament Greek term *Diabolé* (from which we derive our word *devil*) means "accuser" or "slanderer."[15] But this may be the most horrible kind of power a villain can have—which is perhaps why this idea, like the war mentioned above, is a theme taken up in later myth and fantasy. It is a fixture in most modern fantasy to portray an evil force opposing the protagonists, doing so via a power to twist words and minds. It can be argued, for example, that Lewis's White Witch (in *The Lion, the Witch, and the Wardrobe*) accomplishes far more evil by first deceiving Edmund and then accusing him before Aslan than she does with her wand. Likewise, the greatest power wielded by Tolkien's Nazgûl

13. Cf. Exod. 3:14 in the Septuagint translation.

14. In the original Greek texts, Cf. Matt.14:27; Mark 13:6, 14:62–3; John 6:20, 8:24, 28, 58. Also compare the use of the Greek *kurios* to refer to God in the Septuagint and to Jesus in Acts 2:36, 1 Cor. 16:22.

15. From Greek *dia*, "across," and *ballô*, "to throw," meaning one who throws out obstacles and impediments (to cause others to stumble).

in *The Lord of the Rings* is not a physical might exhibited in battle, but rather the power to affect the minds of their enemies by causing them to lose hope, and thereby also to lose the will to resist. "Resist the devil," James writes in his epistle, "and he will flee from you" (James 4:7b).

However, this picture of Satan is not presented all at once. Knowledge of Satan, like that of God, develops over time. In Genesis he appears only as a wily serpent. In Job he is first introduced as "the Satan," or the accuser. But the name is not used only to refer to a single diabolic figure. In Numbers, an angel of God appears to the prophet Balaam "as his Satan,"[16] to tell Balaam not to continue on the road he is traveling. In the New Testament, Jesus calls Peter "Satan" when Peter ignorantly attempts to dissuade him from going to be crucified in Jerusalem,[17] but Jesus also uses the name *Satan* to refer to a single angel who rebelled against God and fell from the sky like lightning.[18] In the Prophets, Satan comes to be known as the greatest of the angels, the bearer of light (whence the Latin name *Lucifer*), who rebelled against God and fell from heaven. Ultimately, the picture of Satan that emerges is of a mocker and deceiver who is supremely unhappy and who wants others to share his unhappiness. He tries to gain this end by urging those who are on the right path to leave it, and to put off the voice of conscience.

The mythic significance of Satan is to underscore that moral strife is no mere question of reasoned ethical inquiry, but a struggle between real yet invisible forces of good and evil in the war. Evil cannot be a physical person; it is always invisible: an idea, a belief, a false and demonic voice. An important consequence of this is that it underwrites the virtues of mercy and forgiveness: if the forces to be battled are invisible, then it follows ipso facto that visible people (like all created things) are always redeemable, and never wholly evil. In modern fantasy, this last idea is probably most clearly illustrated in *The Lord of the Rings* by the treatment of Gollum and Saruman by Gandalf and later Frodo; no matter how far the individual has fallen, the wise also hope (and work) for their redemption.

Images of Heaven and Hell

Heaven and hell are mythic elements in the Bible, inasmuch as they are only vaguely understandable, but significant for comprehending earthly

16. Num. 22. Our translation.
17. Matt. 16:23.
18. Luke 10:18.

life. As we just said, heaven gets no mention in the earliest books of the Bible but eventually is taken to be the place surrounding God, the seat of his power, or his throne. It is perhaps significant that in most European languages, the word for heaven is the same as the word for sky. This does not mean that God dwells in the sky. (The Soviet cosmonaut Yuri Gagarin, upon returning to earth from his historic space flight, announced that he had been to heaven—*the sky* and *heaven* are identical in Russian—and that he had seen no God.) It means rather that the sky has come to signify for us the place of God's dwelling. There is something about lofty places that inspires us, that makes us view the world differently. It is no accident that the Greeks supposed many of the greatest of their gods to dwell atop Olympus. Plato once wrote that "astronomy compels the soul to look upwards and leads us from this world to another."[19] His implication is that contemplation of the visible skies leads us to contemplation of the possibility of further realms and an invisible heaven.

In the earliest book of the Bible, Genesis, there is no mention of either heaven or hell, but there is some "place" where God is, and where God works. It is referred to as the *tohu va bohu,* normally translated as "formless and void." The words in Hebrew do not quite mean absolute vacuity (as is commonly assumed, as in the phrase "creation *ex nihilo,*" or creation from absolutely nothing). Rather, they refer to trackless waste, a place that has real being, but which is indistinct, unformed, and uninhabited. As the literature of the Bible grew, so did the concepts of both heaven and hell. The notion of heaven came into full flower in the teachings of Jesus, who spoke of heaven as the presence of God and the reward of the righteous. The Acts of the Apostles begins with the resurrected Jesus ascending into heaven. Jesus sometimes explained to his disciples that majestic events took place not because they needed to happen that way, but for the sake of those observing them. The implication is that the disciples need visual aids to grasp the significance of certain events. So, for instance, when a voice is heard from heaven speaking of Jesus, Jesus turns to them and says that he didn't need to hear the voice, but it was done for their benefit. The rolling away of the stone from his tomb is another such event (on the assumption that anyone who can conquer death can get out of a tomb without opening the door). So Jesus's ascension into the sky appears to be a visual aid to help the disciples understand that when Jesus leaves them it is to go to his proper place. He did not need

19. *Republic,* 529. Jowett translation.

to go *up* to get there, but his having done so illustrated, in the only terms the disciples could grasp, just where he was going.

References to hell in the New Testament are not intended as accurate descriptions of the climate or content of hell. They are mythic representations of justice and freedom: justice is represented in punishment, freedom in the liberty that humans are given to refuse forgiveness.[20] The biblical representations of hell always rely on imaginable landscapes: either actual landscapes or else other mythological landscapes. Jesus sometimes uses the word *Gehenna,* referring to an actual place outside Jerusalem. Gehenna was the pit where Jerusalemites tossed their refuse.[21] It was a vivid image of a horrible place, a visual and olfactory assault on the senses. And it was a metaphor, an attempt to show the reality of hell by referring to a tangible image of it on earth. The words give a foretaste, nothing more.

The authors of the New Testament similarly sometimes refer to hell as *Hades.* This is a borrowing from Greek culture. Hades was the god of the afterlife, dwelling beneath the earth in the place where there is no light. The name *Hades,* or more properly, *Aïdes* or *a-ides,* means "no-sight" in Greek. The dead go to where they are not seen and where they cannot see. In Homer's *Odyssey,* when Odysseus sails to Hades he finds a land full of shades who cannot speak—only one, the blind prophet Teiresias, can see and speak to them. In the Hebrew scriptures, Sheol resembles the Greek Hades. Both are places where *all* the dead go. Thus, King David laments in the Psalms that "no one praises God from the grave."[22] Only in later times are the dead considered to have a continued living existence, and the place or condition of their existence is distinguished according to their sin or lack thereof.

The sharp *topographical* distinction between heaven and hell is a later conception, a way of visualizing the punishment of the wicked and the reward of the good in the afterlife. These concepts of reward and punishment already existed in germinal form in earlier Jewish thought, but what matters here is the fantastic element of visualizing reward and punishment by visualizing other worlds. In Jesus's moral teaching, he turns the Greek conception of "no-sight" to mean that no mortal has seen what heaven is like. Hell, on the other hand, becomes more distinct as Abaddon or Apollyon, drawing on the Hebrew and Greek words for "destruction."

---

20. "Hell is just a courtesy for those who insist they want no part of forgiveness." Robert Farrar Capon, *Parables of the Kingdom* (Grand Rapids: Zondervan, 1988), 154.

21. Cf. Jer. 31:40.

22. Ps. 6:5.

The upshot of all this for the writing of later myths and fantasies is that it motivates and justifies attempts like Dante's and Tolkien's to re-envisage celestial powers and principles in further myths. Dante's *Divina Commedia,* Tolkien's *Ainulindalë* and *Valaquenta* in the *Silmarillion,* and even the philosophical and theological conceptions of medieval scholastics are examples of this. These imaginings are not idle amusements. In each case, because the "worlds" so envisaged are related to one another, there are always consequences for the moral life of earthly, mortal readers of these stories.

These broad myths that get developed as the Bible is written and interpreted are significant, especially if they are taken not as literal places (in which case they are largely irrelevant for daily life) but as ways of calling to mind real truths about the cosmos: there are invisible principles at work, and they concern us immensely. They should not be taken as mere ideas to be toyed with. If they are true, these ideas are perhaps the most significant that we can imagine, and should be dwelt upon: the idea of there being a personal God who can be understood as both supremely just and unendingly loving; the idea of real moral virtues and real consequences for offenses; the idea that there is more to our existence than meets the eye; the possibility of angels, and powers that cannot be controlled by us, and that are subservient to greater powers still; the idea of a war between good and evil in a world parallel to ours—these ideas are the heart of myth and fantasy, because they translate the invisible into the practical. They should not be concretized but should remain as ideals that spur us to consider our lives and how we should live them. The total displacement of value to the afterlife is antithetical to the gospel. Nietzsche and Kierkegaard both recognized this and lambasted the church in their day for making it seem that this life was of no value, and that only the afterlife mattered. The myths of heaven and hell can be used to make this displacement, but they should not be. Rather, we should use them to keep considering how we should live our lives here and now. The point of the biblical myth is that *both* this life *and* the next life matter, and that they are intimately connected. That heaven and hell are known to us through mythic conceptions does not mean they are not real. If anything, it suggests that they are real in the fullest sense—even if the literal conceptions we may form of them are mistaken. Myths are not false! They contain eternal truth, of the kind that can, perhaps, be told only in story.

Genesis and the Flood

We can now move from images and ideas developed throughout the biblical mythos to some specific important mythic stories within the Bible. The book of Genesis, and especially the story of the flood, is a wonderful example of how a mythic understanding leads us to deeper truth than a mere historic understanding (though the two are fully compatible).

Genesis tells the story of the origin of the nation of Israel. The first eleven chapters tell the story of the origin of the world and the great events in its history until the time of Abraham, the first patriarch of Israel; the remaining thirty-nine chapters tell the story of Abraham and his descendants until Israel's migration to Egypt in the time of Joseph. It is common to charge that the Bible's mythic elements have been taken from the mythic stories of other nations. The first eleven chapters of Genesis are usually cited as prime examples of this.[23] These chapters contain many of the most familiar stories from the Bible: the stories of creation in chapters 1 and 2, the Garden of Eden in chapter 3, Cain and Abel in chapter 4, Noah and the great flood in chapters 5–10, the tower of Babel in chapter 11.

There are several reasons for the charge about Genesis. To begin with, the first eleven chapters read like mythology, while the remaining chapters of Genesis read more like family history. Since, according to the first chapter of Genesis, humans were not created until the sixth day, it seems unlikely that the events of the first five days were recorded by a human witness. The stories of Abraham, however, might well have been first heard by Isaac at Abraham's knee. The Abrahamic stories have a greater (though by no means precise) attention to persons, places, and historical events, while the stories of the first eleven chapters of Genesis show almost no such concern. Second, the events of the first eleven chapters are paralleled in other, often older, myths from the Near and Middle East. Third, these events are fantastic, without equal in modern times. They stretch the imagination and tax credulity. If the stories are taken at face value, they engender numerous difficulties for many modern readers.

Some scholars argue from this and from disputed authorship of the Torah or Pentateuch (the first five books of the Bible) that the Genesis

23. For instance, S. H. Hooke speaks of the "mythical material which the Israelite authors of Genesis borrowed from Canaanite [and] other sources." He adds, "In the form in which we have it now, the Old Testament is the product of editorial activity extending over many centuries. . . . The final editors of the Old Testament collected most of the mythological material into the first eleven chapters of Genesis." *Middle Eastern Mythology* (New York: Penguin, 1983), 104.

stories are edited myths borrowed from other cultures and are therefore neither divinely inspired nor historically accurate. There is certainly good reason to suspect that parts of the Bible have been edited. The Psalms were obviously collected at some point and edited in such a way as to permit repetitions.[24] The Synoptic Gospels (Matthew, Mark, and Luke) plainly draw on a common source. But if the Genesis accounts were edited, there is scant textual evidence of this. Only if we had earlier versions of Genesis could we see just how it was edited, but no such versions exist. The parallel myths found in other Near Eastern cultures are not textually close enough to Genesis to permit anything more than speculation about the genealogy of the stories.

The authorship of Genesis is an open question. Jesus names Moses as the author of Genesis, and if he had divine knowledge about this, he cannot be gainsaid. But what if he was simply speaking in the idiom of scholarly opinion in his day by calling a series of redactors "Moses"? It might be instructive to ask what is at stake in this discussion. Some Christians worry that if the authorship of Moses is denied, then the prophetic stamp on Genesis fails; if so, then Jesus's knowledge of the Old Testament is questionable, and if that is so, they fear, then other more important things about Jesus are also questionable. On the other side, opponents of the Mosaic authorship of Genesis fear that if Moses is acknowledged the originator of the stories, there will follow severe political ramifications. This was what was at stake in the infamous Scopes trials, after all.

But while these may be interesting historical questions to ask about Genesis, they are probably the wrong questions to ask if our goal is to understand the book and the mythic truth that it conveys about God, ourselves, and the world in which we live. Genesis is not a science book, nor is it a history book. This ought to be plain for no other reason than that the academic disciplines of science and history as we know them are modern inventions that were unknown to the author(s) of Genesis. Even if the author were actually many people, this would have no bearing on the divine authorship, since God could just as easily inspire a series of redactors as a single author. Furthermore, if the author of Genesis borrowed myths and recast them in the light of monotheism, this also does not impugn their prophetic nature. The author did not need to invent

24. Cf. Ps. 14 and 53; 40 and 70; 57, 60, and 108. Each of these groups shows that one of the psalms relies on the other or on some common source, indicating some redaction. Psalm 72:20 is another piece of evidence: it states that this psalm is the last of the psalms of David, but it is followed by eighteen more psalms of David. Apparently, the five books of the psalms were once separate, but were joined together by later redactors.

a new language to write the book. To have done so would have been absurd and pointless. Why should he invent stories wholly unfamiliar to his audience? More than likely, he would use the stories they already knew and recast them to emphasize certain points.

For example, if Moses was the man the Bible tells us he was, he would know the mythologies of the Near East: he was raised in the palace of Pharaoh, came to know his Jewish culture, and lived for four decades as the son-in-law of Jethro, high priest of Midian. We would expect that such a man, when writing about God, would do so by relating the truths he had learned in various places and then binding them together in a truer narrative. We see an example of this sort of storytelling in a later figure, Paul of Tarsus. Like Moses, Paul grew up across cultures. He was born a Roman citizen with Jewish parents living in Tarsus, now part of Turkey. He was educated both in the Greek and Roman classics and in the Jewish law. When asked to speak to the Areopagites, he told the story of the gospel—without mentioning the name of Jesus—by drawing solely on the stories familiar to the Greeks who were his audience. This means that when the poet composed the *Heliand* nine centuries later, he was only imitating what Paul—and possibly Moses—did before him.

Consider the flood episode from Genesis. Numerous accounts of floods exist in ancient literature. Significantly, the Babylonians had several versions of the flood story, predating and similar to the story found in Genesis. The *Epic of Gilgamesh* and the later *Epic of Atram-Hasîs* both contain accounts of a cataclysmic flood and of one man who, warned by a god, saves the animals in a boat. In the eleventh tablet of *Gilgamesh* we read of the Noahlike figure Enlil:

> Enlil heard the clamour and he said to the gods in council, "the uproar of mankind is intolerable and sleep is no longer possible by reason of the babel." So the gods agreed to exterminate mankind. Enlil did this, but Ea because of his oath warned me in a dream. He whispered their words ... "Tear down your house, I say, and build a boat. ... let her beam equal her length, let her deck be roofed like the vault that covers the abyss; then take up into the boat the seed of all living creatures."[25]

Edmond Sollberger comments on this that when Abraham's family left Ur, they

25. *The Epic of Gilgamesh*, N. K. Sandars, trans. (London: Penguin, 1976), 108.

did not only take with them their womenfolk and their servants and their cattle and other worldly possessions, but also the far more important riches of the Sumero-Akkadian culture and traditions, literary and religious, which were their heritage and would eventually influence and inspire the authors of the Biblical books.[26]

Does the suggestion that Abraham passed on to his descendants a Babylonian myth undermine the truthfulness or validity of the Bible? Not in the least. The beauty of the story is not its originality, but what arises from the retelling of the myth. The Genesis stories of the flood were likely written down by one who had heard them before. But they were retold in a truer fashion by an inspired reteller. The earlier versions do very little to explain *why* the flood happened or *why* one man was saved. The Hebraic version in Genesis ties the story of the flood neatly into a coherent narrative with a consistent monotheistic worldview. To wit: the story is retold to show that: (a) the flood came for a reason, and from a reasonable God, not simply due to the whim of the gods; (b) the reason pertains to a moral law that is universal, indicating that good and evil have a universal basis; (c) the moral law had been flagrantly transgressed, so the punishment was in some sense both avoidable and to be expected; and (d) God is not merely wrathful, but reasonable and merciful in sparing the righteous. According to this version of the flood, all the flood-myths have some truth, but they miss the point that the world makes moral sense.

This retelling and correction of a common myth also suggests an explanation of why there are two stories of creation in Genesis. Just as Jesus often said "you have heard it said that . . . but I tell you that . . ." so the author of Genesis is retelling familiar stories: "You have heard that the world was created by the gods; I tell you that it was created by one God. You have heard that there was a flood and an ark; I am telling you that the flood came as a result of sin, yet the ark is a sign that God is merciful and gracious, and that he provides salvation for those who love him."

But it would not do simply to state this as a theory, as we will see in the next section. It is not simply the case that suffering and sin go hand in hand. Punishment is not meted out instantly or even fairly in this world. The story embodies ideals, but it does not insist that they will always be seen in the same way in the world. On the contrary, at the end of the flood, we are told that such a flood, as God's retribution against a

26. Edmond Sollberger, *The Babylonian Legend of the Flood* (London: British Museum, 1977), 10.

sinful world, will never be seen again. Rather, instead of swift justice, the world will be marked with silent signs of mercy, like the rainbow. Such things reach us most clearly and deeply in mythic form. The story of the flood becomes not so much a story about an actual prehistoric deluge (if it were only that, who would care about it?) as about the reality of sin and the permanence of God's mercy.

Job, the Great Biblical Myth

Whereas the flood myth in Genesis is concerned with establishing the reality of human moral responsibility, the story of Job is concerned with the question of what that view of morality entails for the apparently innocent who suffer. This story suggests that the relationship between moral virtue and suffering is, in the short run, unfathomable. The most human life is a moral life marked by honesty, concern for others, and truthfulness. These things constitute right religion and are the only sure defense against the invisible powers of evil.

The story is quite simple: there is a man named Job, who is recognized by God and by people as being without fault. One day Satan appears before God, and God asks Satan to consider Job. Satan asks permission to entice Job to sin by causing him suffering, and God grants him permission to do so. Job's children die, he loses both his health and his wealth, and his wife counsels him to kill himself. When his three friends come to mourn with him, they sit in silence for a week with him. Finally, Job cries out to God, and the friends respond to Job. The bulk of the book of Job is taken up with this dialogue, in which Job alternates between calling out to God and responding to his friends. The dialogue takes place in three cycles, in each of which first Job speaks, and then one of his friends speaks. After this, a mysterious younger friend appears and harangues all four of them. Finally, God appears in a whirlwind and questions Job. Job is forced to admit he spoke in ignorance when he challenged God to defend his actions. God says to Job's three "comforters" that, unlike Job, they have not spoken of God what is right. Job prays for them, and they are forgiven. Then Job receives twice the wealth he had before, and his children are restored to him.[27]

27. It is not plain from the text whether these are the same children or new children. What is striking, however, is that everything else is doubled, but the children are restored one-for-one. There is a tacit moral lesson here: two human lives are not worth more than one. Each life is infinitely valuable, and twice infinity is still infinity. There is a second moral lesson here as well: Job sees the face of God

The language of Job, especially in the opening chapters, is the language of fairy tale.[28] It is a "once upon a time in a distant (but not too distant) land" story. The author is not concerned with history or geography. We are told only that Job, the protagonist, lived in the land of Uz. This Uz may have been a cousin of Abraham,[29] and if so, then a Jew reading the story near the time of its composition would have understood that this is a story of a man who is not one of us, but distantly related to us. This is important for two reasons: first, it means that Job cannot be expected to know all the things we know about God from the stories of God's dealings with Israel over the years. Second, it situates Job near enough to the reader to show that Job's story could be her or his story, but far enough away to show the reader that it could be anyone's story.

After giving a few details about Job, the narrator shifts his attention to celestial events. Unlike the Revelation of St. John, where John explains how he came to glimpse the affairs of heaven,[30] the narrator does not attempt to explain how he came to eavesdrop on God. The disturbing dialogue between God and Satan serves to give the divine stamp of approval to Job's virtue. However, Job never finds out what is said in heaven.

The story of Job is particularly difficult to understand if one reads it in an attempt to form a positive theology or to formulate a theodicy. On the surface, it would appear that Job is a good source for such theorizing, since it is chiefly a dialogue about the nature of God and of suffering. Furthermore, Job's friends have a fairly coherent theology, complete with a theory of suffering: suffering occurs to those who sin, in proportion to the sin committed. This is the divine economy of justice, they say. Job, on the other hand, vacillates in his beliefs. Sometimes he speaks to his friends to remind them that the world is not a fair place. "Have you never questioned those who travel?"[31] Job asks. If they had done so, they would know that the just suffer all over the world. Other times Job speaks not to men but to God, begging him to end his life or to appear and explain what Job has done to deserve the suffering. Job does not present us with a consistent theology.

---

and then gives his daughters an inheritance. This was unheard of in biblical times; daughters inherited only when they had no brothers, but Job saw the face of God and knew that his daughters, just like his sons, were made in God's image.

28. Cf. Robert Sacks, *The Book of Job with Commentary* (Atlanta: Scholars Press, 1999), 80.
29. Cf. Gen. 22:21, but also 10:23, 36:28, and Jer. 25:20.
30. Cf. Rev. 1:9ff.
31. Job 21:29.

What Job does give us is a believable story of a man who is suffering, and yet who loves God. "I know that my redeemer lives," he says, and this may be his greatest moment. So what does it mean that Job has "spoken what is right" of God? Not that he spoke theology or correct creed, to be sure. After all, in the end Job repented of his words, and confessed his ignorance about God. We are left to assume that Job spoke correctly in three ways: first, he spoke what was in his heart and did not try to substitute false piety for honesty; second, he spoke *to* God, and not just about God; third, he confessed his ignorance about God. Contrast Job with his "comforters," and the case is made clear. They are concerned only with defending their God, but in the end this becomes a defense of their theology. God does not need their defense, though. They defend their theology at the expense of their friendship. This is tantamount to committing human sacrifice, sacrificing Job to the idol of their creed. Their atheism is proved by the fact that not once do they pray. This is striking: they have the most religious language, but their religion consists only in persuading (or attempting to persuade) others that they are correct. Such religion is really atheism and idolatry. Even more significantly, these "comforters" actually become Job's accusers, seeking to accuse Job of wrongdoing, to present him as guilty. As such, they are doing Satan's job for him, the same job that Satan was doing in the first two chapters of Job. Thus, they also have become satans.

Job, by contrast, becomes a redeemer, and a prefiguring of Christ throughout the book. There are prophetic hints of the Gospel story. Job speaks of the need for someone to arbitrate, or to go between him and God. But he knows this arbitrator or "intercessor" must be more than a man, because God is "not a man like [him] that [he] might answer him."[32] Later Job longs for an "advocate" or "intercessor" to plead his case before God. This advocate must be both a "witness" for Job and also a "friend."[33] And eventually Job speaks his faith in his Redeemer in the passage already mentioned. But the greatest hints of the Gospels come not in vague references, but in the *very story* of Job. Like Jesus, Job is a righteous man who suffers as though he were a sinner. He is disfigured and loses everything he has, much as Jesus did, as described in Philippians 2:5–8 or the Messiah in Isaiah 42:3–4. In the end, however, he is restored to his former glory, and he himself becomes the intercessor to

32. Job 9:32–35.
33. Job 16:18–21.

God for the sake of sinners—the three comforters. Thus, the Gospel story is played out in the story of Job.

All of the above we see not by way of propositional statements, but through story. To some degree, then, it does not matter in the end whether Job and his comforters were historic figures. If anything, the story is strengthened by taking it as myth. Job has often been compared to the Greek stories of Oedipus. The comparison is not exact, since Oedipus is more concerned with his own honor (he kills his biological father to avenge his own honor) than Job. Still, Oedipus's is a powerful myth, one that stirs the human heart to fear and pity, and the comparison is just.

In light of this, one notable aspect of the narrative of Job is its emphasis on speech and words (and hence the near complete lack of physical description). The story takes place in cycles of speeches; Job fears his children might have cursed God in their hearts (the only real sin dealt with in Job); Job's wife tells him to "curse God and [so to] die" when his suffering is at its greatest; Satan only attempts to incite Job to speak ill of God; Job is commended for speaking correctly of God. (It is also worth noting that Job is never aware of Satan's presence or even of his existence.) The universality of the story matters infinitely more than the historical questions of whether there really was a man named Job, and what his address was, and so on. *Fabula de nobis narratur;* the story is told about us, and about everyone.

The Gospels: True Historic Myth

The Gospels contain a constant and subtle mythos that differs from that of Job in the matter of their historicity. In Job it mattered that the characters could be understood as universally standing in for *any* person, and thus (as with fairy tales) any specific historical tie to a particular time, place, and person diminishes the significance. What mattered was not the individuals but their characters. In the case of the Gospel stories, their historicity matters supremely. It is precisely their historicity that makes them significant. The universal element is located here not in general characters, but in the person of Jesus. This universal element contains the reality of all myths. That is, whatever real truth may be found in other myths is ultimately personified in the Incarnation of God. It is the mythic element of the Gospels that makes them comprehensible by permitting us to see the Gospels not as a stale religious doctrine but as a story into which we can enter.

Recall the citation from Peirce that begins this chapter. God could have entered the world as a series of propositions spoken by a prophet;[34] or he could have incarnated and then died in greater obscurity. But from the earliest times, what has mattered to Christian evangelists is the telling of the story of Jesus. Jesus's whole life matters, not merely his death or his resurrection. Mark begins his Gospel by stating that he is writing the *beginning* of the gospel of Jesus Christ, not its entirety. That gospel is not merely a statement; it is a transforming narrative. It has transforming power because it is the unique story of the salvific irruption of heaven into the affairs of earth. It takes place at the boundary between heaven and earth in a way that takes the business of earth just as seriously as it takes the business of heaven. Neither is marginalized; neither becomes a mere echo of the other. Earth is dignified by receiving the exclusive attention of heaven; heaven is validated by its entrance into earth.

The story of Jesus is not an addition to religious law or practice. The gospel "rule" is that no rule can ever suffice to reconcile humanity with God. The gospel is the story of the triumph of grace. This is important: grace is not to be mistaken for some stale doctrine of religious economics, whereby sinful flesh is exchanged for an equal quantity of forgiveness. It is a story, a living story—one might say it is *the* story, the one that validates and energizes all other stories. It is a story in which we all participate, and this is why Mark says that his account is only the beginning. The gospel is not a creed; it is life itself, continually growing, ramifying, fructifying.

Ultimately, all the myths in history—like that of Job discussed earlier—contain smaller versions of the great myth of the Gospels, each one to the degree that it is true. The Gospels are the myth come true. Jesus has been compared with other mythic and historical figures, with the implication that Jesus was the lucky one whose story got told. There is some basis for this: there were in Jesus's time many would-be Messiahs. The New Testament does not attempt to hide this fact, but rather refers to it from time to time.[35] It has also been pointed out that there are mythic figures who are like Jesus. The Greek gods Athena and Zeus are referred to as "saviors" just as Jesus is; and in the ancient mythologies of the Levant region there are similar stories of gods who become incarnate; who are born of virgins; who die as sacrifices for sins; who die unjustly;

---

34. This would have resulted in theo*logy* (the study of God as a science), but what seems to matter more is theo*mythy* (telling true stories about God) and understanding ourselves as part of that story.

35. Cf. Acts 5:34ff.

who are raised from the dead. Versions of the notions of heaven and hell, of judgment and afterlife all predate the writing of the Gospels. In one sense, there is no wholly original element in the Gospel stories.[36]

Nevertheless, Jesus differs from all these in an important way: the claim is made by Jesus's earliest biographers and historians that Jesus's birth, way of life, and death were historical. More to the point: the story of Jesus ultimately hinges on the event of the resurrection, which was predicted and then enacted historically. In this book, we are not interested in trying to prove that this event did or did not actually occur.[37] It suffices to point out that the earliest Christians believed that it did, and, more important, they cited the resurrection as the basis of their beliefs, lives, and willingness to die as martyrs. (The word *martyr* comes from the Greek word for *witness;* many of the early Christians who claimed to have witnessed the resurrected Jesus died simply because they were unwilling to recant.) The apostle Paul comments on this, saying that if Jesus was not literally and historically raised from the dead, then Christians like himself are the most pitiable people.[38]

It might be claimed that the Gospels are mere myth, in the sense of being a pleasant religious fabrication. But this is challenged by the statements and martyrdoms of the earliest Christians. On the other hand, it might be argued that there is no room for the mythical in the Gospels. But if this is the case, then the Gospels become wholly meaningless. If there is no breakthrough from heaven to earth, and if the Gospels are not the truth of all other stories, then the Gospels become either a mere literary pleasantry or a harsh, legalistic dogma with no reality to underwrite it. The Gospel story, ultimately, is a mythos. One does not grasp it by granting assent to doctrines; one grasps it by hearing the story and entering into it. One becomes part of the story. Walter Wangerin has pointed out that the first Christians had no theology, but they had Jesus, and participated in his story, and that's what matters; propositional theology is important, but not as important as knowing and participating in the story. As Wangerin puts it,

> Religions do exist without doctrines and theologies; but no religion has ever existed without a story at its core, not as an illustration of some doctrine, but rather as the very truth, the evidence and the testimony of

36. Cf. Plato, *Republic*, 361e–362a; Alan Watts, *Myth and Ritual in Christianity*.

37. For an overview of scholarship on both sides of this issue, see Paul Copan and Ronald K. Tacelli, *Jesus' Resurrection: Fact or Figment?* (Downers Grove, IL: InterVarsity Press, 2000).

38. 1 Cor. 15.

God's action for the sake of the believers. But a story that goes untold lacks life. It becomes a puzzle to be solved by intellectual analysis alone. And a religion whose story is untold, likewise, lacks life. For if we never have, by means of the sacred story (the gospel), experienced the presence, love, activity of our Christ, then we will fall back upon lesser experience; we will fulfill our natural need of religious experience with mere sentimentalities and silly diminishments of God. And so our religion, too, will be diminished.[39]

To paraphrase John's Gospel, the *logos* of God became a mythos; the reason, the account of God became a human story so that we might grasp the ungraspable—not with our minds alone, but with our whole lives by entering into the story.

The Bible as the Grand Myth

This brings us back to the last way that myth appears in the Bible. The whole Bible fits together as a grand narrative. This grand narrative appears at first to be loosely connected stories about individuals trying to find their way in the world, and trying to understand the cosmos. But viewed as a whole, the story reverses itself, and it becomes apparent that the story of the Bible is the story of heaven courting earth's inhabitants, teaching them its language, seeking them out. This too is an important element in myth and fantasy. The stories always appear at first to be quests or adventures that individuals embark upon with small aims, but in the end, the quest is reversed, and it is seen that the adventure sought out the adventurer for a purpose.

We have so far refrained from strictly defining myth, but recall some of the things we have said are characteristic of myths. Myths are profound stories that speak of the world from the perspective of Faërie. Taken in this sense, it can be readily seen that the Bible contains many passages that qualify as mythic. Myths are also significant, showing the three faces of Faërie, without being purely didactic. So then, the whole of the Bible, the whole evangelium, the whole *kerygma*, the whole story of God shown in the tradition of scripture, is a grand myth. In varying degrees, churches remember this myth and reenact it in cyclical readings of the scriptures, in liturgies, and in the church calendar. At Christmas

---

39. Walter Wangerin Jr., "Making Disciples by Sacred Story," in *Christianity Today*, February 2004. See http://www.christianitytoday.com/ct/2004/002/9.66.html.

they retell and remember the story of Christ's birth; at Easter they retell the story of his passion and resurrection; at Pentecost they celebrate the birth of the church. What matters in all of this is the creative and redemptive *story* of God.

We said earlier in this chapter that stories are helpful because they can grow while retaining their essential shape and structure. The *Heliand* is an example of this, in which the story of the Gospels is translated into Saxon. It grows to fit the Saxon understanding of how a story is told, while retaining the essential core of the Gospels. By using the Saxon language and Saxon elements, it shows that the grand myth of the Bible is not a once-told tale of times long gone, but a vital, ongoing story. The Gospel story, like any other, was meant to be told and retold. It can and should be translated into new idioms, made understandable to those who do not grasp it in its original form.

Myth and fantasy are one type of this retelling. Of course, just as a body can grow poorly, so can a story. The Grimms understood something about telling fairy stories that Perrault or Andersen did not; thus Andersen and Perrault tried to make their stories into moral tales. They were not wholly wrong in doing so, since the tales do communicate "morals," or rather morality; however, in the attempt to translate those morals into propositions they become emaciated and lose some of their vital energy. By contrast, Tolkien's Middle-earth stories are more religious for the lack of explicit religion than they would have been had Tolkien made them into religious allegories. So the stories of the Gospels should not be reduced to mere moralizing, or to mere propositions. They were given to us as stories, and stories they should always remain. They are stories to be told and retold, and ultimately, stories to enter into. The author of the *Heliand* took his job to be the same as that of the original Gospellers: "to chant God's spell." This may sound like dark magic, but it is not. It is, in fact, just the opposite. Were he trying to invoke God by magic powers and use God as a tool, it would be dark magic. Instead, he saw himself as being like the Gospellers Matthew, Mark, Luke, and John: he was telling the great myth, in a new way, translating the language of heaven into Saxon.

4

Homeric Myth
(and the "Epic" Fantasy)

Philosophy (i.e., the love of Wisdom) begins in wonder . . .
even the lover of myths is in a sense a philosopher, for the
myth is composed of wonders.

Aristotle, *Metaphysics* (our translation)

The more alone I am, the fonder I have become of myths.

Attributed to Aristotle,
upon his retirement to his estate
in Chalcis (our translation)

The crowd sat in rapt silence as the old man began to chant, "Sing, O Goddess, of the rage of Achilles, that hurled many great Achaeans down to Hades!" Most of them had heard the tale many times before, but none was bored by it. This was the great ancient story of the heroes and the gods, and of the siege of Ilium, or Troy, by the ancestors of those who now sat listening with attentive devotion. No mere tall tale, this was *their* story. This story gathered together all the great stories of the gods and of history, and showed the Greeks how they fit into it. It was the story that made sense of their world. It is also a story that continues to inspire much of the greatest and most important *epic* fantasy of our time.

We attribute *The Iliad* and its companion epic poem, *The Odyssey,* to Homer, the great ancient poet. Scholars dispute whether Homer was the original author of the poems or merely the editor of previous versions. What is clear is that these two poems became the foundational works of an entire culture, informing every aspect of its private, civic, and intellectual life. Their impact on Western culture even today cannot be overestimated. Alongside the Bible, the other great source of mythos in Western literature is, of course, Greek and Roman mythology, all of which owes a debt to Homer. During the Golden Age of Athens, centuries after Homer, a multitude of dramas, based on the Homeric epics, were penned. Many of the plays of Aeschylus, Euripides, Sophocles, and Aristophanes survive still. The *Oedipus* cycle and the *Oresteia,* for instance, are timeless, and the problems they grapple with remain problems for every age. *The Aeneid,* Virgil's patriotic myth of the founding of Rome, begins where *The Iliad* leaves off. St. Augustine wrote about the Greek plays in the fourth century AD, in his *Confessions.* In the eleventh century, Snorri Sturluson began his compilation of the Norse myths by tying them in to the ancient Greek and Roman myths, connecting his Ásir—the gods Odin and Thor and their family—with the heroes of Troy. The fourteenth-century Anglo-Saxon poet of the English West Midlands who composed *Sir Gawain and the Green Knight,* one of the most beautiful late medieval Arthurian romances, and also one of the few to actually come from England, does the same thing when it begins with the line: *"Siþen þe sege and þe assaut watz sesed at Troy . . ."* ("When the siege and the assault ceased at Troy . . .").[1] When poet Joachim du Bellay (1522–60) needed a grand poetic image of returning home after a journey, he compared himself to Ulysses (the Roman name for Odysseus) and Jason. In occupied France during the Second World War, Jean Anouilh rewrote and produced Euripides' *Antigone* as a protest against the German occupying forces. None who saw it in 1944 in Paris missed the significance of Antigone's willingness to give up her life in defiance of an unjust ruler and for the sake of the gods and her family.

The Atlantis story also comes to us from antiquity, through the Greek philosopher and mythopoet Plato, who grew up under the spell of Homer's

---

1. Translated by J. R. R. Tolkien (*Gawain,* 19).

epics as well. Thus Tolkien also comes under the spell, connecting his Middle-earth *Legendarium* to the Greek myth of Atlantis; when he wrote *The Lord of the Rings,* he identified it as the story of the inhabitants of Middle-earth after the fall of the kingdom of Númenor, a rough parallel to Atlantis.[2] Though Lewis is perhaps most famous for his Narnia stories, his favorite of his own works was *Till We Have Faces,* a retelling of the Cupid and Psyche myth. His source for that was Apuleius's Latin classic *The Golden Ass.*[3] Apuleius in turn drew on Homeric and other Greek myths. Atlantis winds up underwriting any number of other classical and modern myths of paradise lost, from Plato to Lewis's posthumous poem "The End of the Wine," to the more recent *Taliesin,* the first book of Stephen Lawhead's *Pendragon Cycle.* For pagan Europe, Atlantis was a rough parallel to the loss of utopia in the Hebrew story of Eden.

These authors who recast earlier myths are part of a long tradition dating at least back to Homer. Most of the stories of the gods and heroes of ancient Greece and Rome depend on Homer's two epics. This is just the tiniest sampling of the ways in which the ancient myths have mattered to Western civilization throughout the centuries. Since there is no shortage of good reference books and recapitulations of the ancient myths (see the Appendix), in this chapter we will focus on the poet Homer and his epics that are the source for most subsequent Greek and Roman myths. These Homeric myths contain within themselves the kind of literary and speculative richness that makes great works endure. Without them, the cauldron of Western myth would be considerably emptier. On a superficial level, the Greek myths contribute a whole pantheon of characters, from the gods and heroes to satyrs, fauns, dryads, naiads, centaurs, and Cyclopes. On a deeper level, they set the tone for understanding myth as much more than mere tales. Myth for the Greeks meant thinking about everything from the nature of the universe to our deepest moral attachments and obligations. At the deepest level, Greek myths use natural and fantastic characters and settings to probe the questions of who we are and how we are related to the gods—and God. Great early Chris-

2. Tolkien explicitly uses the derivative name *Atalantë* (meaning "Downfallen" in the Elven tongue) as another name for the sunken land of Númenor, even as he uses the name *Avalónnë* (reminiscent of the *Avalon* of Arthurian legend, an important legend touched upon in the next chapter) for the city closest to the undying lands of Valinor. The famed Isildur, who cut the Ruling Ring off the hand of Sauron, was one of the few survivors of the Fall of Atalantë, and Aragorn is described as one of Isildur's descendants in whom the true blood of Númenor (Atalantë) still runs. Tolkien tells a long version of the legend of this fall in the *Akallabêth,* published as part of *The Silmarillion.*

3. See the sixth chapter of Thomas Howard's *The Achievement of C. S. Lewis* (Wheaton, IL: Shaw, 1980) for an excellent treatment of *Till We Have Faces.*

tian thinkers from the apostle Paul to Augustine found in the myths novel and fruitful means of communicating the gospel, from which we continue to benefit today.

Homer's *Iliad*

The storylines of Homer's two great poetic epics are easy to relate. In *The Iliad*, Helen, the beautiful wife of the Greek king, Menelaus, has been stolen by his guest, prince Paris, son of Priam, King of Troy. In response, Menelaus's more powerful brother, King Agamemnon, rallies all the forces of the Achaeans—the people of what is now known as Greece—and they sail in a thousand ships to win back Helen and to punish Paris. *The Iliad* begins when this war is already ten years old. It is only a three days' journey by sea from Achaea to Troy, but the Achaeans have taken ten years to sack and pillage every tributary city along the way, perhaps intending to sap the strength of Troy while lining their own pockets. Meanwhile, Troy has had ample time to call on other allies, so when the Achaeans arrive at Ilium, or the city of Troy, it is well defended from within.

The intrigue, however, involves not only men but gods. Indeed, the gods are deeply involved in the tale.[4] In his plundering, Agamemnon had defiled the temple of Apollo and captured the lovely daughter of Chryses, priest of Apollo. Apollo punishes Agamemnon by striking the Achaeans with a plague until Chryses' daughter is returned. Proud Agamemnon returns her but insists that Achilles give Agamemnon his beautiful prize, Briseis, in order to ensure that no ally of Agamemnon had a lovelier prize than he.

All of this is in the background when the poem begins with the line "Sing, O Goddess, of the rage of Achilles." Achilles was king of the Achaean Myrmidons, and the greatest champion of all the Greeks. His mother was the goddess Thetis, making Achilles a demigod. When Agamemnon insists that he is more worthy of honor than Achilles, Achilles' rage against Agamemnon incites him to respond by refusing to fight for the Achaeans. This gives the Trojans and their allies a strategic advantage over the Achaeans, who suffer heavy losses in the days to come. Achilles sits by impassively, awaiting Agamemnon's apology, immune to the pleas from his men and others to let the Myrmidons return to battle

---

4. This was one of the great weaknesses of the 2004 film *Troy,* which omitted the importance of the gods almost entirely.

with their allies. Only when Achilles' dearest friend, Patroclus, is slain in battle does Achilles return to fight. He challenges Prince Hector, Paris's older brother, to single combat and slays him. Strapping Hector's body to his chariot, Achilles defiles the body in his rage, until Priam comes humbly to beg a temporary cessation of hostilities so he may bury his son. Achilles, moved by Priam's humility (in stark contrast to the arrogance of Achilles' sometime ally, Agamemnon) grants the request. Achilles seems less noble than Hector, who does not delight in killing but who is willing to die for his home and his honor. The poem that began with wonder at the rage of the Achaean hero ends gently, "so they buried Hector, breaker of horses."

The Iliad has captivated audiences for thousands of years. This is partly because it is full of adventure, intrigue, and battles, but it is also because it offers such profound opportunities to reflect on human life and its significance. We discover that Achilles has been told by the gods that he must choose between dying peacefully, at an old age, at home, or dying very soon in battle, and that he has chosen the latter. He has evidently done this because he believes this is the fullest life, and he would rather live a short but important life than a long and wasted life. The story is ostensibly driven by Menelaus's desire to recover his wife and his stolen honor, but Menelaus's allies behave even more despicably toward the towns they pillage than Paris ever did toward Menelaus. The hero of the poem appears at first to be the great warrior Achilles, but at the end we are left to wonder if the gentle, honorable, and noble Hector and his father are not better men than any of the conniving, arrogant, and violent Achaeans. *The Iliad* is the national poem of Greece, to be sure, but it is no sop to patriotism. It continually offers sober reflections on the fragility of human life and the ease with which great men perform terrible deeds. The battles are violent and graphic, but the violence itself is never celebrated. It is not even the case that Homer tells the Greeks that they have divine sanction for all they do. Some of the Olympian gods are decidedly on the side of the Greeks, but others are on the side of the Trojans and interfere in the battle on their behalf.

One of the key features of mythos in Greek and Roman mythology is that, like the biblical myth, it involves several worlds that interact and commingle. Put in the terminology of this book, it takes place near to the borders of Faërie. Olympus touches Piraeus. The gods affect not only the outcomes of the great wars, like the siege of Troy, but the lives of individual men. Thus, even a common fairy tale in which a peasant girl (or boy) is aided by a powerful being and becomes a princess (or king) bears something of the marks of the Greek myth.

We also see that myths are the ground for working out moral questions. This is important to note. Polytheism, such as we have in the mythology of Homer, is often dismissed by association with the allegorical nature-myths discussed earlier: "the Greeks needed a god to explain that natural phenomenon." In fact, the gods do not explain natural phenomena at all. If the phenomena are mysterious, the gods are more mysterious still. But they do interact with mortals, and engage them in great moral issues, and sway the courses of their lives. Perhaps more important, the gods remind the mortals that there is always something far grander at stake in their lives than their own interests. Mortals who think that they are the center of their own universe, such as Prometheus and Narcissus, wind up paying the penalty. Mortals who honor the gods don't necessarily prosper, but they live well and leave a powerful legacy.

Something else needs to be said here about the gods. Ancient European mythopoets were largely (though not exclusively) polytheists. They found reason to worship many gods. Some of them, however, also spoke of God in the singular, as though the many gods were all faces of the one unknown God. The world of the ancient Greeks was, in a sense, an enchanted world, one in which divinity, the transcendent, was omnipresent. Aristotle remarks that it was common usage in some places to call men gods, as in "yon man is god," meaning that he somehow exhibited the virtue of divinity in his very being. Some of the heroes, like Achilles, were taken to be *daemons,* or demigods, offspring of the union of god and mortal. Our point here is twofold: first, that in the Christian story, the myths of the Greeks finally came alive—God became man; God was born of a mortal. Second, in the subsequent marriage of Greek culture and Hebrew Christian theology, there was an adoption of terms that can today cause confusion. We take our word *demon* from the Greek *daemon,* which can mean anything from the inspiration a prophet receives to a demigod, and which may not be sinister.

Homer's *Odyssey*

Homer's other great epic is *The Odyssey,* which gets its name from its protagonist, Odysseus, whom the Romans later called Ulysses. Since most of the book is about Odysseus's travels, it is fitting that his name is related to the Greek word for road, *hodos.* Odysseus was one of the kings who accompanied Agamemnon to Troy. As king of the small island Ithaka, he did not have the military power to resist Agamemnon's call to arms, but Odysseus turned out to be far more clever than Agamemnon. Cleverness is Odysseus's trademark.

There are three main strains to the narrative. The first is the story of Odysseus trying to return home after the war in Troy. The second is the story of Odysseus's wife, Penelope, faithfully and cleverly managing his kingdom during his twenty-year absence. The third is the story of the goddess Athena, who invisibly guides and aids Odysseus through his adventures and perils.

The poem begins when Troy has been razed and plundered. Odysseus and his men begin their journey home, which, once again, should take only three days or so. But Odysseus runs afoul of the gods and winds up taking ten years to return home. Along the way, he must do battle with Polyphemus the Cyclops, navigate between Scylla and Charybdis, resist siren songs and the seductions of a goddess, wrestle with shape-changing Proteus, travel to Hades and back, and resist the temptations of the false paradises of Circe and the Lotus-Eaters. Meanwhile, Penelope is being courted by scores of suitors, each of whom hopes to persuade her that Odysseus will never return and that he should be chosen to be the next king in Odysseus's place. After many years, Penelope's argument that Odysseus will return falls on deaf ears, and she agrees to choose a suitor, on one condition. She is weaving a tapestry, and she will not choose a suitor until she has finished her weaving. Each day she weaves all day long, giving the suitors hope, but then each night she unravels the work she has done that day. As she works, the stories depicted on the tapestry are "written" and "rewritten" each day, symbolizing the way in which clever Penelope and Odysseus are actively trying to write their own story.

Finally, through much travail, Odysseus arrives on the shores of Ithaka. He has lost all his men and all the treasure he accumulated on his journey. He arrives in his own land as a beggar king, in rags and with no retinue to announce and protect him. He must approach his halls with caution. If he declares himself king, the pretenders will surely slay him. Athena leads him to his one true and faithful servant, Eumaeus the swineherd, who has faithfully awaited his lord's return, lamenting the lavish feasting of the suitors that has decimated Odysseus's livestock. Odysseus dares not reveal himself even to the swineherd, but Eumaeus, who has so longed for his lord's return, will not be deceived and quickly pledges his assistance. (Despite his subterfuge, all who love Odysseus recognize him.) Together, they arrange for an interview with his nursemaid, who recognizes him by a scar on his leg. Several others, including his old dog, recognize him and signal their allegiance. Odysseus proves to the kingdom that he is who he claims to be by performing a feat only he could do. Then he and his son and a few faithful servants drive out the suitors, killing many of them. There remains then only one person to persuade of his identity, the woman who has ruled in his stead for two decades. Penelope asks him a question about their bed, which is built from a living tree planted in their bedroom, a fact only he would know. The two schemers are reunited at last. Together with his son, Telemachus, and his father, Laertes, Odysseus battles those who sought to depose him. Laertes strikes down their leader, and then Athena intervenes, urging the combatants to wisdom and terms of peace. Odysseus gladly accepts this advice, and his return to his kingdom, led by Athena, is concluded.

Like *The Iliad*, *The Odyssey* has had many echoes throughout history. Indeed, though *The Iliad* has certainly had a profound influence on Western thought and literature, the influence of *The Odyssey* is much more apparent, especially in later works of myth and modern fantasy. The movie *O Brother, Where Art Thou?* was very loosely based on *The Odyssey*, for instance. Its themes of persistent faithfulness, cleverness, and recognition are timeless. And, unlike *The Iliad*, the title of *The Odyssey* has entered our language as a word describing an arduous and fantastic journey. Moreover, the arduous and fantastic journey has itself become a hallmark of much of modern fantasy literature, and more generally of adventure literature. Consider the number of fantasy titles that center around quests. Both *The Hobbit* and *The Lord of the Rings* are quests (or in the latter case an antiquest) involving arduous and fantastic journeys. So is the tale of Beren and Lúthien, the central story in *The Silmarillion*. Terry Brooks's *The Sword of Shannara* is another such quest. So are *The Horse and His Boy, The Silver Chair,* and *The Voyage of the Dawn Treader*—three of the seven books in Lewis's *Chronicles of Narnia*. And every book in both of Stephen Donaldson's *Chronicles of Thomas Covenant* involves an arduous and fantastic journey. The list is endless.

If we look at something else at the heart of all of these adventures, we will also find them pointing back to *The Odyssey* in yet another way. The very word *adventure* comes from the Latin *advenio*, which means "to arrive." Of course, in order to return, one must first leave home. Why? Because adventures rarely happen at home. One goes away to have adventures. Does this belief that faraway places are where strange things happen and strange people live arise out of xenophobia or an ignorant fear of the outside world? These stories engender wanderlust in all but the most timid and spark curiosity in all but the most insipid. In every one of these stories, the tacit question is, Even when the results are tragic, is it not better to have embarked on the quest than to have stayed at home? Achilles could have lived a long life and died in the comfort of his bed, but he is remembered because he chose a short life and glory. While Penelope's failed and spurned suitors stayed in Ithaka, their king, Odysseus, sailed to war against Troy. The suitors sought glory at home: by courting the queen they hoped to rise on her merits. Their fate is infamy, dissatisfaction, and death. (When Odysseus sailed, he left behind two types of people, and time showed them for what they were: the faithless cowards and the faithful who were too young or too old to fight abroad. The whole tale of *The Odyssey*—and of the myths and tales it inspired—is shot through with the importance of faithfulness.) Adventures are costly, but they are also good. The military exploits are not glorified; Odysseus came home with nothing and lost the whole fighting strength of Ithaka in his return voyage. But he returned to Penelope, and his loyal dog and swineherd, and with the help of grey-eyed Athena.

Which raises another point. Ultimately, the great adventures end with a homecoming. Home is the final "arrival" that defines the *advenio*. And yet it is a homecoming, like Odysseus's, where something has changed; it is not the home that the hero left. It has been correctly argued that the most important imaginative influences for *The Hobbit*—from the names of the dwarves, to the character of the dragon Smaug, to the were-bear Beorn, to the Misty Mountains beneath which lives a monster—are from the Old Norse and Anglo-Saxon. But Bilbo's return to the Shire to find his home taken over, his possessions being ransacked, and his identity questioned bears resemblance to no postadventure return so much as it does to that of Odysseus. Certainly Bilbo's return is described in a much more comic and lighthearted tone than that of his Greek inspiration, but the similarities cannot be missed, and the possibility of an intermediate source between *The Odyssey* and *The Hobbit* only strengthens the argument of the former's influence.

Then, also, Odysseus's quest to find his home again raises the question of what makes any given place a home. Several times, Odysseus is offered wealth, comfort, and permanent lodgings in other lands. When he finally arrives back in Ithaka, he is destitute but glad to have returned. What makes Ithaka so worth returning to, especially at such great cost and after so long? The answer is that it is his home, and no other place will do. Like Bilbo's journey to the lonely mountain, or Thoreau's walks to "Oregon" and "The Holy Land" (he actually visited neither but referred to his walks in the woods as travels to these places), we usually think of our trips as round ones, and the travels are given meaning by the return. As du Bellay wrote, "Happy is he, who like Ulysses—or like him who captured the Golden Fleece—and then returned, full of usage and reason, to live with his family for the remainder of his years."[5] The writer of the book of Hebrews gives a similar account of Abraham, who left his birth home in search of his true home and was willing to endure any hardships and travels in order finally to arrive "at the city with foundations" (Heb. 11:10). The fact that this narrative occurs on three levels makes it even richer. Penelope is a rare strong female lead in ancient poetry, just as capable and clever as her husband. Odysseus would be helpless were it not for the woman and the goddess who assist him along the way, subtly raising the question of whether male political dominance is natural or a perversion of the way things ought to be.[6]

Myth and History in the Ancient World

Hopefully, by this point the persistent influence of Greek myth in general and Homer in particular is clear. "Achilles' heel," the one weakness of the otherwise invulnerable body of *The Iliad's* greatest warrior, is still a catchphrase in today's society. The notion shows up again and again in literature, sometimes in very surprising places, such as in the one bare spot in the otherwise impenetrable armor of a famous dragon named Smaug in *The Hobbit*. There are also certain echoes of Agamemnon and Hector in the characters of Lord Denethor and King Théoden. The former is an overly proud ruler of an ancient kingdom undoubtedly modeled after Rome, while the latter is a humbled ruler and horse lord, or "breaker of horses," who dies in battle before the gates of the ancient city. Of course, Denethor and Théoden are not enemies, but Tolkien's narrative suggests that Denethor is in some way responsible for Théoden's death. Yet even these influences are somewhat superficial. The influence of Greek myth runs deeper and pertains to all of modern thought—especially the ideas that run deepest through much or most of modern fantasy, for isn't all of the discussion of heroism in the Homeric epics shot through by Faërie?

5. Our loose translation of the opening lines of Joachim du Bellay's sixteenth-century sonnet "Heureux qui, comme Ulysse."
6. This is, of course, suggested by Gen. 3:16, where an exclusively male rule is a consequence of the Fall.

Though in modern times we make a sharp distinction between myth and history, it was not altogether plain to the ancients what the difference between them was. We don't often realize how much the science of history has changed since then, or how much it depends on our worldview. In the modern West we have come to think of history as linear and teleological or purposive. That is, it moves in a definite direction and toward some end. But this view is very much influenced by Judaism and Christianity, both of which emphasize the implication of God in history, choosing and directing the course of events for a predetermined purpose. In the ancient world of Europe and the Near East, history was often viewed as cyclical or nonteleological, and many cultures today still retain this view. While Westerners tend to agree that history is linear (so that it makes sense to record history and to number the years, for instance), there is often sharp disagreement in the West over whether there is any purpose to history. Utopian visions of history (Marxism, for instance) often assume that the only purpose in history is the one we give to it; eschatological visions (most Christian views, for instance) conceive of history as being given a purpose from a force or forces outside history; and physicalist views such as are often common among scientists conceive of history as being without purpose and without the possibility of intentional change. (This is a large part of the disagreement between advocates of "intelligent design" and Darwinists.) Without a linear and purposive vision of history, there is little incentive to write history. How, then, does one learn the lessons of the past?

In the fifth and fourth centuries BC, it occurred to several writers that detailed accounts of the arguments and battles between Persians and Greeks and between Athenians and Spartans would be of benefit for later readers. In particular, Thucydides, author of the *Peloponnesian War*, hoped his writings would be a *ktema es aei*, that is, a heritage unto the ages. What distinguishes his writing from other writings is an attention to descriptive detail, especially to speeches and natural events. In such endeavors the discipline of history was slowly born, though it did not come into full flower for many centuries.

Meanwhile, the dominant mode of passing on wisdom remained mythic poetry. It is not uncommon to dismiss this as prescientific ignorance, but it is in fact quite brilliant. It is no surprise that psychology and philosophy in the twentieth century made continued forays into ancient myth for inspiration (witness Freud, Bettelheim, and Camus, for instance). Poetry is easily memorized, especially when sung, and stories are tremendously effective means of transmitting information, especially information that

pertains to the conduct of life. Poems, in short, make excellent moral teaching tools. This practice continues in hymn-singing in modern churches
and in the singing of national anthems, and it is—whether we wish it or
not—a fact about contemporary music. When we sing, we tell stories that
shape our moral lives, for good or for ill. What's more, when the Greeks
wrote down their myths, they captured the truth of both teleological and
nontelic views of history. Cyclical views of history are correct inasmuch
as they emphasize history as a source of wisdom—we can learn from
the stories of those who went before us. Stories generally are not wholly
cyclical, however. The return trip is not wholly a round one, in the end,
since the hero usually returns to find that he has undergone a conversion
while he has been abroad. The home may not have changed, but it never
looks the same again. In a way, the myths are truer than history.

Myth and National Identity

In our times, history and precedent play a large role in shaping our national identities, in jurisprudence, and in international relations. Without
a modern sense of history, ancient peoples needed some way of telling
them who they were. Homer's two epics begin and end in Achaea, or
Greece. They tell the story of who the Greeks were, over against the
peoples to the East. In later times, when Persian armies crossed the
Bosporus to invade Greece, they left from the area around ancient Troy.
By that time Homer's epics were several centuries old, but the story of
the many Greek peoples uniting to fight a menacing people to the East
may well be part of what helped the Greeks to become the first people
to successfully resist Persian military might.

Centuries later, the Roman poet Virgil retold the story of the founding
of Rome by appealing to Homer as well. His *Aeneid* recounts the story
of Aeneas's escape from Troy with a few ships while the Greek armies
destroyed the city, and of his eventual travels (somewhat in the vein of
Odysseus's travels) to the west coast of Italy, where he eventually founded
Rome. In turn, centuries later Dante made Virgil his guide through his
Inferno and *Purgatorio,* until he finally reached his heavenly home. Dante
wrote his fantastic *Divine Comedy* while he was living in exile. For Dante,
Virgil's epic continuation of Homer could be wedded seamlessly to the
Abrahamic longing for "the city with foundations."

So even in Dante's time, when history writing had begun to flourish, the myth gave a sense of what one's place in history is. Myths show

the world to be charged with meaning, and they convey the weight and wisdom of the ages to new generations.

Ancient Myth, Religion, and Morality

In ancient Athens, myth-making and myth-celebrating were part of the religious life of the community. There was very little difference between the religion of the state and the state itself. The plays offered in the Golden Age of Athens were staged in competitions that were both dramatic and religious festivals, and playwrights competed for prizes before a panel of judges. The whole population of the city would attend the plays, and the actors and choruses (actors or groups of actors who would act as narrators) would often speak prayers to the gods as part of the dialogue. These plays helped to pass on the ancient myths by retelling them in often novel ways, and always with an eye to celebrating the strengths of the community or urging the community to move in a new direction. For instance, Aristophanes' often bawdy comedies contain trenchant and barbed political commentaries that urge Athens not to lose sight of its strengths in their wars against Sparta.

The consistent element in the plays is that they nearly all derive from episodes in Homer. His epics were the "Bible" of Athens. This analogy should not be understood too strictly, however. By it we mean that his poems were the source of nearly all other mythology and were not to be lightly tampered with. However, their authority is nowhere near the authority ascribed to the Bible by post-Reformation Protestantism. It is more like the precanon scriptures in the very early church: authoritative, but subject to additions as other texts were written.

These plays often attempted to illustrate dramatically the importance of moral decisions, and of the moral heritage of Athens. Sophocles' famous *Oedipus* cycle, for instance, has been frequently compared to the biblical book of Job. (Some scholars suggest that they share a common literary source.) The question raised by all three of the plays in the cycle is, What constitutes human legal and moral obligation? Is a man guilty who commits a crime or a sin unwittingly? Can anyone mediate between humans and the gods when sins have been committed? Aeschylus's *Oresteia* asks a similar question and points to the importance of the famed Athenian respect for rational law.

Ancient Myth and the Rise of Science and Philosophy

Just as the myths helped to shape the way nations and peoples understood themselves, they also spurred the rise of philosophy and science. Plato and Aristotle, the great Athenian philosopher-scientists, spent considerable time dwelling on the myths, and Plato wrote and retold a number of myths in his philosophic writings. Aristotle devoted one of his treatises, *The Poetics,* to a study of dramatic mythopoeisis. Aristotle spent his life studying the rational principles of the cosmos and wrote extensively on medicine, theology, political science, ethics, physics, astronomy, biology, and metaphysics. His thought and Plato's have become deeply wedded to modern theology and serve as much of the basis of modern science. Yet when he retired to his estate at Chalcis, he wrote to a friend that as he became older and more alone, he became more and more fond of myths, which provided for him a solace that other texts apparently could not.

Ancient Myth and Early Christianity

Although we could say much more about ancient myth (and, indeed, have given it only a summary treatment here), we will limit this chapter to just one more point. We've just mentioned that contemporary Christian theology owes a tremendous debt to Platonic and Aristotelian thought. It is also the case that Christian thought owes a debt to ancient myth, though this debt is not so easily traced. We do not mean to say that Christian thought is dependent on pagan mythical conceptions of the divine, or anything of that sort. Rather, Christianity grew up in a world that was infused with pagan Greek and Roman myths, and much of Christian thought developed as a response to it. When Paul entered Athens, and especially when he spoke to the educated elites atop the Areopagus (Acts 17), he drew on what he knew of Athenian culture to present the Christian message to the pagan Athenians. What he saw there was that even in their myths the truth of the Gospels was already largely present.

When Augustine, the great fourth-century African bishop, wrote his famous *Confessions,* he changed the face of Western literature forever. His style was unique and unparalleled, and his first-person prayerful autobiography became the model for all confessional literature that followed it. Augustine frequently mentions the ways in which Roman and Greek myths formed his preconversion moral life and how he rejected the pagan myths when he became a Christian. All this is fairly well known. What is not so well known is that the story itself has a parallel in the *Golden Ass* of Apuleius, a story Augustine knew and read before he wrote his own *Confessions*. Apuleius's early Roman novel is, like Augustine's *Confessions,* a story of conversion. The protagonist, Lucius, sneaks into a witch's house and uses one of her potions to turn himself into a bird, for a little fun. He chooses the wrong potion, however, and instead turns himself into an ass. He is soon stolen by thieves and forced to labor for them (a strong parallel to Collodi's later *Pinocchio,* and one of the main sources, along with Ovid's *Metamorphoses,* of stories of transformation). After many adventures, he finally succeeds in turning back into a man, and he offers worship to the goddess Isis for having saved him.

Augustine's autobiography tells a story that imitates many of the themes of Apuleius's tale. As a youth, Augustine also sought only his own pleasure and became (figuratively) an ass who did evil for its own sake. When he chose to sin, he too was taken and enslaved by his sin and by forces beyond his control. He too was constantly in peril, until God came to save him. Although Apuleius was not a Christian (and mocked Christianity), his praise to Isis is not wholly unlike the praise a Christian like Augustine would ascribe to his God. Augustine was a brilliant rhetorician. Although he does not openly claim to have imitated Apuleius, it seems at least possible that he saw in Apuleius's bawdy tale an inkling of the truth. Recognizing that Apuleius's fantasy was a popular story that many people would read, Augustine may have combined his love of the gospel and his brilliance for preaching with Apuleius's formula. The result was a novel way of telling the gospel in the first person. Augustine's story is so powerfully and beautifully told that it is still a staple in college classrooms. There may be a lesson there.

5

Beowulf to Arthur

Medieval Legend and Romance

It seems fairly plain that Arthur, once historical (but perhaps
as such not of great importance), was also put in the Pot.
There he was boiled for a long time, together with many other
older figures and devices, of mythology and Faërie, and even
some other stray bones of history . . . until he emerged as a
King of Faërie.

J. R. R. Tolkien, *On Fairy-Stories*

There are many things in the Cauldron, but the Cooks do not
dip in the ladle quite blindly.

J. R. R. Tolkien, *On Fairy-Stories*

Michael Drout, editor of the *Journal of Tolkien Studies*, began
a recent lecture (Drout) with an interesting reminder. He
pointed out that scholars of J. R. R. Tolkien have long held the belief that

Beowulf (the heroic Scandinavian figure from the Old English poem of the same name) must appear somewhere in *The Lord of the Rings;* the problem is that nobody has been able to find him. What Drout and these other scholars mean is that Tolkien was so powerfully influenced by the poem *Beowulf,* and his works so deeply rooted in the Germanic and Norse legend, that he *must* have incorporated the poem's main character *somewhere* in his famous trilogy.

Consider first that Tolkien was a noted scholar of Anglo-Saxon, the language of this poem. One of his most famous scholarly works was his essay "Beowulf: The Monsters and the Critics." This essay is considered by many to be the most influential essay ever written on the poem, and one of the things the essay argues for is the importance of the superhuman aspects of its hero. Tolkien argues that fantasy *ought* to contain not only monsters, such as the giant Grendel, Grendel's mother, and the dragon, but heroes like Beowulf.

> We do not deny the worth of the hero by accepting Grendel and the dragon. Let us by all means esteem the old heroes: men caught in the chains of circumstance or of their own character, torn between duties equally sacred, dying with their backs to the wall. (*Monsters,* 17)

Beowulf the hero was also one of the three central subjects of another of Tolkien's more important essays: "The Homecoming of Beorhtnoth Beorhthelm's Son." In that latter essay, Tolkien discusses both the glory and the shortcomings of the "northern heroic spirit, Norse or English" (see *Homecoming*). Gawain, Beorhtnoth's loyal retainers, and the *young* Beowulf are examples of the finest of this northern Germanic heroic spirit. King Arthur, Beorhtnoth, and the *old* Beowulf, by contrast, are examples of the excessive desire for glory that is the downside of Germanic chivalry. Beowulf is the only character in the essay appearing as an example of both aspects of the Germanic hero. Given what Tolkien as a scholar said of the importance of Beowulf as hero, one would thus expect that Tolkien as a writer of heroic fantasy would include a Beowulf figure.

In addition to Tolkien's scholarly pursuits, we must take into account his passions. From as long as he could remember, Tolkien was a lover of Norse myth and of heroic Germanic (including Old English) literature, and more broadly of anything capturing the essence or atmosphere of Northern Europe. He writes, in "On Fairy-Stories," of his own early love for this material: "But the land of Merlin and Arthur was better than [that of pirates and American Indians], and best of all the nameless North of

Sigurd of the Völsungs, and the prince of all dragons. Such lands were pre-eminently desirable" (63). Not surprisingly, therefore, when seeking to create a mythology for England, Tolkien explicitly aimed to capture something of that Norseness. He wrote of his *Legendarium:*

> It should possess the tone and quality that I desired, somewhat cool and clear, be redolent of our "air" (the clime and soil of the North West, meaning Britain and the hither parts of Europe: not Italy or the Aegean, still less the East), and . . . [possess] (if I could achieve it) the fair elusive beauty that some call Celtic (though it is rarely found in genuine ancient Celtic things). (*Letters*, 144)

The poem *Beowulf,* whose heroes are Scandinavian but which was written in Old English, provides a wonderful mix of these northern traditions. Again, if Tolkien sought to capture that tone in his own *Legendarium*, what better way than to include a character analogous to Beowulf?

Then, too, we have the unmistakable presence of Beowulfian plot devices in both *The Hobbit* and *The Lord of the Rings.* The whole quest in *The Hobbit*—the quest to rid a once fair kingdom of an evil monster that now plagues it—is lifted directly from *Beowulf,* as is the device of having the dragon awoken to a rage by a thief stealing a cup. This is just one of the more obvious examples in *The Hobbit;* Tolkien and Beowulf scholars have found several more. There are some examples in *The Lord of the Rings* as well. In *Following Gandalf,* Dickerson comments that the welcome "given to Gandalf, Aragorn, Gimli, and Legolas by the guards at the gates of Edoras . . . is borrowed almost directly from the welcome given to Beowulf and his warriors by the beach-guards when they arrive at Heorot" (Dickerson, 31). Indeed, this is evidence (along with names, linguistic issues, and poetry in Rohan) to support Drout's assertion that despite Tolkien's protestations to the contrary, the Rohirrim are Anglo-Saxons. Drout's conclusion is the obvious one.

> Since *Beowulf* is in Old English, and since there is Old English in Lord of the Rings, and since Tolkien was such an expert on *Beowulf* . . . it stands to reason that *Beowulf* would have been an important influence on The Lord of the Rings. (Drout)

In fact, this conclusion is understated. Drout expects to find not only *Beowulf* the poem in *The Lord of the Rings* (it can be found at least in the guard's speech) but to find Beowulf the hero there as well.

However, every attempt to identify *one particular* character from *The Lord of the Rings* as *the* Beowulf figure has failed. The attempts to analogize have failed in much the same way that attempts to impose an allegorical interpretation have failed; although several characters—Théoden, Éomer, Aragorn, and Boromir, to name a few—share *some* traits in common with Beowulf, each one taken separately and individually also differs from Beowulf in substantive ways.

Nonetheless, that this assumption is so widely held by so many scholars is powerful testimony to the influence of the poem *Beowulf* on Tolkien, and hints more generally to the influence (direct or indirect) of medieval Germanic legend and romance on all of modern fantasy literature. This chapter explores that influence by examining a handful of important pieces of that literature focusing primarily on *Beowulf*, but including also the Scandinavian *Edda* recorded by Snorri Sturluson, and the famous legend of King Arthur.

The Cauldron of Story and Beowulf in Tolkien

To begin this exploration, we must return to Tolkien's essay "On Fairy-Stories" and examine the notion of the Cauldron of Story that we mentioned in our second chapter. Borrowing an image from Dasent's *Popular Tales from the Norse,* Tolkien refers to story as a *soup containing bones:* the soup is "the story as it is served up by its author or teller," and the bones are "its sources and material."[1] This Pot of Soup, also called the Cauldron of Story, is that massive kettle that contains all of Story that has ever been told, especially Story that borders on myth and Faërie. Tolkien writes that the pot "has always been boiling, and to it have continually been added new bits, dainty and undainty." What are these bits? Certainly the soup contains some history. But it also contains legends, fairy tales, and myths. And once a bit of history has been thrown into that pot, it becomes bigger and more important by virtue of *having been in the pot.* To be thrown into the pot (as a historical character), Tolkien explains, is "a considerable honour, for in that soup [are] many things older, more potent, more beautiful, comic, or terrible than they were in themselves (considered simply as figures of history)" (*Essay,* 29–30).

1. As with many other sources, Tolkien borrowed the image of soup but then improved upon it. For Dasent (according to Tolkien) the "soup" was the "mishmash of bogus pre-history founded on the early surmises of Comparative Philology," and the "bones" were the "workings and the proofs that led to these theories." (See *Essay,* 22–23, 28–32)

One example Tolkien gives is Charlemagne's mother, Bertha Broadfoot. Four centuries after Bertha's life, stories were told of her that resemble Grimms' tale "The Goose-girl." This doesn't mean that the stories are false but suggests instead that "Bertha was turned into the Goosegirl." Bertha, and various stories about her, were "put into the Pot, in fact got into the Soup [as] new bits added to the stock." What went into the pot was a real figure of history, Bertha; what came out, after the stories of Bertha had simmered in the Cauldron of Story itself, was the Goose-girl of the Grimms' fairy tale. But if a once-historical figure comes out of the pot with the flavor of Faërie—if she becomes "more potent, more beautiful, comic, or terrible" than she was as a historical figure, then we know that something more than mere history is in the pot to impart its flavor. What is in the pot is Faërie itself, myth and fantasy, the most important and potent of all Story. This "fairy-tale element," Tolkien argues, is always there in the cauldron, "waiting for the great figures of Myth and History, and for the yet nameless He or She, waiting for the moment when they are cast into the simmering stew, one by one or all together, without consideration of rank or precedence" (*Essay*, 29–30).

Perhaps the best example of the simmering of history and fairy—of the nameless He becoming the famous Hero—is King Arthur, the King Arthur who has been served out of the pot by countless authors over the past millennium. Tolkien writes:

> It seems fairly plain that Arthur, once historical (but perhaps as such not of great importance), was also put in the Pot. There he was boiled for a long time, together with many other older figures and devices, of mythology and Faërie, and even some other stray bones of history (such as Alfred's defense against the Danes), until he emerged as a King of Faërie. (*Essay*, 30)

The point, as Tolkien makes clear, is that what goes into the pot is not necessarily what comes out. There is a flavor imparted to these bits by the broth, and by all of the bones that are simmering in it. The longer something stays in the pot, the more it takes on this flavor. The various King Arthurs who have been served out of the pot—those of Thomas Mallory, Wolfram von Eschenbach, Chrétien de Troyes, and the *Gawain and the Green Knight* poet, as well as the more modern Arthurs of Marion Zimmer Bradley, Mary Stewart, Roger Lancelyn Green, Stephen Lawhead, and T. H. White—are among the most flavorful and influential figures of legend in all of Western literature.

Of course as soon as we use the word *served,* we imply that the cook—the writer or teller of the story—is also an important figure in the process, almost though not quite as important as the broth itself. "But if we speak of a Cauldron," Tolkien tells us, "we must not wholly forget the Cooks." He goes on to explain:

> There are many things in the Cauldron, but the Cooks do not dip in the ladle quite blindly. Their selection is important. The gods are after all gods, and it is a matter of some moment what stories are told of them. So we must freely admit that a tale of love is more likely to be told of a prince in history, indeed is more likely actually to happen in an historical family whose traditions are those of Golden Frey and the Vanir, rather than those of Odin the Goth, the Necromancer, glutter of the crows, Lord of the Slain. Small wonder that *spell* means both a story told, and a formula of power over living men. (*Essay,* 31–32)

Returning to *Beowulf,* we note that the poem's hero was added to the cauldron the moment his story was first sung at the end of the day in some Germanic mead hall. Indeed, *Beowulf* the poem and Beowulf the hero are very important ingredients in the soup. It would be difficult—probably impossible—for a modern fantasy author to ladle out a bowl of soup without getting any bones from *Beowulf,* at least as difficult as getting a ladle that had no Tolkienian bones and bits.

Nonetheless, the dipping isn't blind. As mentioned earlier, the story-teller is weaving a spell. The effective *spell*—that which really carries power over the living men and women and children who hear the tale—must be carefully ladled. Does the spell-maker wish to tell a tale of love? If so, he will be careful to ladle out the bones of some prince like Arthur, and not those of one of Odin's Berserkers, even if both have been simmering together in the same broth. This makes it more difficult to find *exactly* where various bits occur, as is the case with Tolkien and *Beowulf.*

As Drout notes, the obvious place to look for Beowulf is in Rohan, where Tolkien's Anglo-Saxon warriors live. Théoden and Éomer are the best choices here. King Théoden is like Beowulf in that he lives a long life as king, and at the end of his life goes into battle against a monstrous enemy (the Lord of the Nazgûl) and is defeated and killed. As with Beowulf, Théoden's enemy is also vanquished thanks to the bravery of a loyal retainer and kinsperson (his niece Éowyn) who refuses to flee from the terror. His hall, Meduseld (an Anglo-Saxon word for "mead hall"), is very much in the tradition of the Danish mead hall Heorot that the hero Beowulf rescues, and the Anglo-Saxon mead halls in which the poem *Beowulf* would have been sung. However, a very important aspect of *Beowulf* is that the death of King Beowulf results in the destruction of his kingdom and the end of the Geatish people. In sharp contrast to this, King Théoden's brave ride into battle, though costing him his own life, results in the *salvation* of his nation of Rohan. Thus Théoden departs from Beowulf in at least one very significant way. Éomer works even less well. He faces no monstrous enemy alone, and the story concludes long before his death.

Aragorn and Boromir also share some of Beowulf's heroic traits, including his prowess in battle. Boromir, like the medieval hero whose name alliterates with his (an important feature in Old English poetry) has strength bordering on superhuman, shows pride in his battle prowess, and dies in battle against monstrous orcs. Éomer even comments that Boromir was "more like to the swift sons of Eorl" (Tolkien's Anglo-Saxons) "than to the grave men of Gondor" (Tolkien's Classical Romans) (III/ii). Boromir seeks personal glory, and he seeks it largely on the battlefield, much like Beowulf. However, Boromir does not live a long life and never rules as king. Aragorn is more like the Old English hero in that he also rises from obscurity to become a king. In the process, Aragorn must also endure the scorn of a better-known warrior, who is close in counsel with the current ruler of his kingdom; for Aragorn it is Boromir, the son of the steward, while for Beowulf it is Unferth. However, Aragorn does not show Beowulf's desire for glory, nor does Aragorn's death come in battle.

Before giving an answer to this riddle, we return for a moment to Tolkien's earlier work. Though the figure of Beowulf may be difficult to find in *The Lord of the Rings,* he is not at all difficult to locate in *The Hobbit.* In *J. R. R. Tolkien: Author of the Century,* Tom Shippey makes a good case for understanding Beorn as an obvious Beowulf figure. The clearest hint can be found in Beowulf's name. As Shippey points out, the name *Beowulf* is translated literally to "bee-wolf," but *wolf* is another name for a thief (Scandinavian Vikings were sometimes called "Sea-wolves"); hence, Beowulf is a robber of bees, which, as readers of *Winnie-the-Pooh* will tell you, is a bear (Shippey, 31–32). Beorn, of course, is literally a bear, or bear-man, or were-bear. Like Beowulf, he possesses superhuman strength and dwells in a perfect model of a medieval mead hall. That such a clear and unmistakable Beowulf figure is present in *The Hobbit* is another reason why so many scholars expect to find him in the trilogy.

Indeed, it has been argued that there are several Beowulf characters in *The Hobbit.* Bilbo and Thorin, lacking the strength of Beowulf (and

Beorn), are less obvious models but are still well worth considering. With Bilbo, the hint is again in the names. As Dickerson argues in *Following Gandalf,*

> Bilbo lacks Beowulf's superhuman strength, but he gains through the Ring some measure of superhuman abilities. . . . It is also Bilbo . . . who aids Bard in slaying the dragon. Finally, Bilbo is himself a bee-thief like Beowulf—though with a little twist typical of many of Tolkien's philological jokes. Rather than being a thief *of* bees as Beowulf the bear is, Bilbo is a thief (a burglar to be exact) who is a bee (he carries a Sting). (Dickerson, 205)

We could add to this list the fact that Bilbo, like Beowulf, refuses to slay his monstrous but unarmed enemy Gollum (whose name alliterates with *Grendel*) with a sword, because it would not be a fair fight. Thus, Bilbo represents something of Beowulf's heroic attributes devoid of his larger-than-life size; that is, Bilbo shows how the common man can be a hero like Beowulf. Lastly, Thorin himself is yet another sort of a Beowulf character.[2] Here the connection is made through the plot, rather than through philology. Thorin, like Beowulf,

> is the descendant of the great kings of old, who leads a group of fourteen companions (if you count Gandalf) on a quest in which they face several monsters, culminating with the dragon who is woken to a rage by a thief. The dragon is slain, but Thorin also dies and is buried with his great sword and with treasure taken from the worm's hoard. (Dickerson, 204)

Both Thorin and Beowulf die and are buried as kings. As Bilbo represents the courage and heroic virtue of Beowulf apart from the superhuman strength, so Thorin represents the excessive pride of Beowulf devoid (until the very end of his life) of the heroic virtue. When Beorn, Bilbo, and Thorin are taken together, we have the strength, fearlessness in battle, courage, cunning, and also the excesses of the hero Beowulf.

It is the threefold presence of Beowulf in *The Hobbit*—the character of Beowulf *spread out* among Beorn, Bilbo, and Thorin—much more than in the one strong Beowulf figure of Beorn alone, that gives us the strongest hint of where to look for him in *The Lord of the Rings*. Michael Drout gives one other important hint as well; he notes that Tolkien in *The Monsters*

---

2. Here again we comment that Thorin, even more so than Beorn, owes much more to Old Norse than to *Beowulf* and Old English. This will be touched upon in the next section on the *Prose Edda*.

and the Critics draws an important parallel between the fairy-tale hero Beowulf and the historical figure of Oswald.[3] Oswald may have been one of those historical characters who simmered in the Pot and contributed to Beowulf. So to see where to find a Beowulf character in *The Lord of the Rings*, we must understand what Tolkien thought were the important elements of the hero in the poem, and we understand these by looking at the parallels Tolkien made with Oswald. To say this all more simply, we can look for Beowulf by looking for Oswald. As Drout summarizes, Oswald returned from obscurity in exile in the monastery at Iona to unite two kingdoms and defeat (against great odds) a pagan king who had been terrorizing Northumbria, but eight years later "is killed in a dramatic battle against a horrible foe." Putting these two hints together, Drout effectively argues that Beowulf can be found in the trilogy not by exploring any one character, but only when several characters—Aragorn, Théoden, and Éomer—are taken as a whole. (We would add to that list Boromir, for reasons stated above.)

> I think [Tolkien] took the attributes of Beowulf the character and spread them through Aragorn, Eomer and Theoden. Each character in *Lord of the Rings* has some key similarities to Beowulf, but each is also different. Thus Tolkien can with a straight face deny the influence of Beowulf on *Lord of the Rings* when at the same time make use of all his Anglo-Saxon source material—which includes Beowulf. (Drout)

As a final note, Drout's suggestion of why Tolkien took this approach also gives insight into our broader understanding of modern fantasy and how it uses its roots:

> This technique of taking the attributes of medieval characters and dividing them among multiple *Lord of the Rings* characters is necessary, I believe, in order to make a modern audience accept the characters in *Lord of the Rings*. A true analogue of Beowulf, with all of Beowulf's bravado, fearlessness, and legalistic perfection, would be too scary to a Modern audience. We wouldn't trust him. (Drout)

Having seen that one Germanic poem (*Beowulf*), written in Old English with Scandinavian heroes, is an important source for a pair of works (*The*

---

3. Drout discovered just how important this parallel was when he edited an earlier, longer draft of the essay and saw that Tolkien's original parallel was not to Oswald but to Alfred. See *J. R. R. Tolkien's Beowulf and the Critics*, ed. Michael Drout, *Medieval and Renaissance Texts and Studies* 248 (2002).

Hobbit and *The Lord of the Rings*), we now have a strong model for how to explore the cauldron for further influence. We would like to generalize this observation in two directions: from *Beowulf* to the bones and bits added to the soup by a broader array of Norse and Germanic myth, legend, and romance; and also from Tolkien as cook to what has been ladled out by other modern fantasy authors. The latter task will largely be taken up in the second part of this book. The first task we take up in the remainder of this chapter. We look at what a Christian poet did with the Germanic source material in composing *Beowulf,* and then at the later medieval romance of Arthur (also by and large the work of Christian imaginations), but first it is helpful to explore some other aspects of Germanic myth and legend.

The *Prose Edda* and Scandinavian Myth

Just as there is no doubt that Tolkien was strongly influenced by *Beowulf,* it is also clear that he was influenced by Norse mythology, and especially by the *Prose Edda* and the work of Snorri Sturluson.[4] Sturluson, a twelfth-century Icelandic Christian, is one of the main sources of our knowledge of Norse myth. Sturluson wrote his *Edda* and *King Harald's Saga,* apparently, in an attempt to preserve the ancient Scandinavian myths that were already dying out in his time. The Norse world had so warmly embraced Christianity that the stories of the old gods were no longer being told. Sturluson seems to have recognized that these stories, though incomplete without the Christian revelation, were nevertheless an important part of the great Story. His opening lines of the *Prose Edda* indicate as much, tying the Norse myths together with the Greek and Roman myths and with the Gospels. The Norse myths could be seen as advance messengers of the Gospels, preparing the Norse to receive the Good News when it arrived.

While Beorn of *The Hobbit* is certainly a Beowulf character, he also has aspects derived from the Old Norse *Böthvarr Bjarki* from *The Saga of Hrolf Kraki.*[5] Tom Shippey explains that Böthvarr is "a clear analogue

4. In a personal letter written in 1967 to W. H. Auden, Tolkien suggests that his own earliest work in writing alliterative poetry was an attempt to unify the lays based on the *Poetic Edda,* written in old eight-line *fornyrðislag* stanza (*Letters,* 379). Sturluson's *Edda*s were composed in the twelfth and thirteenth centuries, drawing on much older material.

5. This may be an instance of the older tales having themselves drawn source material from the Pot, as well of Tolkien's skill in synthesizing and improving upon material. As Shippey notes in *Author of the*

to Beowulf in what he does. . . . His nickname Bjarki means 'little bear.' . . . It is pretty clear that Böthvarr is in some ways or other a bear: in fact, a were-bear." He goes on to add that Beorn's name "is the Old English 'cognate,' or equivalent, of Böthvarr's father's, Bjarni, and in Old English it means 'man': but it used to mean 'bear,' taken over and humanized" (Shippey, 31–32). Likewise, the dwarves of *The Hobbit* are directly inspired by the *Prose Edda*. The list of dwarf names in "The Deluding of Gylfi" (part of the *Prose Edda*) includes: Dvalin, Bifur, Báfur, Bömbör, Nori, Óin, Fili, Kili, Glóin, Dóri, Óri, and Thorin. As most readers of this book recognize, these (with a few minor changes in spelling) are the names of all but one of the dwarves who go questing with Bilbo Baggins. (Only *Balin* appears as an original name in Tolkien's work.) Also in the Eddic list are Thrór and Dáin, other important dwarves in Tolkien's Middle-earth. Of course, Durin, one of the two most important dwarves in the *Prose Edda*, is the name of one of the Seven Fathers of the Dwarves in Tolkien's *Legendarium*, and the most renowned of their race. As for the character of the dwarves, it is told in "The Deluding of Gylfi" that "they acquired human understanding and the appearance of men, although they lived in the earth and in rocks" (*Edda*, 41–42). In that way, at least, Tolkien was drawing upon the Eddic tradition, though in other ways his dwarves are his own creations.

Perhaps more interesting is another name that appears in the list: *Ganndálf.* The appearance of the name *Ganndálf* in this list of dwarves is a riddle, for the name means *Sorcerer-elf*, or perhaps more literally *Staff-elf* or *Wand-elf*. Tolkien must have wondered how the name of an elf (or sorcerer-elf) got mixed up with a bunch of dwarves. *The Hobbit* is Tolkien's explanation of this riddle raised by the *Edda*. Shippey suggests a scenario something like this, when he writes,

> Tolkien seems to have concluded at some point that "Gandálfr" meant "staff-elf," and that this must be a name for a wizard. Could it be that the reason the *Dvergatal* [the list of dwarves] had been preserved was that it was the last fading record of something that once had happened, some great event in a non-human mythology, an *Odyssey* of the dwarves? This is, anyway, what Tolkien makes of it. *The Hobbit*, one might say, is the story that lies behind and makes sense of the *Dvergatal*. (Shippey, 17)

Century, "[Tolkien] took fragments of ancient literature, expanded on their intensely suggestive hints of further meaning, and made them into coherent and consistent narrative" (Shippey, 35).

The Bones of Beowulf

So far we have only scratched the surface of *Beowulf* and the *Edda* and their influence. It is not so much what some of the characters look like, but what they mean. We can now return to Beowulf, and ask what else the *Beowulf* poet tossed into the simmering cauldron to be drawn from by later writers. The first obvious answer—the one we began to explore at the start of this chapter—is the hero himself: Beowulf. What are the attributes that make up such a hero?[6] Of course, we've already seen some of these as we explored how to find a Beowulf figure in Tolkien's work. But we have only begun. R. E. Kaske breaks the list into two traditional categories: *fortitudo* and *sapientia*, which roughly translated are *prowess* and *wisdom*. The former category includes physical might and courage. The latter category is harder to pin down. "It is an eclectic concept including such diverse qualities as practical cleverness, skill in words and works, knowledge of the past, ability to predict accurately, and ability to choose rightly in matters of conduct" (Kaske, 123).

So what do we make of this? These characteristics are not unique to Beowulf. They can be found in many heroes. After all, Beowulf, for all he added *to* the pot, himself had to be taken *from* the cauldron by the *Beowulf* poet (or poets) before he could be put back in. The story, for example, has a close parallel in the much earlier Greek foundational myth of Theseus, who travels with a company of fourteen to conquer the labyrinthine Minotaur that has plagued his people. These would appear to be some of the "bones" in the "cauldron." Tolkien comments on this aspect of the poem, especially with respect to the Danish king, whom Beowulf rescues at the start of the story. "King Hrothgar and his family have many manifest marks of true history . . . yet even in the older (English) accounts of them they are associated with many figures and events of fairy story: they have been in the Pot." This simmering in the pot, according to Tolkien, probably accounts for "the turning of the bear-boy into the knight Beowulf" and "the intrusion of the ogre Grendel into the royal hall of Hrothgar" (*Essay*, 30). As we saw earlier, the historical figure of Oswald may have been one bit put into the pot, which simmered and flavored Beowulf. There was also the basic concept from Germanic literature of the heroic ideal. Kaske explains:

6. Any attempt at a quick answer to this question will risk oversimplification of years of valuable *Beowulf* scholarship. As with many other works discussed in this book, the reader is encouraged to read the poem.

In the Germanic tradition as we have it, the ideal appears several times in poems of the *Edda* as well as in Old English poems like *Widsið* (138–41) and the *Gifts of Men* (39–43, 76–77). There seems small room for doubt, then, that *sapientia et fortitudo* as a heroic ideal was familiar in the literature and the ways of thought most likely to have been available to the poet of *Beowulf*. (Kaske, 123)

Thus, much of what we see in the poem *Beowulf*, and in the hero Beowulf, was already in the pot and had been used (and contributed) by other writers before our poet told his story. At first glance this might seem to diminish the significance of *Beowulf's* contribution. After all, if all of these elements were already simmering, why did we need this new poem? In answer to this last question, we argue that *Beowulf* brought something unique. For whatever had gone into the pot before, two very important things emerged with *Beowulf* (and thus were immediately added back in), which were not previously present in such a developed form, and yet which have dramatically influenced later works. The first is the synthesis of the Germanic heroic spirit with a Christian sense of morality, and the second is the overarching sense of moral purpose in the great War that defines so much of fantasy.

Let's first consider the merging of the Germanic heroic spirit with a Christian sense of morality. For simmering in the pot with Oswald and the bear-boy was the Great Fairy Tale itself, the gospel. We might call Beowulf the *Christianized* Germanic hero (or perhaps the *Germanicized* Christian hero). There are numerous other virtuous heroes of earlier Germanic legend, but the *Beowulf* poet takes the step of associating Beowulf's virtue with *eternal* values. To the categories of *wisdom* and *prowess* is added the category of *moral integrity*. It is no longer enough that the ideal hero has foresight, knowledge, and skill with words in addition to his great strength and courage. It is now necessary that he act morally. Or, if you prefer to use the category of *sapientia*, then the Christianized Beowulf hero redefines the term "rightly"—the "ability to choose *rightly* in matters of conduct"—in moral terms and not merely in terms of political savvy or prudential foresight.

Contrast this vision of a hero, for example, with that of Odin's Berserkers. Malcolm Todd explains:

Odin's aspect is always grim and sinister. His magic could strike panic terror into his enemies and make their weapons useless. His own warriors could be inspired with a mystic rage, the rage of the *berserks*, which made them fight with the ferocity and strength of wild animals, but his protection did not extend over all those who served him. Strife between kinsmen was his especial delight. Odin was the arch-deceiver, as well as the lord of battle. In him men saw the horror and futility of war, and nothing of the nobility and courage of the ideal soldier.[7]

Or contrast Beowulf with the greatest of Norse heroes: Sigurd/Sigurth of the *Edda* and the *Volsungasaga,* or the later closely related Sifrit/Siegfried of the Germanic (Austrian) *Nibelungenlied.* Beowulf and these heroes undeniably share certain heroic elements taken from the pot. Both Beowulf and Sifrit/Sigurd are powerful warriors of superhuman strength. Both are dragon slayers—Sigurd at the start of his heroic career and Beowulf at the end. And yet, despite the similarities, we cannot imagine Beowulf being presented as hero because he used a cloak of invisibility in order to deceive the Valkyrie Brunhilde and win her as a bride for a friend, and then again used the cloak to help his friend overpower her in the bedroom in order to consummate the marriage against her will.[8] Yet these were some of the actions of the hero Sifrit. There is no issue of fairness in the *Nibelungenlied;* Sifrit is a hero because he succeeds; his success comes from a combination of cleverness, strength, and possession of magic. It is the Beowulf model, and not the Sifrit model, we see in Faramir when he speaks (and lives out) the principle: "I would not snare even an orc with falsehood" (IV/v).

This is at the heart of the question Kaske is asking about *Beowulf.* What virtues define the *sapientia* of the hero, "Christian *sapientia* or pagan Germanic *sapientia?*" Indeed, Kaske comments that the *most important* critical question one might ask about the poem pertains to the poet's attitude toward his hero. "To what extent is he an ideal heroic figure (possibly bearing some relation to Christ), and to what extent a somber portrayal of the inevitable doom that attends even the noblest of non-Christians?" The very phrasing of this question implies that both aspects are present in the poem—a proposition difficult to deny. Certainly the poem *Beowulf* reflects some of the customs of the days, the inherited Germanic *sapientia et fortitudo,* but according to the poet the morality of the hero is transcendent of local mores and customs. Kaske is clear. "The poet has used this old ideal as an area of synthesis between Christianity and Germanic paganism" (Kaske, 122–23).

7. Malcolm Todd, *Everyday Life of the Barbarians* (New York: Dorset Press, 1988), 126–27.

8. Some of the details of the contest to win the Valkyrie differ between the *Nibelungenlied* and the *Volsungasaga,* but in both cases the hero uses magic and deceit to win the bride for his friend.

Just how important is the Christian contribution? F. A. Blackburn notes,

> When the hero continues, "In all this I may rejoice, though sick with mortal wounds, for when my life hath left my body, the Ruler of men may not charge me with the murder of my kindred," we may properly recognize the Christian coloring. (Blackburn, 2)

Beowulf is acting here not only for the glory he will receive from a people steeped in Germanic culture—though that aspect is also certainly involved, even in his foreswearing the use of a weapon—but also for the reward he will seek in the afterlife, in a Christian understanding of the world.

And this is not the only instance of such "Christian coloring." Blackburn goes on to list some sixty-eight passages "in which the form of expression or the character of the thought seems to suggest something in Christian usage or doctrine" (Blackburn, 3). There are places where Christian *sapientia* and the pagan Germanic *sapientia* are compatible, and places where they are not. Courage and strength are compatible, as are loyalty and many other virtues. But the lists are not identical, and even where some Germanic virtues are compatible with Christian ones, in the Christian hero they must take subsidiary roles to other, greater virtues. The Christian hero *can* be strong, and *ought* to be courageous; and he may show this courage (a virtue) in the context of battle, but the actual prowess in battle (especially the ability to kill others) is certainly not a Christian virtue. Mercy, by contrast, is a Christian virtue. On the other side, the Germanic hero may behave at times in ways compatible with Christian morality, but it is not for transcendent moral reasons. For a Christian hero, choosing rightly at the deepest level meant "seeking eternal gains" even at the expense of earthly ones. For the pagan Germanic hero, victory and glory in battle were higher ends.

Beowulf, then, gives us a hero who is strong and courageous, wise in speech, and court-savvy, but also acknowledging a transcendent morality above the pagan *sapientia.* Adding to the list of virtues that define "acting right" in this new tale *Beowulf* told by a Christian poet, we see also fairness (illustrated by the hero's refusal to use a weapon in his fight against Grendel), loyalty (both to those he serves and to those who serve him), faithfulness (in the sense of keeping oaths), and unselfishness (the last of these illustrated in Beowulf's refusal to marry Hygd and usurp the Geatish throne, choosing instead to wait until Heardred's death before taking up the kingship). Kaske goes on to explain this "co-existence of eternal salvation and earthly glory as the goals of human life." He states,

> If Beowulf is deliberately made to behave wisely and bravely according to both codes, then the very ambiguity of both the . . . "judgment of the righteous" and the earthly . . . "praise, fame, glory" is not only relevant but in a way demanded. (Kaske, 122)

Thus, two worlds have come together.

In associating Christian morality with the Germanic virtue and superhuman strength of the hero, the *Beowulf* poet also adds to the pot one other important aspect that is ladled out by most modern fantasy authors. The battle that takes place is not merely between two human powers, Sifrit against Gunther, or the Danes against the Heathobards. There is a larger battle at stake. In the language of Aragorn, it is that of Good against Ill. If all that matters is the outcome of a battle between two human foes, then political savvy would be a higher virtue than mercy or fairness. But if the hero is waging a battle against evil itself, then the rightness of his choices must be weighed on moral scales.

To explore this, we must address yet one more thing that the *Beowulf* poet put into the pot. Perhaps even more important than its hero are the monsters *Beowulf* gives us: Grendel, Grendel's mother, and the dragon. Dragons, as we know, are very important monsters and villains in modern fantasy—and occasionally, as with the Ann McCaffrey's *Pern* books or the *My Father's Dragon* books, may even be benign characters. Contrary to popular opinion, however, there are very few dragons in medieval literature. It was Tolkien, with Smaug in *The Hobbit,* who really brought the dragon as we now know dragons into modern fantasy literature. "For Tolkien's taste," Tom Shippey points out, "there were too few dragons in ancient literature, indeed by his count only three" (Shippey, 36). Nonetheless, there were dragons in the pot, and we must start by acknowledging the writers who put them there, including the *Beowulf* poet. These three are Miðgarðsormr, "which was to destroy the god Thor at Ragnarök"; Fafnir, "who is killed by the Norse hero Sigurð"; and the dragon of *Beowulf.* Unlike Miðgarðsormr, the *Beowulf* dragon is appropriate in size and strength for a heroic tale. As Shippey explains, "he had some good touches but remained speechless and without marked character." Admittedly, it is more from Fafnir that Tolkien took his idea of a dragon. "However, as often, Tolkien took the hints, but felt he could improve on them" (Shippey, 37).

More than just a dragon, however, what *Beowulf* reemphasized was the important notion of having a monstrous evil (and not mere human foes) as the enemy. This is a hallmark of modern fantasy, and the importance of it to Tolkien can be seen in the title of his famous essay on *Beowulf*—"The Monsters and the Critics." Tolkien's works have Morgoth and Sauron and the dragons (as well as Ungoliant, Shelob, Balrogs, Ringwraiths, trolls, and orcs); Stephen Donaldson's Thomas Covenant books have the Worldhater and the ur-viles; C. S. Lewis's Narnia books have the White Witch and the Emerald Witch (as well as giants, a sea serpent, and the god Tash); Le Guin's *Earthsea* trilogy has dragons as well as the Nameless Ones; Patricia McKillip's *Hed* trilogy has the Shape-Changers. Further back, the ancient poems frequently pit heroes against monstrous powers like the Minotaur, the Gorgon, Scylla and Charybdis, Polyphemus, and Harpies. These monsters are important devices in fantasy, but they are more than devices. The presence of monsters returns us to the notion that the battle fought by the heroes who must show both courage and moral virtue cannot be compared to mere mortal conflicts. It is a monumental conflict of Good and Ill. Thomas Cahill brings this together in his comment that

> Beowulf, the great Germano-English hero, is a pagan warrior, sure enough, but he is presented as a model of Saxon manhood—loyal, courageous, generous; and as the poet told the tale, the English Christian audience would have picked up the hints, concealed within the poet's text, that Beowulf grappling with the monsters was a type of Christ grappling with Satan.[9]

Tolkien summarizes the importance of this as follows.

> Most important is it to consider how and why the monsters become "adversaries of God," and so begin to symbolize (and ultimately to become identified with) the powers of evil, even while they remain, as they do still remain in *Beowulf,* mortal denizens of the material world, in it and of it. (*Monsters,* 20)

Having monsters, Tolkien tells us, brings transcendent values to War in fantasy literature—transcendent values that matter immensely to this world.

9. Thomas Cahill, *How the Irish Saved Civilization* (New York: Nan A. Talese, 1995), 203.

Arthurian Legend

If we acknowledge the influence of *Beowulf* on modern fantasy, we must also acknowledge a legend—or rather, a set of legends—that has an even more noticeable influence: the body of work known collectively as Arthurian romance.

Earlier in this book we discussed what Tolkien felt were shortcomings in Arthurian Romance, as least when it is read *as fantasy* or *as a legend for England.* Nonetheless, one cannot deny the influence of Arthur even on Tolkien. We see in Aragorn and Gandalf something of King Arthur and the wizard Merlin. Tolkien even acknowledges this in his naming of the outermost city of the undying lands of Valinor. Avalonnë, it is called. One can give an etymological explanation for the name that has nothing to do with King Arthur: the name in Elvish is a reference to the gods, called the Valar (singular, Vala), and to their city Valinor. However, the similarity to the famed Avalon of Arthurian myth is unmistakable. Other comparisons could be (and have been) made between the works.

To understand the influence and development of Arthurian romance, let us return for a moment to the explicit Christianization of Germanic heroic legend, begun in Anglo-Saxon heroic literature with *Beowulf* and in the *Heliand.* These two poems come from the same era and add similar bits and bones to the broth.[10] If the synthesis of *Beowulf* can be seen as a Christian coloring of Germanic heroic tradition, the *Heliand* is something of a Germanic heroic coloring of the Christian Gospels. G. Ronald Murphy writes of the *Heliand:*

> By the power of his imagination the unknown poet-monk (perhaps ex-warrior) created a unique cultural synthesis between Christianity and Germanic warrior-society—a synthesis that would ultimately lead to the culture of knighthood and become the foundation of medieval Europe.

Roland Bainton summarizes the impact of the Germanic hero on the portrayal of Christianity:

10. *The Heliand* was composed in the first half of the ninth century. The date of composition of *Beowulf* is unknown. The earliest *Beowulf* manuscript dates from the eleventh century, but most scholars agree that it was composed at least two centuries earlier (during the same period as *The Heliand*) and possibly as much as four centuries earlier. Some scholars conjecture a single Christian poet, making use of earlier source material from the Pot. (This would argue for a later composition.) Some conjecture a Christian poet revising old lays. Some conjecture a heathen poet, whose work was later revised by a Christian. It is possible, however, that the *Beowulf* poet and the *Heliand* poet were contemporaries.

This is evident in many instances, starting with Clovis himself. Jesus was for him a tribal war god, a new Yahweh of hosts. The Franks martialized St. Peter, whose noblest exploit in their eyes was that to protect the Lord Jesus he had wielded his broadsword and sliced off the ear of the high priest's servant. The Archangel Michael of the flaming sword became a Heavenly champion and his name was given to the Norman citadel, Mont St. Michel.[11]

The Spanish did the same with Saint James (Santiago) of the Bible, renaming him "Matamoros," or "Moor-Killer," and Spanish legends depict him descending from heaven to lead the Christian Spaniards to victory against the Muslim Moors. Annually, thousands still make the pilgrimage to the city of Santiago de Compostela in northern Spain.

The Arthurian legends, similarly, are martial stories with a strong spiritual dimension. It is sometimes argued that this shows an inconsistency in Christianity, whose founder was peaceful and whose followers are violent. We wish simply to point out that there is another way to read these legends, in which the martial aspects serve the spiritual, and not the other way around. The martial and magical struggle is an image of one of the faces of Faërie. As in the *Heliand,* the Arthurian struggle uses heroic storytelling to point to a deeper and more telling struggle.

We tend to think of the Arthurian legend as an English story but it is not uniquely so. The oldest sources are in fact from the European continent. Like the Spanish stories of *El Cid,* the Swiss *William Tell* legend, and the French *Song of Roland,* the Arthurian legends tie together ancient figures with recent struggles to unify and preserve European nations from non-Christian invaders, European tyrants, and, most important, from the ignobility lurking in the hearts of all people, waiting for a chance to rule us.

Although most of the famous Arthurian sources are French and German, the myth of Logres came to be connected to English soil and the English soul. Toward the end of C. S. Lewis's "modern fairy-tale" *That Hideous Strength,* Dimble attempts to explain the relevance of Arthurian legends to contemporary England. "It all began," he said, "when we discovered that the Arthurian story is mostly true history. There was a moment in the sixth century when something that is always trying to break through into this country nearly succeeded. Logres was our name for it—it will do as well as any other" (*Hideous,* 369). For Dimble, the

11. Roland H. Bainton, *Christendom,* vol. 1 (New York: Harper Torchbooks, 1964), 147.

great struggle of British history is not between Great Britain and her political and military foes, but "really the struggle between Logres and Britain." Britain is "haunted" by its better and truer self, and the Arthurian legend of Logres is a representation of that. It functions as a goad, as an irritation on the conscience of a nation, that it might be much more than it is. "'So that, meanwhile, is England,' said Mother Dimble. 'Just this swaying to and fro between Logres and Britain?'" "'Yes,' said her husband. . . . 'If we've got an ass's head, it is by walking in a fairy wood. We've heard something better than we can do, but can't quite forget it'" (371). The "ass's head" harks back to Apuleius's *Golden Ass*—and the possibility of its Augustinian reworking. The English are enchanted, as Apuleius's Lucius was, by their own ignoble desires. These desires threaten to undo them, but there is around them the constant possibility of redemption. Augustine knew that the only hope for freedom from this asinine enchantment lay in pledging allegiance to the side of Goodness, that is, in confession and conversion. The Arthurian legend is similarly about the peril that constantly threatens England from within its own heart, and the possibility of salvation by turning toward what is true, good, and beautiful. Of course, this is not just true of England, but of all places, all people. In a sense, every work of fantasy that comes after the stories of Logres depends on this same struggle. Each ladle, no matter how small or large, brings up the bones of Arthurian legend.

6

NINETEENTH-CENTURY FAIRY TALE AND FANTASY

The Brothers Grimm and George MacDonald

> *I have never concealed the fact that I regarded [George Mac-*
> *Donald] as my master; indeed I fancy I have never written a*
> *book in which I did not quote from him.*
>
> C. S. Lewis, Preface to *George MacDonald*

Fairy-tales have been told throughout history and have been an important part of the cultures in which they have been told. So central are they to the oral traditions of much of the world that the terms *fairy tale* and *folk tale* have at times been nearly synonymous. The nineteenth century was a particularly important time for fairy tale. It saw numerous successful efforts throughout Europe and Scandinavia to gather the tales of various countries and language groups, in part for the beauty of the tales themselves, but also to help preserve those languages and distinctive cultures.[1] It was also a century when many gifted writers were successful at

---

1. Jacob and Wilhelm Grimm in Germany, Peter Christen Asbjörnsen and Jörgen Engerbretsen Moe in Norway, Elias Lönnrot in Finland, and Andrew Lang in England, to name just a few.

writing new fairy tales. This latter group of fairy tales weren't "folk tales" in the true meaning of that word; though they followed the *patterns* of these traditional tales, they were *original* stories, not handed down orally from generation to generation.

There are several factors involved in the resurgence of the fairy tale in the nineteenth century. As we mentioned in the first chapter, the romantic era was ushered in on the wings of growing disillusionment with the Enlightenment. People were realizing that the Enlightenment emphasis on rationality was insufficient to answer many of life's biggest questions, including questions of ultimate meaning: What is life about? How are we to live it? What is our place here on earth? As we mentioned in chapter 2, Enlightenment science was made possible by divorcing scientific research from discussions of meaning and purpose. But dismissing such questions from the laboratory does not make them go away. The fairy tale—unlike scientific study, propositional definitions, and rational philosophy—provided a way of looking at the world that answered these questions. By reaching us at the level of our moral imagination, the fairy tale could speak to us in ways that the language of science could not. Put another way, fairy tales are a repository of wisdom, though not necessarily of knowledge. And while science and rational inquiry are wonderful tools for the acquisition of knowledge, on their own they provide little in the way of wisdom. But knowledge without wisdom is not only bankrupt; it is dangerous.

W. H. Auden, writing in a century dominated by modernism (the twentieth), describes this bankruptcy of a culture that has science and technology but not the literary imagination nurtured by the fairy tale:

> Half of our troubles, both individual neuroses and collective manias like nationalism, seem to me to be caused largely by our poverty of symbols, so that not only do we fail to relate one experience to another but also we have to entrust our whole emotional life to the few symbols we do have. (Auden-2)

His comments could have applied to the Enlightenment, as well as to modernity or to any culture that accepts only the rational approach to knowledge and denies the validity and power of story and imagination. Auden goes on to suggest that a solution to this bankruptcy can be found in fairy tales. As we earlier quoted him: "So let everyone read these stories till they know them backward and tell them to their children with embellishments—they are not sacred texts." Whether the people of the nineteenth century saw fairy tales as a solution or not, they were certainly drawn to them, and the collections of the Brothers Grimm proved popular and were duplicated in many other cultures and languages.

Hand in hand with the reaction against rationalism, the nineteenth century was also a period of growing nationalism and interest in national identity. The empires of the previous centuries as well as the Napoleonic Empire of the current century were a threat to the regional identity of the conquered peoples. Thus, sociologists, historians, and philologists became interested in the folk tales of their own culture as a way of preserving that cultural heritage.[2] In 1806, not long after Jacob and Wilhelm began their collecting work, Napoleon's armies conquered the Grimms' homeland of Kassel,[3] thus adding urgency to their task. After Kassel fell to Napoleon, Wilhelm complained that the streets of his regions were full of "foreign persons, foreign manners, and a foreign loudly spoken language." Part of his work was simply a way of escaping the troubles of his day by withdrawing to the comparably peaceful world of scholarship. But Wilhelm also wrote: "Not only did we seek something of consolation in the past, our hope, naturally, was that this course of ours should contribute somewhat to the return of a better day."[4] Thus, they went about the painstaking work of gathering together not only oral folk tales (from friends, local storytellers, and family members), but also material found

2. There is a certain irony in this. Today we fear excessive nationalism, rightly observing its dangers. Those living in the mid-twentieth century were particularly sensitive, as the term *Nazi* was short for *Nationalist*. Auden, as we just read, suggested that nationalism was one of the *troubles* of his culture: a "collective mania" he called it. However, a growing sense of national identity was one of the influences that gave rise to the resurgence of fairy tale. It may even be that folk culture actually provided fuel for growing nationalism. Yet both Auden and Tolkien saw fairy tale not as the *cause* of the problem but as part of a *cure*. In *The Two Towers*, it is old fairy tales (about Ents) that connect Rohan to the wide world outside. In a memorable dialogue (III/viii), Gandalf refers to the truth in "tales by the fireside" and "twisted threads of story" as he helps King Théoden break free of his inward-focused nationalistic vision so that he can see (1) that he is not alone and "without allies" (as he had thought); (2) that other peoples and cultures are also endangered; and (3) that Rohan needs to unite with other peoples and other cultures for the defeat of a common enemy. Or again, as mentioned in the chapter on Greek and Roman myth, Homer's epics became not only the founding myths for the Greeks, but also the source of Virgil's founding myth for the Romans. Virgil in turn became a source of inspiration for Dante. The "nationalism" that arises in mythic context is plastic, and not inherently xenophobic or racist. We see the same principle at work today: story, especially the commonalities of the timeless fairy story, can draw people together from many disparate cultures and places. If fairy stories are dangerous—we have already said they are perilous—they're also very helpful. We cannot say as much for many of the political and philosophical ideologies of the last two centuries.

3. This is the region of modern-day Germany where the Grimms lived and from which they collected many of their stories. At the time, however, Germany did not yet exist as a nation but was simply a collection of autonomous local principalities.

4. Wilhelm Grimm, quoted by Joseph Campbell in Campbell, 835–36.

in manuscripts from the Middle Ages. And a large number of these folk tales, as mentioned earlier, were fairy tales. These were the tales that forever became associated with the name Grimm.

The nineteenth century was also the century of the beloved Hans Christian Andersen (1805–75, best known for his fairy tales, including "The Ugly Duckling" and "The Snow Queen"), and of the first significant American writer of fairy tales, Frank Stockton (1834–1902, author of "The Griffin and the Minor Canon," "The Bee-Man of Orn," and more than twenty other tales). It was late in the century that the Oxford-educated Andrew Lang (1844–1912), a well-known poet, novelist, journalist, and literary critic of his day, began his extensive work that involved collection of traditional tales, writing of original fairy tales, and commentary *about* fairy tale and resulted in his *Blue Fairy Book, Red Fairy Book, Yellow Fairy Book, Lilac Fairy Book,* etc. Though Tolkien would later disagree with many of Lang's ideas given in his commentary and introductions, Lang's fairy tales themselves were timeless. Lastly, the nineteenth century was the time of perhaps the greatest modern creator of original fairy tales, George MacDonald, author of *The Princess and the Goblin, At the Back of the North Wind,* and *Phantastes.* MacDonald, also a prolific and successful Victorian novelist, in addition to writing several fairy tales of traditional length, took some of the usual devices of the fairy tale genre and spun from that material several book-length works of Faërie. That is, he blended the fairy tale with the novel—two forms with which he was very familiar—and in crossing that frontier, the predecessor of the modern fantasy romance was born. In many ways, then, the nineteenth century became *the* century of the fairy tale, as well as an important time in the development of modern fantasy.

Here many of those familiar with the Grimms' tales might ask, with no small amount of incredulity: "What could the likes of Little Red-Cap and the Goose-girl have to do with the heroic figures of J. R. R. Tolkien?" A great deal, it turns out, though the connections might not be immediately obvious. Whereas it is easy to see the influence of the *Edda, Beowulf,* and King Arthur on Tolkien's *The Lord of the Rings,* the direct influence of these nineteenth-century fairy tales is less immediately evident. It comes through more clearly in stories like *Farmer Giles of Ham* and *Smith of Wootton Major* and, to some degree, *The Hobbit* (as well as in C. S. Lewis's *Chronicles of Narnia*). This influence needn't be merely surmised. In a letter written in 1937, Tolkien said of *The Hobbit:* "Mr. Baggins began as a comic tale among conventional and inconsistent Grimms' fairy-tale dwarves, and got drawn into the edge of it—so that even Sauron the terrible peeped over the edge" (*Letters*, 26). Even *The Silmarillion*, as we shall see, draws some inspiration from some of the Grimms' tales.

Now, as with the mythic and Arthurian material discussed earlier, these fairy tales are worthy of considerable attention on their own merits. Consider that some of the most famous psychologists of the twentieth century (including Bruno Bettelheim, Sigmund Freud, and Carl Gustav Jung) saw fairy tale as important and influential enough to offer their commentary, in addition to the folklorist research and commentary of scholars like Joseph Campbell. Even for those not interested in fairy tale itself, if we are to explore both the meaning and importance of modern fantasy, and more broadly the literature of Faërie, we must spend some time with the fairy tales of this influential era. We will do so by looking first at the collected tales of the Brothers Grimm and then at the original tales of George MacDonald. [5]

Fairy Tales and the Nineteenth Century

In once sense, the fairy tales associated with Jacob and Wilhelm Grimm are not nineteenth-century works at all, but merely carefully compiled collections of much older works. That these "Germanic" fairy tales are much older and have sources ranging as far away geographically and chronologically as ancient India to the southeast and pre-Roman Ireland to the northwest is part of the reason for exploring them in this book. Nonetheless, the Grimms' own nineteenth-century voices are undeniable even in stories dating to a much earlier period.

The introduction to one popular and extensive (over 800 pages long) collection of *The World's Best Fairy Tales* states: "The first systematic recording of *ancient* tales was done early in the nineteenth century by the Grimm brothers, who set down the stories *word for word* as the German peasants told them" (emphasis ours).[6] Joseph Campbell makes a similar

---

5. We probably could have written this chapter instead making use of Andrew Lang's various collections, or even the early work of Perrault. We might even have been able to make use of other European collections that followed the Grimms, such as famous Finnish collections, or even fairy tales from other parts of the world (India, Persia, Africa, pre-Columbian North America). However, the Grimms' collection is extensive, and in the opinion of the authors of this book it is the most characteristic such collection. It is certainly very influential, as we will illustrate later in this chapter, and perhaps most importantly it remains the most famous of the nineteenth- and early-twentieth-century fairy-tale collections.

6. *The Worlds Best Fairy Tales: A Readers Digest Anthology*, ed. Belle Becker Sideman (New York: The Reader's Digest Association, 1967).

comment with regard to one of the Grimms' most important sources, the now famous woman from Kassel from whom they first heard many of the tales.[7]

> Anyone believing that traditional materials are easily falsified and carelessly preserved, and hence cannot survive over a long period, should hear how close she always keeps to her story and how zealous she is for its accuracy; never does she alter any part in repetition, and she corrects a mistake herself, immediately she notices it. (Campbell, 833)

We can rightly conclude that most of these stories had almost certainly circulated in some form among the Germanic peoples for several centuries. There is overlap, for example, with some of the stories earlier collected in the late seventeenth century from the neighboring region of France by Charles Perrault (1628–1703).[8] Accepting that the stories really are old, this is not surprising; though the language spoken in adjacent France had centuries earlier become latinized, the German and French peoples shared common Germanic roots: the Gauls who occupied France fifteen centuries earlier were Celts romanized in the first century BC, eventually conquered or displaced by the Franks (another Germanic tribe) and thence by a whole succession of various Germanic tribes. We should *expect* the same fairy stories to keep reemerging. Indeed, a few of the stories told by the Grimms likely predate *Beowulf* and the Norse mythology discussed earlier. Why, then, do we include them in a chapter labeled (or mislabeled) as nineteenth-century?

The question is legitimate. The Germanic fairy tales presented to us by Jacob and Wilhelm are, indeed, much older. So old that they and the oral tradition that kept them alive were in danger of being lost. Nonetheless, it is also true that the brothers—especially Wilhelm—performed a substantial amount of revision and "editorial work" on these tales from the 1810 manuscript to the first edition in 1812, and then to the final edition of 1857.

Consider, for example, the opening story "The Frog-King, or Iron Henry" in *The Complete Grimm's Fairy-Tales*. In the 1810 manuscript it is the frog who speaks first. After the princess becomes sad at dropping her ball into the well, the frog offers her the bargain of fetching the ball in exchange only for being brought home with her. In the published edition

---

7. Frau Katherina Viehmann (1755–1815).
8. See *Histoires ou contes du temps passé avec les moralités* and *Contes de ma Mère l'Oye*.

of 1812, though the characters and the sequence of events remain largely the same, the telling of the tale changes, as do the details of the dialogue. The edited version is over twice as long, and is much more elaborate in the telling. As well as adding the now famous fairy-tale beginning, "Once upon a time," the published version also adds considerably to the princess's words—it is now the princess who speaks first—including an explicit promise of clothes, jewels, and pearls for any who can help her. The frog's response is conspicuously augmented with the condition of eating at the princess's table and *sleeping in her bed*. The princess, eager to get her bauble back, concedes to all of this.

Then we come to the 1857 final edition of the same story, which is more than half again longer than the 1812 edition: "In olden times," it begins, "when wishing still helped one, there lived a king whose daughters were all beautiful, but the youngest was so beautiful that the sun itself, which has seen so much, was astonished whenever it shone on her face." Now it is back to the frog who speaks first, and the opening dialogue is even more elaborate with an increased tension between the two: "What ails you, King's daughter? You weep so that even a stone would show pity." To which the princess replies: "Ah! Old water-splasher, is it you?" The frog also adds yet another condition to his bargain: the princess must agree to "love" him and let him be her "companion" and "play-fellow." Again the princess agrees, assuming that a frog can't possibly really want any of this (*Grimm's*, 17–18).

It should be noted that Jacob was at first opposed to this reworking. Clemens Brentano, a friend of the brothers, had undertaken a similar collection of German folk songs but had reworked the material more aggressively. At one point Jacob and Wilhelm considered turning their work over to Brentano, but, as Campbell writes, "Jacob mistrusted their friend's habit of reworking traditional materials—shooting them full of personal fantasy, cutting, amplifying, recombining, brilliantly, and always flavoring to the contemporary palate" (Campbell, 837). Nonetheless, despite Jacob's demurring, between the 1812 and 1857 editions the tales were indeed reworked, primarily by Wilhelm. Wilhelm's *goal* was to be faithful to the original voices. Again, as Campbell explains, it was the work of a "careful, loving, improving hand . . . inspired by his increasing familiarity with the popular modes of speech." In fact, the Grimms must have heard numerous different versions of most of the stories, from different people at different times. So rather than there being some definitive version, it was more a task of finding the essence of the story itself. Only after much labor and study of the speech and storytelling patterns,

Wilhelm "chiseled away the more abstract, literary, or colorless turns and fitted in such characteristic, rich phrases, as he had gathered from the highways and the byways" (Campbell, 838). Still, as the example from "The Frog Prince" illustrates, the Grimms' voice could be "increasingly discerned" (Campbell, 838).

So does it matter how old the stories are, and how much they have changed? In some sense, our appreciation of the stories as stories is independent of their history. And fairy tales—as much as or more than any type of story—must be enjoyed simply as story. Thus, the discussion of Wilhelm's editing and adaptation is not intended as a criticism of their work. Even as collectors or mythologists, they *might* be criticized for corrupting the oral tradition and the "word for word" accounts from German peasants *only* if there were some one definitive version of the stories (there wasn't), or if all of the stories were presented as those of one particular storyteller (they weren't). But as writers and storytellers themselves, we can instead praise the Grimms for improving on the work or for finding the essence of the story and style amid all the different versions. Indeed, as Auden suggests, the story *ought* to be retold and embellished. What we are pointing out is the nature of fairy story to change and adapt over time and to incorporate new material—an important feature of Faërie that will carry over to modern fantasy.

In considering the nature of fairy story to change and adapt, we return to the Pot of Soup, both what went into the soup to become these fairy tales and also what the Grimms contributed back to the Cauldron. The Grimms' fairy tales are identified as coming from a Germanic folk tradition. But just as the stories are both old and yet are retold, so too they are German and yet also far more than German, descending from roots in fairy tale all over the world as well as from the spread of Christianity in Europe (largely at the hands of Irish missionaries). Joseph Campbell points out numerous influences, old and new:

> In 1859, the year of Wilhelm's death, a Sanskrit scholar, Theodor Benfey, demonstrated that a great portion of the lore of Europe had come, through Arabic, Hebrew, and Latin translations, directly from India—and this as late as the thirteenth century AD. . . .
>
> A quantity of Late Classical matter was being imported from the Mediterranean by the itinerant entertainers, minstrels and pranksters, who came swarming from the sunny south to infest the pilgrim routes and present themselves at castle doors. And not only minstrels, missionaries too were

at work. The fierce, warrior ideals of earlier story were submitting to a new piety and sentimental didactic. . . .

There seems to have prevailed a comparative poverty of invention [in Germany] until the twelfth century, when the matter of India and the matter of Ireland found their ways to the fields of Europe. This was the period of the Crusades and the Chivalrous Romance, the former opening Europe wide to the civilization of the Orient, the latter conjuring from the realm of Celtic faërie a wild wonderworld of princesses enchanted in sleep, castles solitary in the forest adventurous, dragons steaming in rimy caverns, Merlin-magic, Morgan le Fay, cackling hags transmuted by a kiss into the damsel of the world. . . .

A wonderful period opened in the thirteenth century . . . A tumbling, broad, inexhaustible flood of popular merry tales, misadventures, hero, saint, and devil legends, animal fables, mock heroics, slap-stick jokes, riddles, pious allegories and popular ballads burst abruptly into manuscript and carried everything before it. Compounded with themes from the Cloister and the Castle, mixed with elements from the Bible and from the heathenness of the Orient, as well as the deep pre-Christian past . . . This was the first major flourishing in Europe of a literature of the people. (Campbell, 847–49)

Thus, in the Grimms' tales we have a voice most familiar to twentieth and twenty-first-century English-language authors—a voice most closely associated with the very name *fairy tale*—and yet also a collection of specific fairy tales representing ancient stories, traditions, and themes from cultures as diverse as Ireland and India, Christianity, and Scandinavian mythology.

The Fairy Tale Collections of Jacob and Wilhelm Grimm

And we are back again at the basic questions. So what do we make of these fairy tales and of their influence? It would be tempting to try to take each story, one at a time, and find a summarizing moral or lesson that we are supposed to learn from that tale. All of the fairy tales of Charles Perrault, for example, already have explicit morals stated at the end, such as that from *Little Red Riding Hood* (who in Perrault's version is not rescued, but comes to her end in the wolf's belly):

> From this story one learns that children,
> especially young lasses,
> pretty, courteous and well-bred,

> do very wrong to listen to strangers,
> And it is not an unheard thing
> If the Wolf is thereby provided with his dinner.[9]

Perrault has wrapped the story up in a tidy little message.

If we applied this approach to Grimms' fairy tales, however, it would fail miserably. The Grimms' tales have no such explicit "message." Not only do they require no moral, most times they defy even the attempt at moralistic summary. The message, we might say, is the story itself. Which is to say, they are true fairy tales. Perrault's stories (or at least his presentation of them), by contrast, are closer to fable or parable than to fairy story. His kind of explicit moralizing is an easy mark for modern parody and satire, such as the moral tales of Edward Gorey. Sadly, the modern mind has come to assume that all fairy tales aim at moralizing, which may be one reason many of us do not read them.[10]

Nevertheless, if the *individual* stories in the Grimms' collection transcend or defy simplistic summaries, there are numerous important threads that run through the stories as a whole, and when taken as a whole they have their effects. Thus one way to start answering this question, "What do we make of them?" is to look at some of the oft-occurring character types, devices, patterns, and symbols. The repetition of similar ideas will communicate something to the reader that does not necessarily come through in a single story. Likewise, to answer the question, "What is their influence?" we can look at how many of these devices and character types remain in common use in modern fantasy.

have The so-called *simpleton* is one such oft-occurring character. He doesn't appear smart or clever, and yet he has some other important virtue, usually moral virtue, or perhaps wisdom rather than craftiness, and as a result of that wisdom or virtue becomes the successful hero. Consider "The Three Languages," which begins, "An aged count once lived in Switzerland, who had an only son, but he was stupid, and could learn nothing." As it turns out, the youth isn't as stupid as his father thinks, and he learns to understand the speech of dogs, frogs, and birds. He rescues a country from a horrible bewitchment, is adopted by the lord of the castle, and becomes the pope (*Grimm's*, 169–70). Similarly, in "The Good Bargain," the simpleton fares well in one trial after another, benefiting by his simplicity even from the seeming

---

9. *Perrault's Complete Fairy Tales* trans. A. E. Johnson et al., (New York: Dodd, Mead, 1961).

10. This is more a criticism of the appended morals of Perrault's fairy-tales than of the tales themselves. Many of the tales do stand on their own, and would be better without the summarizing morals.

whims and injustice of the tyrant king. Perhaps the classic example of the simpleton is "The Story of the Youth Who Went Forth to Learn What Fear Was."

In many stories, the *simplicity* of the simpleton is exaggerated by contrast with others (frequently, siblings) who appear shrewder, craftier, more intelligent, or in some other ways more gifted. Yet the simpleton still proves the hero. "The Queen Bee" begins:

> Two kings' sons once went out in search of adventures, and fell into a wild, disorderly way of living, so that they never came home again. The youngest, who was called Simpleton, set out to seek his brothers, but when at length he found them they mocked him for thinking that he with his simplicity could get through the world, when they two could not make their way, and yet were so much cleverer. (*Grimm's,* 317)

It is Simpleton, however, and not his brothers, who rescues a kingdom from enchantment and becomes the king. Such a contrast can also be found between the two brothers in "The Singing Bone," one of the few stories in which the "innocent and simple" one is killed and never restored to life:

> Now there lived in the country two brothers, sons of a poor man, who declared themselves willing to undertake the hazardous enterprise; the elder, who was crafty and shrewd, out of pride; the younger, who was innocent and simple, from a kind heart. (148)

Here the elder brother kills the younger, but justice is eventually served, and the elder brother receives death as a punishment.

Like many of the elements, characters, and devices appearing so often in the Grimms' stories, the simpleton makes his or her way into some important modern works of Faërie. We can see echoes of the simpleton in the *Lord of the Rings* character Samwise son of Hamfast; the very name *Samwise* means "dim-witted," while *Hamfast* suggests a "stay-at-home."[11] A modern version of such a simpleton rustic Grimms' fairy-tale hero can also be found in the bears of C. S. Lewis's *Prince Caspian* and *The Last Battle.* J. K. Rowling was drawing on something similar with her

---

11. We can see the meaning of the Old English name *Sam* in the modern cognate *Semi;* it means "half." Thus, *Samwise* is *Half-wise,* or *Dimwit. Ham* is Old English for *Home,* and thus *Hamfast* (not only the name of Sam's father, but the name he gives his son) refers to one fast-bound, or stuck at home.

character Neville Longbottom.[12] Lloyd Alexander's Prince Rhun (from *The Chronicles of Prydain*) is the clumsy but good-hearted and courageous simpleton.

The opposite side of the coin is that, of the characters who think themselves clever, most fare poorly. This is the case with the two older brothers in "The Queen Bee." Likewise, in "The Singing Bone," the shrewd but prideful older brother is quite confident of his cleverness when he kills the younger and takes his reward. Then there are those who hold the title "Clever," but aren't, and are doomed to disaster (e.g., the title characters in the stories "Clever Hans" or "Clever Elsie"). These characters are even more common in modern works of fantasy. At the end of *The Lord of the Rings,* Saruman continues to cling to an overly inflated view of his own cleverness, and we see the result. Bill Ferny and Ted Sandyman have similarly inflated opinions of their cleverness, and they both contrast and enter conflict with the simpleton Sam Gamgee.

Fairy-tale villains are also important: witches, tyrants, evil stepmothers, ogres, and dragons, and even the devil. Witches, like the famed owner of the candy house in "Hansel and Gretel," appear with some frequency. The witch who with her wand turns one brother and his talking animals to stone in "The Two Brothers" reappears as the White Witch in C. S. Lewis's *Chronicles of Narnia,* also turning many of the talking beasts of Narnia to stone, until (as in the Grimms' tale) one of two brothers destroys the wand. Hand in hand with evil witches are the greedy kings and evil stepmothers who make numerous appearances in the nineteenth century and return to us in the twentieth and twenty-first. "The Two Brothers" also presents us with yet another staple in the genre of fantasy: the dragon who must be appeased with a yearly sacrifice of a virgin.

Another recurring plot device is the animal or inanimate object speaking up for justice, often on behalf of a murdered or at least wronged (and now silent) victim. In "The Singing Bone," it is the bone of the innocent brother, buried in a river by his murdering older brother, which resurfaces and sings of the injustice; only when the king hears the bone sing does the older brother suffer a just fate. Talking beasts are likewise common in the Grimms' tales and are often companions of the hero or heroine, giving needed advice or aid at a critical moment. Again, "Faithful John" and "The Two Brothers" are classic examples. Sometimes the animals are

12. At the time of this writing, book 7 of the *Harry Potter* series had not yet been released, but the authors cautiously anticipate an end for Neville in keeping with that of the simpletons of so many of the Grimms' stories.

people who have been enchanted—like Apuleius's Lucius the ass—and that is yet another important recurring device.

In modern fantasy also, talking objects and animals continue to make an appearance.[13] In Lloyd Alexander's *Chronicles of Prydain*—a retelling of tales from the Welsh *Mabinogion*—Caw the crow is an important companion of the hero Taran. Even more important is the oracular pig Hen Wen, who speaks through magical sticks. The climax of the final book of the series hinges on the prophecy of a rock crying out (though when it happens, it is explained by the wind). In Lewis's *Narnia* stories, the spirits of inanimate objects (naiads and dryads) visit kings and cry out for justice.[14] In Tolkien's *The Silmarillion*, Turin's sword Gurthang speaks to Turin and says it will gladly take his blood because of the innocent blood of Beleg and of Brandir unjustly slain. In *The Hobbit*, it is an old thrush who tells Bard, in the thick of battle, how he can slay the dragon Smaug.

Impossible tasks are also common fare, usually demanded by the aforementioned oft-appearing wicked kings. In "The Devil and the Three Golden Hairs," consider the words spoken by the king to the beautiful youth who wants to be married to the king's daughter, and also the task the king assigns the youth:

> The King said in a passion: "You shall not have everything quite so much your own way; whosoever marries my daughter must fetch me from Hell three golden hairs from the head of the Devil; bring me what I want, and you shall keep my daughter." In this way the King hoped to be rid of him for ever. But the child of good fortune answered; "I will fetch the golden hairs, I am not afraid of the Devil." Whereupon he took leave of them and began his journey. (*Grimm's*, 154)

Those who know Tolkien's tale of "Beren and Lúthien" from *The Silmarillion* (also told in brief by Aragorn in *The Lord of the Rings*) may find this tale of the Grimms startlingly familiar. In *The Silmarillion* King Thingol also begrudges the hand of his daughter Lúthien to one of lesser race, and assigns to Beren the task of removing one of three Silmarils (pre-

13. Some modern fantasy series, such as Walter Wangerin's *The Book of the Dun Cow* and *The Book of Sorrows*, and Brian Jacques's *Redwall* books, are based entirely on talking animals. In some of these instances, however, the animals really seem to be humans in the shape of animals: they wear clothing, use sewing machines, and fight with swords. Closer to the heart of fairy story is the real animal that by enchantment speaks to a human, or the human who learns the language of the animals.

14. Though the concept of naiads and dryads come from the more ancient source of Greek mythology, Lewis's use of them seems to draw as much from fairy tale as from the more ancient source.

cious jewels) from the head of Morgoth in Utumno: a person and place mythically akin to the devil in hell. Beren replies in a fashion much like the youth and (in a fashion) also succeeds—though in Tolkien's tale his task is accomplished only with the aid of others, including King Finrod and eventually Lúthien herself. Similar tales are found in the stories of Heracles, Theseus's Jason and the Argonauts, Orpheus and Eurydice, Odysseus, and Demeter and Persephone, illustrating again the centrality of fairy tale to the soup.

We could also talk about: rings and cloaks that make their bearers or wearers invisible; heroes who unselfishly give aid to animals (or beggars) in need and then later are able to accomplish impossible tasks only with the aid of those animals (or beggars); people learning the speech of animals; or babies appearing out of nowhere and bringing with them good fortune. These are things associated not with one story, but with numerous tales old and new. This is all well and good. We have reappearing simpletons, wicked witches and evil stepmothers, greedy kings, and impossible tasks (accomplished by the hero). So what? What does it all mean? Can we get beyond a tedious grocery list of recurring themes?

Consider the examples discussed above, such as the simpleton. We see not so much in a single tale but in the whole body of stories that the simpleton or rustic, despite lacking of sophistication, can prosper if he or she has noble character traits such as moral virtue, courage, or perseverance. In "Cinderella," it is Cinderella's piety, expressed in devotion to her dead mother, which brings forth the hazel tree from which comes her redemption out of oppressive circumstance. In "The Story of the Youth Who Went Forth to Learn What Fear Was," it is through perseverance that the simple-minded youth, thrown out of his own home because of his stupidity, wins a castle, treasure, and the hand of the queen's daughter. In "The Three Languages," the youth shows both piety and perseverance before becoming pope. In "The Queen Bee," Simpleton succeeds (marries the youngest and sweetest princess and becomes king), in part because of his mercy to helpless animals. There is an overall effect of this repetition through numerous tales that helps certain ideas sink in, where a single tale with a stated moral might not. In repeatedly *showing* moral virtue to be heroic (rather than simply stating that it is), the teller draws the hearer toward a life of such virtue. The important lesson in the combined weight of all of these stories: it is better to be wise than to be clever; and it is better to do good to others than to seek mastery over them. Those who are willing to lay themselves down for others' sake usually wind up gaining much; those who seek to be lords usually wind up getting what they deserve. It is also good not to think too highly of one's own cleverness.

Not surprisingly, then, this pattern exists in the best fairy tales today. Tolkien's simpleton Sam, through both his loyalty (to Frodo and the Quest) and his courage, becomes the ultimate hero of *The Lord of the Rings*—"ultimate" not necessarily in the sense of greatest but in the temporal sense: he is the final hero whom we are left with at the end of the book, when all the others are gone. Thus, Samwise, the rustic but virtuous simpleton, is a perfect nineteenth-century fairy-tale hero.

It is rarely without pain and suffering, however, that the redemption and victory occurs, and this is another "lesson" that comes to us through repetition. In the story "Faithful John," it is, as the title suggests, the faithfulness of the king's servant John—faithfulness to the point of death—that saves the young king. "I will save my master," John says, "even if it bring destruction on myself" (*Grimm's*, 48). (Here is another statement that might well have been echoed by the rustic Sam about his master, Frodo.) As foreseen, John's faithfulness does bring about his own death even as it spares the king, but then he is restored to life by the returned faithfulness of the king. Still, it is a gruesome faithfulness, reminiscent of the command to Abraham to sacrifice his son Isaac in the stories of Genesis.

Likewise, Rapunzel finds her true love, the king's son, only after years of searching and hardship; the king's son himself is blinded by the witch, and his sight is not restored until he is found by the searching Rapunzel. In "The Twelve Brothers" the sister must endure seven years of silence and be nearly burned at the stake before her brothers are restored from their enchantment. As Joseph Campbell summarized with wonderful simplicity: "Slandered Virtue is triumphant, Patience is rewarded, Love endures" (Campbell, 847).

Violence, Virtue, and Grace

But is it all the merit of the hero that overcomes the adversity? As important as is the noble character of the hero, many of the fairy tales also have something else at work: something Tolkien referred to as "eucatastrophe," but that in this context might best be described simply as grace. Very few of the characters succeed *on their own*. Cinderella has the aid of the magical hazel tree. Faithful John has the aid of the three ravens. The Two Brothers are faithful, merciful, and brave, but find success largely through the aid of their traveling companions: a lion, bear, wolf, fox, and hare that have taken up with them. And on and on. There are exceptions, of course. Hansel and Gretel are saved largely by Gretel's quick thinking; there does not *appear* to be any miraculous intervention, except perhaps in the duck who aids their return journey and the fact that they return home to find their wicked stepmother dead. But there is enough of a pattern that it is unmistakable. W. H. Auden commented on these aspects of the tales:

> From the formula of the three brothers [the reader] will learn that the hero . . . is not a superman with exceptional natural gifts. The third son succeeds, not through his own merit, but through the assistance of Divine Grace. His contribution is, firstly, a humility which admits that he cannot succeed without Grace; secondly, a faith which believes that Grace will help him, so that, when the old beggar asks for his last penny, that is, when, humanly speaking, he is dooming himself to fail, he can give it away, and lastly, a willingness, unlike his elder brothers who always carry aspirin, to accept suffering. He is, in fact, one who is not anxious. (Auden-2)

It would seem here that by "merit" Auden is primarily referring to strength, intellect, or other natural abilities (or "natural gifts") and not to moral virtue. The third brother is lacking in the former, but not in the latter. Charity, as the brother shows to the beggar, is one of the chief virtues. Nonetheless, it is ultimately upon grace that the hero relies, and that grace often comes after hardship.

But what of the violence? One of the first things that strikes many modern readers of these fairy tales is how dark they are, and grim. (The last name of the brothers who collected them is a very appropriate co-incidence.) Tolkien observed that these fairy tales often drew out of the Cauldron some rather gruesome bones—and he is *thankful* for it! "I do not think I was harmed by the horror *in the fairy-tale setting*," he writes, "out of whatever dark beliefs and practices of the past it may have come." He even complains that many modern versions of the stories—what we might think of as "Disneyfied" versions—are "mollified" for children (*Essay*, 56). In his *Poetics* Aristotle complained about theater in his day, observing that the best dramatic works arouse real fear and pity in the observer. He argued that this has cathartic effects on both the individual and society. Tales that rely too heavily on visual "spectacle" to make us feel good without taking us first through the fearful and pitiable parts of life cheat us of the real value of stories at their best.

Consider, for example, the nineteenth-century version of "Cinderella" told by the brothers in contrast with popular versions circulating in the twentieth century. The modern version is far more different from the latest Grimm version than the latest Grimm version is from the earliest. There is no fairy godmother figure in the Grimm version. Instead, Cinderella weeps every day by the tomb of her mother, her tears water a young hazel branch, causing it to grow into a great hazel tree, and her wishes are granted by two doves who nest in the tree. At the end, Cinderella's two wicked stepsisters have their eyes pecked out by the same birds who helped Cinderella go to the ball. "And thus, for their wickedness and false-hood, they were punished with blindness all their days" (*Grimm's,* 128). It is hard to imagine such an ending in any Disney film! However, these endings, especially the cruel punishments for the tormentors of the hero or heroine, are common in the Grimms' versions. In the brothers' version of "Snow White," the story ends with the wicked queen "forced to put on the red-hot shoes, and dance until she dropped down dead" (258). Or consider the end of "The Twelve Brothers," a less well-known story but one quite representative of the collection: "The wicked step-mother was taken before the judge, and put into a barrel filled with boiling oil and venomous snakes, and died an evil death" (64). "The Singing Bone" ends: "The wicked brother could not deny the deed, and was sewn up in a sack and drowned" (150).

Nor is the harshness reserved for the cruel endings of villains. There are numerous tales in which the hero or heroine loses eyes, or hands, or feet, or in some cases, heads (though the heads are often miraculously restored). In "The Frog-King, or Iron Henry," the enchanted prince is restored not by the *kiss* of a princess, but by a much more violent means: the princess hurls the prince in the form of a frog "with all her might against the wall." When he falls down, "he was no frog but a king's son with kind and beautiful eyes" (20). Is there a simple, satisfying explana-tion—or summary message—of this violence in one tale? It doesn't seem so. But is there something in the pattern? Yes. While the more modern versions of these fairy tales are softer, less severe, and less rigid—and some would say more merciful—they are also less intense; as Tolkien would argue, they are less powerful and less moving.

Tolkien has a point. We can agree that it is a good thing that we don't put people in barrels full of spikes and roll them down hills as punish-ment, or use heated iron shoes to kill people. If "mollification" means that cruelty is replaced by grace and mercy, we can rejoice. Even Tolkien's hero Frodo shows mercy to Saruman and refuses to let the other Hobbits kill him, though such a killing would surely be just. But something good is also lost in any modernization of the tales that lose their nerve and their ability to recognize evil for what it is, and don't see the need for rectification of wrong situations. In the same breath that Gandalf praises Bilbo for showing mercy to Gollum, he also acknowledges that Gollum *deserves* death. Likewise, at the same time Gandalf says he will not seek to punish Saruman or Wormtongue, he mentions that a cruel fate likely awaits them both, and that they *deserve* it: "the punishment is just."[15] Furthermore, Gollum, Saruman, and Wormtongue all do get their just desserts in the story, though it is not the wise who mete out those punishments.

There is yet another point that is simple, but important. The gruesome ends that so many characters meet are a vital reminder of what so many today have forgotten: there are, in fact, taboos in the world—things that we must not do, or must not touch, or must not say, because the consequences of that doing, or touching, or saying are horrendous. Tolkien writes of these taboos in his essay:

> The things that are there must often have been retained (or inserted) because the oral narrators, instinctively or consciously, felt their literary "significance." Even where a prohibition in a fairy-story is guessed to be derived from some taboo once practiced long ago, it has probably been preserved in the later stages of the tale's history because of the great mythical significance of prohibition. A sense of that significance may indeed have lain behind some of the taboos themselves. Thou shalt not—or else thou shalt depart beggared into endless regret. The gentlest "nursery-tales" know it. Even Peter Rabbit was forbidden a garden, lost his blue coat, and took sick. The Locked Door stands as an eternal Temptation. (*Essay*, 57)

Fairy tales remind us of these taboos and warn us (often vividly) of the danger of breaking them. In this way, they function much like myth.

And yes, as Thomas Howard points out, fairy tales can function even like the myth of the Bible:

> There was a common thread, if we may so speak, running through ancient paganism, Judaism, Christianity, and Islam. It was the idea that God, or the gods, are there, and that we mortals, far from being autonomous, are below these gods who are not only higher than we are, and more powerful, but most unsettling of all, call us to account. . . . There *is* a divine order,

---

15. See *The Lord of the Rings*, I/ii and III/x.

and . . . we mortals are under the most somber obligation to get in tune with, or in step with, that order.[16]

Fairy Tales contain taboos

There is the point. Fairy tales tell us that "there *is* a divine order," even though they give no theological statement about where or who that divine order comes from. And the very horror of the tales helps build that notion. Great trouble comes to those who disobey or try to ignore that order. There are consequences if we stray, if we don't stay in tune and in step with it.

This last point may well be the biggest modern objection to the fairy tales, for if a society denies the very existence of a divine order or divine authority, then it will rebel against any thought of punishment inflicted on those who break such an order, or disobey the authority. A result is that fairy tales will be mollified. As one popular bumper sticker ironically (and authoritatively) commands us, "Question authority." This objection can also be phrased in terms of taboos, which are often (in the thoughts of the cultures that originated them) human responses to some divine order and authority. It may be argued that since fairy tales pass along and perpetuate taboos, and since taboos are sometimes unjust, therefore fairy tales are purveyors and promulgators of injustice and therefore worthless, and the taboos as well as the fairy tales should be forgotten.[17] Certainly, some taboos should be broken, as for instance taboos that oppress people of lower castes. (Sadly, these taboos exist in every society.) But are all taboos evil? Or can some taboos be true reflections of a divine order that is good? One of the main taboos of fairy tales is that against injustice. This is a taboo that ought to be upheld.

A third effect of the stories, as the Grimms told them (in contrast with the modern Disneyfied versions), has to do with the whole mythic tradition. In the modern "mollified" versions, we lose some of the aura of antiquity. The nineteenth-century versions give a sense of "distance and a great abyss of time." As Tolkien goes on to explain:

> Such stories have now a mythical or total (unanalysable) effect, an effect quite independent of the findings of Comparative Folklore, and one which

16. Thomas Howard, "Cardinal Newman and C. S. Lewis on the Limits of Education," a lecture presented at Middlebury College in 1997.

17. Another problem with this logic is that it is self-contradictory. It is, in fact, a taboo against taboos—the replacement of an old taboo with a new one. If we destroy all taboos, we must also destroy the taboo against taboos. We may do well to question authority, but this should include questioning the very authority that tells us to question authority.

it cannot spoil or explain; they open a door on Other Time, and if we pass through, though only for a moment, we stand outside our own time, outside Time itself, maybe. (*Essay,* 56)

What Tolkien is saying is that even these romantic fairy tales—not despite their hard edges but precisely because of them—can accomplish something akin to what is accomplished by the "higher" or more cosmogonic and cosmological myth. They are also equally hard to nail down, with respect to any explanation of what exactly causes the effect. Joseph Campbell summarizes this aspect (and several others) of the importance of the Grimms' collection:

> Through the vogues of literary history, the folk tale has survived. Told and retold, losing here a detail, gaining there a new hero, disintegrating gradually in outline, but re-created occasionally by some narrator of the folk, the little masterpiece transports into the living present a long inheritance of story-skill, coming down from the romancers of the Middle Ages, the strictly disciplined poets of the Celts, the professional storymen of Islam, and the exquisite, fertile, brilliant fabulists of Hindu and Buddhist India. This little mare that we are reading has the touch on it of Somadeva, Shahrazad, Taliesin and Boccaccio, as well as the accent of the story-wife of Niederzwehren. If ever there was an art on which the whole community of mankind has worked—seasoned with the philosophy of the codger on the wharf and singing with the music of the spheres—it is this of the ageless tale. The folk tale is the primer of the picture-language of the soul. (Campbell, 864)

The Fairy Tales of George MacDonald (and Their Influence on Tolkien and Lewis)

Whereas the Grimms' fairy tales remain to this day the most famous—the name *Grimm* is synonymous with fairy tale—and Hans Christian Andersen is also a household name, the influence of the lesser-known George MacDonald on the genre of modern fantasy is arguably equally great or even greater, and is also easier to trace than any of his fellow nineteenth-century writers. Between 1855 and 1895 MacDonald wrote nine original short fairy tales,[18] plus five book-length works that belong

---

18. *The Complete Fairy Tales of George MacDonald* contains eight short fairy tales, but does not include "The Lost Princess," a fairy tale that has appeared both as a self-contained book and also in collections of fairy tales. Adding this brings the total to nine. Some give a larger number, taking into account that

to the literature of Faërie: *Phantastes* (1858), *At the Back of the North Wind* (1871), *The Princess and the Goblin* (1872), its sequel, *The Princess and Curdie* (1883), and *Lilith* (1895).[19] While the two *Princess* books are considered to be children's stories, and have a similar tone to his shorter fairy tales, *Phantastes* and *Lilith* are fairy tales for adults and belong more in the realm of fantasy (or Victorian fantasy, as it has sometimes been called).

A good deal is known about the life of George MacDonald (1824–1905), largely through his biography, *George MacDonald and His Wife*, written by his son Dr. Greville MacDonald and published in 1924. We will say little of his life. It was a very difficult one, full of poverty (he was often on the edge of starvation), disease (he spent much of the last two decades of his life in Italy because of lung disease), and tragedy (his mother died when he was only eight years old, and he lost four of his eleven children at young ages). Yet it was also a joyful life, rich in relationships though not in material possessions. By all accounts, he had a wonderful relationship with his father despite theological differences that would deepen as the younger MacDonald matured. Though death—a frequent visitor to the MacDonald house—is a common theme of many of his works, it is usually portrayed as merely another step in life toward something greater and more wonderful: an escape not *from* life, which MacDonald enjoyed, but to a better and richer life.

Of MacDonald's shorter works, most are from a mold similar to that of the tales of Grimm, Andersen, and Lang, and use devices familiar to that romantic mode of fairy tale, which resides on the lighter side of the spectrum of Faërie, opposite of myth. Of these, "The Golden Key" is the exception. Its symbolism is profound, and also very mysterious. Though the mysterious *key* to some unknown treasure is a device that appears in the Grimms' tales, what MacDonald makes of it is very different from anything found in Jacob and Wilhelm's collection. (Not coincidentally, "The Golden Key" is also widely considered his best fairy tale. We will discuss it in greater length at the end of this chapter.) MacDonald's two books about Princess Irene take a few tentative steps—both in length and in tone—from traditional fairy tale toward the middle ground in the literature of Faërie: the subgenre of romance and fantasy. *Phantastes*

"The Carosyn" was originally two stories that MacDonald later merged. And there are also other short stories (such as "The Gift of the Christ Child") that the editor of the collection (rightly, we think) exclude as being something other than a fairy tale.

19. He also wrote some twenty conventional novels, set primarily in the Scottish Highlands of his youth. Many of these are still in print today, as are collections of his sermons.

and *Lilith,* his adult works of serious fantasy move even further in that direction, paving the way for the twentieth century's major works of heroic fantasy in a way that the short fairy tales of the Grimms and Andersen could not. C. S. Lewis writes that shortly after he began reading *Phantastes* he knew that he "had crossed a great frontier" (*Preface,* xxxiii). Some measure of the "frontier" of which Lewis speaks is surely that of book-length modern fantasy, the distinctive union of fairy tale with the novel, and taken as a serious form of literature. It was a frontier that many other writers of modern fantasy would cross with Lewis.

C. S. Lewis's affinity for George MacDonald's writing is well known. He once wrote: "I have never concealed the fact that I regarded [George MacDonald] as my master; indeed I fancy I have never written a book in which I did not quote from him" (*Preface,* xxxii). Considering just how many books C. S. Lewis wrote, it is easy to assume he was exaggerating. When you begin to read Lewis carefully, however, you quickly realize that he was not. We cannot think of one major work of Lewis in which there is not a clearly discernible trace—and often a direct quote—of MacDonald's thought. MacDonald even appears as a character (in heaven) in Lewis's *The Great Divorce.*

Likewise, Tolkien, early in his career, acknowledged his own debt to George MacDonald. In a letter written in 1938 denying one critic's comment that he derived many of his ideas for *The Hobbit* from Victorian fairy tales, he made one notable exception. "As for the rest of the tale it is ... derived from (previously digested) epic, mythology, and fairy story—not, however, Victorian in authorship, as a rule to which George MacDonald is the chief exception" (*Letters,* 31). Later in Tolkien's life, he distanced himself a little more from MacDonald and criticized some of his work. Even then, however, he was quick to praise what he considered George MacDonald's *best* fairy tales. In a letter written in 1964, he states: "I am not as warm an admirer of George MacDonald as C. S. Lewis was; but I do think well of this ["The Golden Key"]" (*Letters,* 351). In "On Fairy-Stories" he describes both "The Golden Key" and *Lilith* as "stories of power and beauty" (52). Tolkien's own story *Smith of Wootton Major* began in 1965 as a preface to a new edition of "The Golden Key." As Tom Shippey accounts, "The story grew and the Preface was abandoned" (Shippey, 297). Nonetheless, it was thinking about George MacDonald that inspired Tolkien's own last and greatest fairy tale.

Thus, two of the most important writers of fantasy in the twentieth century both look to MacDonald as an important influence on their own writing. What was that influence? Some of MacDonald's contributions to modern fantasy, though mundane, are easy to see. Tolkien attributes the concept of goblins in *The Hobbit* largely to the portrayal of goblins in *The Princess and the Goblin*. In a letter written in 1954, he describes the origin of his orcs:

> They are not based on direct experience of mine; but owe, I suppose, a good deal to the goblin tradition (*goblin* is used as a translation in *The Hobbit*, where *orc* only occurs once, I think), especially as it appears in George MacDonald, except for the soft feet which I never believed in. (*Letters*, 178)

By the writing of *The Lord of the Rings*, Tolkien's MacDonald-inspired "goblins" had fully evolved into the darker orcs. In a different letter of the same year, he also describes the shift from the term (and concept) of *goblin* to that of the *orc*. "Personally I prefer Orcs (since these creatures are not 'goblins,' not even the goblins of George MacDonald, which they do to some extent resemble)" (*Letters*, 185). In writing this, Tolkien is referring to perceived deficiencies in the image of goblins: the "goblin tradition" he calls it. He realized that as soon as he used the term *goblin*, it would immediately conjure certain images in the minds of any readers steeped in Faërie.

This was a problem. In our discussion of the differences between myth, heroic fantasy, and fairy tale, we saw that one usual difference is in the might and nature of the main characters. The myths are about the gods; heroic fantasy is about heroes (larger than life, but not gods); while fairy tales are about the simpleton, the tailor, the younger brother, the good-hearted and virtuous peasant who accomplishes some great task despite a lack of heroic strength. While goblins, as we know them in our collective imagination, are appropriate villains for a romantic fairy tale, Tolkien's orcs are both more wicked and more powerful, and thus more fitting as villains of a work of heroic fantasy. Goblins, for all their potential wickedness, are too silly to provide a worthwhile adversary to a legendary hero. And yet, as we suggested in the previous chapter in our discussion of *Beowulf*, such an adversary is necessary; appropriate monsters deepen the meaning and significance of works of Faërie. Thus, while the term *goblin* at least partly sufficed for *The Hobbit*, it did not for *The Lord of the Rings*. So Tolkien invented orcs, taking the name from a little used Old English term Tolkien glossed to mean "demon." Still, Tolkien felt that MacDonald's treatment of goblins was the best, and even his orcs owe much to them.

Tolkien also owes something to MacDonald's portrayal of the wandering explorer in the land of Faërie. MacDonald gives us such a character in Anodos,[20] the narrator of *Phantastes*, who through opening a hidden chamber in an old heirloom desk is granted permission to enter Fairy Land.[21] Tolkien explores the same idea in his story *Smith of Wootton Major*, where Smith is given a fay-star that comes from "an old black box with several different compartments" (*Smith*, 15) that had been tucked away on a high shelf in the storeroom. The fay-star proves to be a passport into Faery: a setup very similar to that of Anodos's many-compartmented desk. Once in the realm of Faery, Smith's adventures also bear resemblance to those of Anodos. Both explorers encounter watchful trees, and there are great knights passing through both tales. These are important images of fairy tales. The tree has myriad connections to myth and fairy (some discussed earlier in the book), but Tolkien's use bears closest resemblance to that of MacDonald; in both stories the trees serve as images of grace, with symbolic connections to the cross. The knights suggest something of a greater battle in the realm of Faërie, which humans like Anodos and Smith know little about, and are irrelevant to.

In his essay "On Fairy-Stories," Tolkien even speaks of *himself* as an Anodos figure: a wandering explorer in the land of Faërie, full of wonder but not of information. He also borrows directly from MacDonald's line in "The Golden Key"—another fairy tale about wanderers in the realm of Faërie—that "if a wanderer gets in among [the mischievous creatures of Faërie], the good ones will always help him more than the evil ones will be able to hurt him" (*Complete*, 215). Again, both authors are referring to a battle that takes place among unseen powers.

MacDonald's influence on C. S. Lewis is even easier to see. The representation of the underworld creatures in *The Silver Chair* is reminiscent of the beast-creatures in *The Princess and Curdie*, who are in the process of becoming human. Likewise, Lewis's depiction in *The Last Battle* of moral, rational, talking beasts returning to mute animals can be seen earlier in *The Princess and Curdie* in the many humans who are in the process of becoming beasts (but don't know it).

Indeed, the connections go much deeper. In *The Princess and the Goblin*, Princess Irene finds a secret and enchanted doorway that leads

20. *Anodos* probably comes from the Greek *ana* ("up") and *hodos* ("road"), describing one who travels upward, or who is on the upward road.

21. We use "Fairy Land" here, and "Faery" in the next sentence to be consistent with the particular usage of the two stories being discussed.

her up to the garret room of her great-great-grandmother. With its fire of roses, and its healing bath, it is a room that surely exists within the borders of Faërie even as the great-great-grandmother is a being from Faërie. Others, however, are not able to find that room (or the grandmother), and even Irene cannot find it at will, but only at certain moments when she is called. As a result, these others (most notably her nurse and, early in the story, Curdie) disbelieve Irene's account. When Curdie finally does find his way into the garret, because of his disbelief he can see nothing of the beautiful room; instead of the grandmother, the "lovely fire of roses," or the moonlight hanging from the roof, he sees only "a big, bare, garret-room" with "a tub, and a heap of musty straw, and a withered applet, and a ray of sunlight coming through a hole in the middle of the roof." Instead of hearing the grandmother talking, he hears only "the cooing of a lot of pigeons." As a result, the prince accuses Irene of making up a story. He says, very condescendingly, "I think you had better drop it, princess, and go down to the nursery, like a good girl" (*Goblin*, 150–51).

Borrowing from his avowed "master," Lewis employs the same sort of devices both in *The Lion, the Witch, and the Wardrobe* and in *The Last Battle*. In the former, youngest sister Lucy finds her way through a magic wardrobe into the land of Narnia—also a land within the confines of Faërie. But when Lucy tries to bring her three siblings (Peter, Susan, and Edmund) through the same door, she finds that it doesn't work, and thus her siblings don't believe her story. "Come, Lu," Peter says to her, when she insists upon her story, "That's going a bit far. You've had your joke. Hadn't you better drop it now?" (*Lion*, 22). In *The Last Battle*, the dwarves are flung through the magical door of the stable and into the eternal realm of the new Narnia, but because of their disbelief they see nothing at all. They are, quite literally but also by their own choice, blind. Where there are fresh flowers, they smell "filthy stable-litter." When they are given a "glorious feast," including pies, trifles, and goblets of fine wine, they are unable even to taste it properly, and they eventually conclude that they are eating hay, old turnips, and cabbages—"the sort of things you might find in a Stable"—and the wine they imagine to be dirty water from the donkey's trough (*Battle*, 145–47).

Lewis's borrowing—which is to say, MacDonald's influence—goes well beyond the devices themselves and includes what is made of them. The whole notion of the enchanted door into the realm of Faërie (which in the case of *The Last Battle* is a clear analogy for heaven) becomes a vehicle for a profound discussion of faith. Lewis, a Christian apologist as well as a writer of fairy tale and fantasy, wrote abundantly about faith. One of his best-known apologies for Christianity is his so-called trilemma argument that Jesus must be either a liar (on the same level of evil as the devil), or a lunatic (on a par with somebody who claims to be a poached egg), or who he claimed to be, namely, the Son of God.[22] This argument appears in *Mere Christianity* in the form of essay as an argument for Jesus's divinity, but it also is presented in story in *The Lion, the Witch, and the Wardrobe* as an argument for the truth of Lucy's claims. "There are only three possibilities," Professor Kirk tells Lucy's concerned oldest siblings. He goes on to explain: "Either your sister is telling lies, or she is mad, or she is telling the truth. You know she doesn't tell lies and it is obvious that she is not mad. For the moment then and unless any further evidence turns up, we must assume that she is telling the truth" (*Lion*, 45). This argument is eminently reasonable. It comes from the lips of Professor Kirk, who is the wisest and most respected character of the tale (other than Aslan himself). Of course, if we also were inside the story, we would probably have our doubts about Lucy's claims. Like Lucy's siblings, we might acknowledge the reasonableness of the argument itself but still deny its conclusion. But as readers of the book, we also know that the conclusion is true, even though the characters within the story do not.

And all of this comes directly from George MacDonald. It is Peter's mother, the wisest character in *The Princess and the Goblin* (with the exception of the great-great-grandmother herself) who presents the exact same form of argument to Peter that he should believe Princess Irene's story. It is clear, Mrs. Peterson argues, that Irene isn't lying. That she isn't crazy—or at least that there is *some* mysterious power behind her stories—is evidenced by the fact that she was able to rescue Curdie from the goblins and lead him out of the mountain following an invisible thread that she can see and feel but he cannot. Thus the conclusion that she is speaking the truth, or least that Curdie should not accuse her until he knows better. "You have no right to say what she told you was not true," Curdie's mother tells him. "There is something you cannot explain, and her explanation may be the right one" (*Goblin*, 157). Again, the reader knows the whole story and sees not only that Mrs. Peterson's argument makes sense, but also that it is true.

22. See the end of book 2, section 3 ("The Shocking Alternative") of *Mere Christianity* (New York: Macmillan, 1945), 55–56.

The Significance of MacDonald

Now, at one level we can see the emphasis on rationality in these arguments. Lewis's formulation takes the logical form known as a *disjunctive syllogism*. On the surface the argument itself (though probably not the conclusion) could have come right from the Enlightenment,[23] and Lewis certainly had some leaning toward rationalism. "Logic!" the professor says to Peter and Susan, before he explains his argument. "Why don't they teach logic at these schools?" (*Lion*, 45). So here we have a strange irony. Fairy tale, whose resurgence in popularity came in part as a reaction *against* the rationalism of the Enlightenment, is used as a vehicle in the *defense* of reason—or of the reasonableness of a rational argument. But here is the double irony. Fairy tale justifies the validity of the rationalistic argument only to turn around and use the rationalistic argument to defend the truth claims of the fairy tale. A rational argument is used to support a very fantastic claim that almost any Enlightenment rationalist would be sure to deny. The syllogism is not alien to the fairy tale. In a sense, it is most at home there, where it can have life in a story.

As soon as we say this, however, we must turn again to the story and realize the limits of reason. Reason, in the stories of Lewis and his predecessor MacDonald, can lead to faith. But even while Mrs. Peterson argues very *rationally* to Curdie that he ought not disbelieve the princess—thus relying on reason and, more specifically, rational discourse as a way of knowing—she and her husband also point out (almost in the same breath) that there are many things that *cannot* be known by reason or science. As Curdie's mother tells Curdie, "There is something you cannot explain," meaning there are things whose explanation goes beyond the natural. That being the case, we might also look to other means of knowing, not to replace science or reason but to add to it. "Her explanation might be the right one" (*Goblin*, 157). When Curdie still struggles to understand this principle, his mother tells him a story about an experience of her own. And it is through her story, more than through her reasoned discourse, that Curdie comes to understand her. In George MacDonald's world, the deepest kind of knowing comes not through the brain but through the heart. Several times we are told that some people can see things that others can't. The same goes for belief. "Curdie is not yet able to believe

23. The logic of syllogism was first articulated by Plato (e.g., in the *Charmides*) and more completely by his student Aristotle in his *Organon*, in the fourth century BC, and it was a constant presence in medieval thought. Disjunctive syllogisms are, after all, not an invention of Enlightenment or other logicians, but more precisely a *discovery* of logicians—a discovery of something we all already possessed.

some things," Grandmother tells Irene. "Seeing is not believing—it is only seeing" (*Goblin*, 152). MacDonald is not arguing for mindless romanticism, and he is certainly not rejecting logical argument. Rather, he is reminding us of the proper place and limitations of logic. Deductive reason cannot deliver all that the Enlightenment promised it could. Often, we know things in other ways. As Viktor Frankl once put it in his criticism of Sartre's existentialism, "the meaning of our existence is not invented by ourselves, but rather detected."[24] Or as the logician Charles Peirce wrote, "reasoning can supply the mind with nothing in the world except an estimate of the value of a statistical ratio. . . . As to God, open your eyes—and your heart, which is also a perceptive organ—and you see him."[25] We are not merely thinking machines; we can often feel the truth when we cannot logically articulate it. Divorced from logic, reliance on feeling is dangerous, just as dangerous as logic divorced from love.

These ideas can also be seen in Lewis's Narnia tales, and the influence is unmistakable. The professor does not suggest any scientific arguments to discover the truth or falsity of Lucy's claims; he knows such an approach would be completely inadequate to discover a truth of this nature. And as Lucy discovers in *The Last Battle* when she tries to rescue the dwarves from their blindness, you cannot force belief via reason and evidence. Not even Aslan can do this. "Dearest," Aslan tells Lucy, "I will show you both what I can, and what I cannot, do" (*Battle*, 147). What Aslan cannot do, it turns out, is force the dwarves to believe in him. So while Enlightenment rationalism denied the epistemological importance of imagination and fantasy, imagination and fantasy do not deny the validity of the rational or scientific; they only deny that these are the *only* ways of knowing.

We could show the influence of George MacDonald on many other modern authors as well, though perhaps in no other case quite so clearly as with C. S. Lewis. However, if once we acknowledge the influence of Tolkien and Lewis on the rest of modern fantasy, then this is unnecessary.

Of course, MacDonald himself was drawing upon many types and symbols found in earlier-tradition fairy tales, such as those of the Grimms' collection. This can be seen especially in most of MacDonald's nine short fairy tales. "The Light Princess" and "Little Daylight" use the device seen in the Grimms' "Little Briar Rose" of an offended witch placing an enchantment on a young princess, who must then be rescued by a prince.

24. Viktor Frankl, *Man's Search for Meaning* (New York: Pocket Books, 1972), 157.
25. Charles S. Peirce, *Philosophical Writings of Peirce*, Justus Buchler, ed. (New York: Dover, 1940), 377–78.

They even follow the same pattern of having one of the good witches offer a blessing after the curse of the evil witch in order to partly offset the severity of the curse. Also in "The Light Princess," the prince's offering of his life for the sake of the unappreciative princess bears considerable resemblance to Faithful John's own sacrifice at a time that his king does not understand him.

In MacDonald's final fairy tale, "The Day Boy and the Night Girl," the boy Photogen and the girl Nycteris are from birth captives of a witch. As is the case in "Hansel and Gretel," it is largely through the girl's humility, wisdom, and bravery that the two are rescued and the witch killed, despite the boy's initial insensitivity and cowardice. In "The Giant's Heart," MacDonald makes simultaneous use of the old device of sending children into the home of a giant, whose wife tries to save them from the pot, and that of removing one's heart and placing it in safekeeping. Readers familiar with MacDonald's short tales and those of the Grimms could make a long list of such debts.

The devices of traditional fairy story can also be seen in MacDonald's longer works. In *The Princess and the Goblin* we have a commoner—Curdie Peterson, the son of a poor miner—who through his perseverance, wit, bravery, and moral virtue rescues a castle and countryside. In *The Princess and Curdie,* Curdie rescues the entire kingdom, weds the princess, and becomes the king. In both stories, he must endure hardship en route to his success. For a time he is a captive of the goblins and later, after being shot in the leg by an arrow and suffering delirium, is a captive of the king's own soldiers. And for all his virtue, his final success is achieved only eucatastrophically through the miraculous aid (and grace) of the grandmother. What MacDonald (along with Hans Christian Andersen) showed was that one could write *original* fairy tales, drawing upon the traditions but also making them better. Put another way, George Mac-Donald went well beyond embellishment; his *fairy tales* were not *folk tales* in the real sense of that term.[26]

So while MacDonald's Curdie is somewhat like the "child of good fortune" in "The Devil and the Three Golden Hairs," or the youngest son in "The Queen Bee"—or indeed the peasant-hero of any of a number of Grimms' fairy tales—he is also very different. For all of Curdie's virtues, early in the first book he lacks in faith. He makes mistakes of judgment

26. This is an important point. It has sometimes been assumed that there was once an age of myth, then an age of fairy tale, and then an age of romance, and that we have finally outgrown these genres. Part of the importance of MacDonald, Lewis, and Tolkien is that they have shown us that there are still stories, "from the cosmogonic to fairy tale," to be told and retold.

(getting captured by goblins and shot by the king's soldiers) as well as moral errors (in his treatment of the princess early in the book). The heroes in the tales collected by Jacob and Wilhelm Grimm almost always make virtuous choices from the start; such a character transformation as that undergone by Curdie is very uncommon in their tales. What we are really seeing is that George MacDonald has taken the fairy tale form a step closer to heroic romance.

At the simplest level, it is a step upward in length from traditional fairy tale in the oral tradition toward the novel. With this step, however, come several other features. Curdie's character is more fully developed than those of the traditional fairy-tale hero. Perhaps most important, though, is the movement along the spectrum of significance. In the *Princess* books, MacDonald shows us a real battle going on between what we might call forces of light and those of darkness. It is a prolonged war, and all that happens is an instance of that war: a battle or skirmish on one front or another. In *The Princess and the Goblin,* the goblins are doing something more than mere impishness (though we see signs of that also, such as in the teasing of the princess and Lootie, or the harassment of Curdie's mother); they are in a war, intent not only on the destruction of the king's castle but on the perversion of his order (especially regarding his daughter.) MacDonald shows that even supposed servants of the king can be doing the work of the enemy: the small-mindedness of the nurse, Lootie, and others of the castle servants (including a few soldiers) is work on the side of the goblins. The battle is even more apparent in *The Princess and Curdie,* where we get glimpses of the insidiousness of the enemy, who in this case are humans motivated by greed and lust, and lacking in nearly all moral virtue.

Mystery, Holiness, and "The Golden Key"

Perhaps the most compelling feature of MacDonald's tales—both short and long—is the sense of holiness, and the pervading presence of death. Colin Duriez wrote, "The most important meaning of MacDonald's myths or marvelous stories is holiness, which nearly always conveys joy." He also wrote that the "distinctive magic" of MacDonald's stories is "only what it is by being full of holiness." One aspect of holiness is simply "wholeness," and in that sense everything we have been saying about George MacDonald so far reflects holiness. There is a wholeness—a completeness, unity, and integration both within his stories and in the ways his stories work in us. There is the wholeness of logic *plus* love, especially in the wisdom of Curdie's mother; the wholeness of the moral fabric of our lives being animated by powerful stories; the wholeness of participating in the stories and having more life; the wholeness of being ourselves storytellers and retellers; and the wholeness of our connection to the whole human race through these archetypal tales that get told and retold, and inspire new tales.

More specifically, though, to be holy is to be set apart, reverent, and especially devoted to service. This type of holiness is deeply spiritual, and also fundamentally of the earth, for it impacts every aspect of one's life as it is lived in the flesh. (In that way, it is also wholeness: an integration of the spirit and flesh.) We see this holiness in everything about the great-great-grandmother of the *Princess* tales. We see it in the spare simplicity of her room.

> There was hardly any more furniture in the room than there might have been in that of the poorest old woman who made her bread by her spinning. There was no carpet on the floor—no table anywhere—nothing but the spinning-wheel and the chair beside it. (*Goblin*, 16)

Such simplicity, and her devotion to her spinning, suggests the deeper devotion to her spiritual purpose. We also see it in her clean and simple dress, and in her simple lifestyle. We see the analogy from spiritual cleanliness to physical cleanliness in the silver-basin in which she washes the princess when they first meet, and later in the great silver oval bath.

This sort of holiness, like the silver bath, is bottomless. It is a holiness that is so clean that it is not afraid of getting dirty, as Irene discovers one night when she comes in soiled from a terrifying encounter with goblin creatures:

> "But, grandmother, you're so beautiful and grand with your crown on; and I am so dirty with mud and rain! I should quite spoil your beautiful blue dress."
>
> With a merry little laugh the lady sprung from her chair, more lightly far than Irene herself could, caught the child to her bosom, and, kissing the tearstained face over and over, sat down with her in her lap.
>
> "Oh, grandmother! You'll make yourself such a mess!" cried Irene, clinging to her.
>
> "You darling! do you think I care more for my dress than for my little girl? Besides—look here."

As she spoke she set her down, and Irene saw to her dismay that the lovely dress was covered with the mud of her fall on the mountain road. But the lady stooped to the fire, and taking from it, by the stalk in her fingers, one of the burning roses, passed it once and again and a third time over the front of her dress; and when Irene looked, not a single stain was to be discovered. (*Goblin*, 98–99)

The grandmother's holiness cannot be stained by anything on earth—or, rather, no earthly stain can long blemish such holiness.

Yet such holiness does not come without cost. One such cost is that borne by the one who speaks the truth and is not believed. Young Irene suffers first as a result of the disbelief of her nurse, Lootie, and then more painfully from the disbelief of Curdie. "What *shall* I do, grandmother?" the princess sobs. But even in her anguish, her concern is not with herself but with helping Curdie, and on the obligation of morality upon her actions, hence the "shall" (MacDonald's emphasis, not ours.) As the grandmother tells her: "You must be content not to be believed for a while. It is very hard to bear; but I have had to bear it, and shall have to bear it many a time yet" (*Goblin*, 151). In bearing this burden herself, Princess Irene comes better to understand her grandmother, even as her own previous doubts can give her greater sympathy for Curdie. Here, then, is perhaps the most profound "lesson" in holiness in all of the book—a lesson seen also in Grimm characters such as Faithful John, or the sister in "The Six Swans," but told in a new way by MacDonald. Holiness involves persevering belief even when everybody around you is in doubt. To be holy, one must be willing to endure a pain that cleanses. We see this also in the burning roses with which the grandmother purifies herself; they are so hot that they would burn young Princess Irene (not to mention, set her frock on fire).

Holiness is also expressed in true worship. In "The Day Boy and the Night Girl" MacDonald gives us—in the midst of fairy story—a very moving picture of worship. It comes when Nycteris sees the moon for the first time, at the age of sixteen, and the passage is worth quoting:

"No, it is not my lamp," she said after a while; "it is the mother of all the lamps."

And with that she fell on her knees, and spread out her hands to the moon. She could not in the least have told what was in her mind, but the action was in reality just a begging of the moon to be what she was—that precise incredible splendour hung in the far-off roof, that very glory essential to the being of poor girls born and bred in caverns. It was a resurrection—nay, a birth itself, to Nycteris. . . . the greatest of astronomers might envy the rapture of such a first impression at the age of sixteen. Immeasurably imperfect it was, but false the impression could not be, for she saw with the eyes made for seeing, and saw indeed what many men are too wise to see. (*Complete*, 252–53)

The falling down on her knees with her hands spread is an obvious expression of worship, emphasized by MacDonald's use of "glory" and "incredible splendour." Likewise, "begging of the moon to be what she was" is a wonderful description of the essence of worship; when we worship God, we are simply acknowledging him as he is and for who he is (as far as we mortals can know these things!). It must be noted here that Nycteris is not worshiping the moon itself, but that which it represents, namely the light. This is not a pagan worship of a celestial object, like a sun goddess or a moon goddess. Rather, Nycteris sees the moon as "the mother of all the lamps"—that is, as a *symbol* of Light—and she is worshiping the Light itself. Even if Nycteris does not understand this ("she could not in the least have told what was in her mind"), the author makes this clear to the reader. Light is a strongly spiritual image throughout the story, representing truth and eternal life, and the Christian reader will eventually think of the apostle John's proclamation that God is Light (1 John 1:5–7), and that Jesus is the Light that came into the world (John 1:4–9).

MacDonald also contrasts knowledge *of* the moon, such as astronomers have, with pure devotion, and in doing so contrasts *dry theology* with *living worship*—a contrast very similar to that between truth in abstract proposition and truth in story. It is far better to have an imperfect image of God but a wholehearted devotion than it is to have great knowledge without love. In making such a contrast, MacDonald is defending fairy story itself—even the pagan fairy stories of his Celtic ancestors and Germanic tradition. Such stories may not start with a correct doctrinal understanding of the Christian God that MacDonald believed in, but are still based on some Truth in the universe, and all true stories will to some degree or another eventually point back to this Truth. Thus, even to the extent that Nycteris might, in her own mind, be worshiping a moon goddess, such a worship would be closer to Truth than would be the worship of one who expressed a correct doctrinal understanding of God but never fell on his or her knees before him. This is a message of the entire story. Watho the witch is a consummate pursuer of knowledge for its own sake. As the first sentence of the story tells us, she was "a witch who desired to know everything." She was also evil. "She cared for nothing in itself—only for knowing it" (*Complete*, 241). Better the wisdom that comes through fairy story, MacDonald tells us, however imperfect the knowledge, than a knowledge that comes through rational pursuits (cold religious doctrine, or science without story, or purely rational philosophy) but is devoid of love. The former may be imperfect, but it is not false.

It is appropriate to end our discussion of George MacDonald with "The Golden Key." If some of MacDonald's fairy tales—especially "The Lost Princess"—can be faulted for occasional lapses into moralizing or even didacticism (a criticism that can also be made of some of Andersen's tales, like "The Snow Queen"), no such criticism can be made of "The Golden Key." It compares with MacDonald's other fairy tales much as Tolkien's *Smith of Wooten Major* compares with his *Farmer Giles of Ham*. Its symbolism is both deep and profound, and also very mysterious. Of this story, Tolkien wrote:

> Fairy-story . . . may be made a vehicle of Mystery. This at least is what George MacDonald attempted, achieving stories of power and beauty when he succeeded, as in *The Golden Key* (which he called a fairy-tale); and even when he partly failed, as in *Lilith* (which he called a romance). (*Essay*, 52)

The symbolism of the story is something like the balls of various colors and sizes being "played with" by the Old Man of the Fire (the oldest and wisest man of the three Old Men, though he appears in form as a young naked child). When Tangle spends seven years watching him, there comes a point when: "She understood it all, and saw that everything meant the same thing, though she could not have put it into words again" (*Complete*, 234). There is only one Truth, MacDonald is suggesting, and though good science and good reason may all point to that Truth, the Truth is higher and greater than the ability of mere propositions to capture it. The closest we come is through symbol, art, and story.

The inspiration for MacDonald's story can be found in a fairy tale of the same name—the final fairy tale in the last edition of the Grimms' collection. Both tales begin with a boy finding a mysterious key, and wondering what lock it fit. In the Grimms' tale, the story ends there. The boy finds the small keyhole: "He tried it, and the key fitted it exactly. Then he turned it once round, and now we must wait until he has quite unlocked it and opened the lid, and then we shall learn what wonderful things were lying in the box" (*Grimm's*, 812). D. L. Ashliman interprets the Grimms' "The Golden Key" as a fairy tale about fairy tales. "By closing their collection with this enigmatic tale without an end, the Grimms seem to be saying that folktales, too, are endless."[27]

George MacDonald's "The Golden Key" also seems to be a fairy tale about fairy tales. The first sentence begins: "There was a boy who used to sit in the twilight and listen to his great-aunt's stories." Soon after, he begins to comment on qualities of Fairy Land and its creatures, and about the truthfulness of the stories about it. MacDonald's story, however, does not stop abruptly. He asks the question of what those "wonderful things" are. In doing so, he takes the image of the golden key and lets it become an image for the key to the greatest treasure that he could imagine. To understand what that treasure is, and what it has to do with holiness, we must look at the imagery through the tale, and at the journey itself.

The first things we learn about the golden key are that it is the subject of many stories and that it lies at the end of the rainbow. The next thing we learn is that nobody knows what it will open; whoever gets the key has to find out for himself. We also learn that it would be better never to find the key than to find it and sell it. Whatever value it has, its value is far greater than any material wealth. We are reminded of Jesus's parables likening the kingdom of heaven to a treasure of such great worth that we would do well to sell everything we have to find it. "What good will it be for a man," Jesus asks, "if he gains the whole world, yet forfeits his soul?" (Matt. 16:26).

When the boy, Mossy, discovers the rainbow under which the golden key is hidden, the narrative moves from declarative statements about the key to imagery of the rainbow. MacDonald uses many spiritually laden terms. The rainbow is described as both "glorious" and "mysterious." It extends into the heavens. Though it is not until the very end of the story that we learn that the key opens a door into the rainbow itself, the reader nonetheless gets the impression that the rainbow is as important as the key beneath it. When Mossy first arrived at it, "he stood gazing at it till he forgot himself with delight—even forgot the key which he had come to seek" (*Complete,* 212). Like that of Nycteris and the moon, this is an image of worship and rapture. Then the imagery gets more specifically religious, as the rainbow is compared with the column of a church. Once again, we have hints that MacDonald is speaking of the kingdom of heaven. Seek that kingdom, Jesus tells us, and you will find it

27. Commentary following a translation by D. L. Ashliman, 1999, found at http://www.pitt.edu/~dash/type2250.html.

and everything with it (Matt. 6:33, 7:7). "You must look for the keyhole," Grandmother tells Mossy. "I can only tell you that if you look for it you will find it" (*Complete*, 222).

The most peculiar aspect of the rainbow, however, is the forms that are ascending within it: "beautiful forms slowly ascending as if by the steps of a winding stair . . . men and women and children—all different, all beautiful" (*Complete*, 212). Later, Mossy and his companion, Tangle, come upon another gathering of shadows—a great valley of beautiful shadows. These shadows do not lie on the ground, but are "heaped up above it like substantial forms of darkness, as if they had been cast upon a thousand different planes in the air." And they are forms so beautiful as to be breathtaking: exquisite shadows of gamboling children, the loveliest females forms, wonderful forms "half bird-like half human" and even the grand strides of "Titanic" shapes, "each disappearing in the surrounding press of shadowy foliage." When Mossy and Tangle descend from the mountains to cross this plain, or valley—a journey which seems to take a lifetime and leaves them grey and wrinkled—nothing is brought to the mind of the reader quite so clearly as Psalm 23: "Even though I walk through the valley of the shadow of death," the psalmist writes, "I will fear no evil" (v. 4). The valley in MacDonald's tale—the valley in which Tangle and Mossy must also learn not to fear—has shadows, rather than the singular shadow. Are they the shadows of the dead, a poetic twist of the psalmist's shadow of death? The whole imagery of the story seems to point to this understanding. But what a glorious image it is! If an image of death, then it is also an image of heaven. Certainly the wonderful forms remind us of heaven: Titanic shapes recall the gods (the Titans were, after all, progenitors of gods), while the winged human forms bring to mind angels. It is not surprising, then, when Mossy says, "We *must* find the country from which the shadows come," and Tangle replies "We must, dear Mossy. What if your golden key should be the key of *it*?" (*Complete*, 227).

As the reader learns, that is precisely what the golden key *is* to: it is the key to the staircase within the rainbow from which the forms are visible, which leads to the country from which the shadows fall. Mossy and Tangle become separated, and between them encounter the trinity of the Old Man of the Fire, the Old Man of the Earth, and the Old Man of the Sea. Before Mossy reaches the door to the country, the imagery is confirmed:

"You have tasted of death now," said the Old Man. "Is it good?"
"It is good," said Mossy. "It is better than life."

"No," said the Old Man; "it is only more life.—Your feet will make no holes in the water now." (*Complete*, 238)

The journey to the country is the journey of life, and beyond life into death, and through death into what? Into the glory that comes after death for all who hold the key—namely, the glory of heaven. The whole story is full of this imagery. Consider the fish that fly into the pots, are cooked, and then are resurrected as the angelic aëranths. Or consider the baths that provide the deep, timeless sleeps from which Mossy and Tangle awake refreshed and young. These are both images of death and resurrection unto a fuller life. "They were younger and better, and stronger and wiser, than they had ever been before" (*Complete*, 239–40).

The golden key is thus the key to heaven itself. Does MacDonald's golden key, then, stand for Christ, the key to heaven in MacDonald's Christian understanding of the world? Or does it, like the key of the Grimms' tale, stand for fairy tale itself? Or does the image do both? Tolkien described the Gospel story as the greatest and truest fairy story ever told, thus linking Faërie with Christ. In both "On Fairy-Stories" and "Leaf by Niggle," he suggests that the subcreative act of fantasy—the writing and telling of fairy tales—may work alongside the great Shepherd to lead people to heaven. Tolkien's predecessor, George MacDonald, may well have been suggesting the same thing.

PART 2

SOME MODERN WORKS
OF FANTASY

7

Ursula Le Guin's *Earthsea* Trilogy and Balance as the Highest Good

Most things grow old and perish, as the centuries go on and on. Very few are the precious things that remain precious, or the tales that are still told.

Ursula Le Guin, *The Tombs of Atuan*

Ursula K. Le Guin is unquestionably one of the most important modern authors of fantasy (as well as of science fiction). Her original *Earthsea* trilogy—composed of *A Wizard of Earthsea* (1968), *The Tombs of Atuan* (1971), and *The Farthest Shore* (1972)—was one of the earliest modern works of fantasy, and remains one of the most beloved. Long before Harry Potter found his way to Hogwarts to be tutored by the great wizard Dumbledore, a young, headstrong lad named Ged from the isle of Gont was learning the ways of the mage at the wizards' school on the isle of Roke in the Inmost Sea, near the heart of the archipelago named Earthsea. These books were no passing fancy. Most readers steeped in fantasy are familiar with them, and have likely returned to them for multiple rereadings. The books are still in print, more than thirty-five years after their initial publication, and thanks to their continued success

Le Guin has been able to return to the world of Earthsea and publish several more books in the Earthsea cycle. And though they didn't make it to the wide screen (as Tolkien's and Rowling's works did), the first two books of the original *Earthsea* trilogy were recently combined into a four-hour made-for-television adaptation[1]—aired at about the time that the extended edition of Peter Jackson's *Return of the King* was released, and between the releases of the third and fourth Harry Potter films.

Not only is it important to discuss Le Guin in a book on modern fantasy, but there are two features of her career and works that also make it particularly worthwhile to address her works in this book. First, in addition to a large number of science fiction and fantasy novels, she has also written a considerable body of essays and critical works *about* the genres. And in these essays, she often discusses (among other things) her own writing. Thus, as with Tolkien and Lewis, we can use her own writing about fantasy as a guide to understanding what she accomplished (or sought to accomplish) in the *Earthsea* trilogy.[2] Second, though Le Guin for the most part successfully avoids didacticism in her fantasy—as all good fantasy authors must do—her stories nonetheless reveal a fairly consistent and discernible underlying worldview.

The Power of Myth and Legend, and the Stories within the Stories

One of the things that Le Guin clearly understands is the universal power and importance of story, and especially story in the tradition of myth, legend, and fairy. Of her own life, she writes, "I read a lot, and a lot of my reading was myth, legend, fairy-tale; first-rate versions, too." She goes on to add, "I had also heard my father tell Indian legends aloud, just as he had heard them from informants, only translated into a rather slow, impressive English; and they were impressive and mysterious stories." She was excited when she learned that people were "still making

1. "Adaptation" is perhaps a generous term; the story line of the books was barely recognizable in the 2004 television movie, and the characters were recognizable only by their names. The entire nature of the priestesses of Atuan was dramatically altered. The movie was both more simplistic and more didactic. Nonetheless, the investment in the films gives some evidence of the long-lasting importance of books published thirty-five years earlier.

2. For reasons of space, we focus our attention on the original trilogy of better-known works: *A Wizard of Earthsea* (1968), *The Tombs of Atuan* (1971), and *The Farthest Shore* (1972). We will not deal with the later *Wizard* books. We do note, however, that some of Le Guin's views may have changed in the intervening decades, and readers may find in the later books some different answers to issues we address in the first three.

up myths"—not just for kids, but "for grownups, without a single apology to common sense"—and that she could make up stories herself (Le Guin, 20–21). She expresses much of the same liberation that Tolkien does in "On Fairy-Stories," or Lewis in "Sometimes Fairy-Stories Say Best What Is To Be Said": that fairy tale and myth are not primarily for children. Le Guin also evidently understands the profound differences between science fiction and fantasy. Though she is at home writing in both genres, she comments, "Along in 1967–8 I finally got my pure fantasy vein separated off from my science fiction vein, by writing *A Wizard of Earthsea* [a fantasy novel] and then *Left Hand of Darkness* [a sci-fi novel], and the separation marked a very large advance in both skill and content" (Le Guin, 25).

That Le Guin was steeped in story, and that she has a thorough understanding of fantasy and its roots in myth, is evident not only in her essays and nonfiction, but in her fiction as well. It comes to light in numerous ways throughout the *Earthsea* trilogy. Near the beginning of *A Wizard of Earthsea,* the first book of the cycle, the wise mage and teacher Kurremkarmerruk tells the protagonist, Ged, that the same language that gives power to "spells, enchantments, and invocations" is also "the language of our lays and songs" (*Wizard,* 47). In other words, just as there is power in a wizard's invocations, there is also power in stories, or in Story. Even though the focus of the stories is the power of Ged's spells, enchantments, and invocations, the remainders of the books are also replete with references to stories within the Story.

Of the classical devices of fantasy and Faërie, the two upon which Le Guin most clearly draws are wizards and dragons. The three most powerful forces in Earthsea are wizards (or mages), dragons, and the Old Powers (demonic powers to which our discussion will return later in the chapter). In all three cases, Le Guin draws enough on the common aspects of old myths to feed our imagination with their familiarity, while simultaneously working something new and original with them. For example, the whole trilogy is about one particular mage, Ged, whose common-use name is *Sparrowhawk*. We follow Ged's life from when he is a young lad first learning about his powers (in *A Wizard of Earthsea*) to when he is the Archmage who must rescue all of Earthsea (in *The Farthest Shore*). Ged must battle dragons (*Wizard*), Old Powers (*Wizard* and *Tombs*), and a corrupt wizard (*Shore*). When Ged first meets a dragon, we read that his heart swells "at the sight of the creature that was a myth to his people" (*Wizard,* 87). This suggests both that there is truth in myths—Ged cannot deny the actuality of the mythic dragon when he faces it—and that myths can inspire us. By the second book, Ged has been named a *Dragonlord;* at this point dragons are no longer enemies to be battled, but rather creatures to be respected, and with whom he occasionally speaks. At times Ged even seeks wisdom from dragons, and in the final book of the trilogy the two mightiest of dragons both seek aid from Ged and offer aid to him. The most famous dragon in Norse mythology is Fafnir, and it proves a fatal mistake when the dragon-slayer Sigurd reveals his name to him; with his dying breath, Fafnir uses that name to lay a curse on Sigurd. Tolkien's Bilbo very wisely and cleverly avoids making the same mistake with the dragon Smaug. While Le Guin's dragons certainly owe some debt to the dragon lore created by Fafnir and Smaug, she also introduces her own twists. In Earthsea, it is also very dangerous to tell someone your true name. Ged, however, while hiding his name from almost everybody else, reveals his true name to the most powerful dragons of Earthsea.

In addition to drawing upon myths from our world, the world of Earthsea has its own myths and legends, and these stories are important for the characters within the story to know. At the school on Roke there are official chanters, whose job it is to tell the old stories as part of the training of young wizards. Among other tales, we are told that these chanters "sing the long *Deed of Erreth-Akbe*," one of the most famous legends of old (*Wizard*, 55). As the reader later learns, Erreth-Akbe is one of Earthsea's greatest heroes, and his legend is especially important to *The Tombs of Atuan*, and arises also in *The Farthest Shore*. By showing us the great importance of stories within her Story—and making the point that the wise of her tales are those who must highly value myth and legend—Le Guin suggests that stories are also vitally important in our world.

We also note that it is not only the mages and the wise of Roke who understand the value of myth and story. Even far away in Kargad—the traditional enemy of Gont and Roke, and a land of raiding war bands and oppressive kings, where wizards are disdained or disbelieved—there are still those wise enough to value stories. In *The Tombs of Atuan*, the sympathetic old servant Thar tries to explain to the heroine, Tenar (known at the time as the priestess Arha), just how precious old stories are. One such old story is the tale of Erreth-Akbe, which surprisingly enough lives on even in Kargad. "And yet still the story is known and told, both here and in the West," he tells her. He goes on to make a profound comment about the values of these old stories. "Most things grow old and perish, as the centuries go on and on. Very few are the precious things that remain precious, or the tales that are still told" (*Tombs*, 49). Though many of the people of Kargad—including, it would seem, many of the priestesses—have ceased to believe the old legends, the *reader* is well aware that the legend of which Thar speaks is true. Thus, Le Guin again builds upon the idea that myths and legends contain truth, even though they are often dismissed or forgotten altogether.

Perhaps the clearest account of the value of old stories comes in the third book of the trilogy. Ged, now Archmage of all of Earthsea, is training young Prince Arren, who will eventually become the great King of All. "Fortune-telling and love-potions," Ged tells him when they first meet, "are not of much account, but old women are worth listening to" (*Shore*, 5). These words are not far different from what Gandalf tells Théoden when they first meet Ents:

> Is it so long since you listened to tales by the fireside? There are children in your land who, out of the twisted threads of story, could pick the answer to your question. You have seen Ents, O King, Ents out of Fangorn Forest, which in your tongue you call the Entwood. Did you think that the name was given only in idle fancy? . . . For not only the little life of Men is now endangered, but the life also of those things which you have deemed the matter of legend. (III/viii)

Shortly after, when Ged introduces Arren to the other mages of Roke, he presents him as the descendant of the legendary hero Morred of the House of Enlad, who died two thousand years earlier. Arren is not sure what to think, for Morred's "deeds were matter of legends, not of this present world. It was as if the Archmage had named him son of myth, inheritor of dreams" (*Shore*, 20). Arren, like Théoden, mistakenly believes that legends do not have to do with "this present world." But he, like Théoden, learns differently: that myth is not merely a dream, and that it can be very important to this world. In other words, Le Guin is saying what we have been saying throughout the book: myth can be true. Not only was Morred real, but Arren himself will become an even greater hero.

So important is this idea, and yet so difficult for the modern mind to grasp, that Le Guin shows Arren learning the lesson throughout the book. Late in the story, when he and Ged are rescued by folk who were to Arren a matter of legend, he finally comes to the realization: "Long ago I heard tell of the Raft-Folk, but thought it only one more tale of the South Reach, a fancy without substance. Yet we were rescued by that fancy, and our lives saved by a myth" (120). At almost the same time, Le Guin also shows again just how potent story is, and how important to society. For Arren must rescue the very Raft-Folk who had just rescued him. From what? From the loss of story—or, rather, the loss of the ability to tell story. When their chanters lose the ability to sing, when they forget the words and cry out in despair, "There are no more songs. It is ended," and all their life's meaning is in danger, it is Arren who steps forward and sings a story in order to preserve their festival of the Long Dance. The song he sings, the narrator tells us, "was that oldest song, of the Creation of Éa, and the balancing of the dark and the light, and the making of green lands by him who spoke the first word, the Eldest Lord, Segoy" (129). That is, he retells an ancient myth.

At the end of the book, when Ged and Arren have finally reached Selidor, the farthest shore, from which the book derives its title, and have accomplished their deed and saved Earthsea from destruction, Arren reflects: "'As far as Selidor,' they used to say in Enlad. The old stories told to children, the myths, began, 'As long ago as forever and as far away as Selidor, there lived a prince . . .'" And then a moment later it dawns on him that he, himself, "was the prince. But in the old stories, that was the beginning; and this seemed to be the end" (190). Of course, it really is the beginning even for Arren—the beginning of his kingship. And so the old stories told to children are proved true. Arren has learned the lesson, and hopefully so have Le Guin's readers.

Ultimately, we see modeled in Le Guin's fantasy a principle she explained in an essay in 1974:

> The great fantasies, myths and tales . . . speak *from* the unconscious *to* the unconscious, in the *language* of the unconscious—symbol and archetype. Though they use words, they work the way music does: they short-circuit verbal reasoning, and go straight to the thoughts that lie too deep to utter. They cannot be translated fully into the language of reason, but only a Logical Positivist, who also finds Beethoven's Ninth Symphony meaningless, would claim that they are therefore meaningless. They are profoundly meaningful, and usable—practical—in terms of ethics; of insight; of growth. (Le Guin, 57)

Names, Words, and Language

So Ursula Le Guin takes myth, legend, and fantasy seriously. She sees them as vehicles for truth and joy and inspiration. We thus ask, what truth do *her* stories convey? Or, using her own words, what is their "profound meaning"? What "insight" do they give us? How do they spur our "growth"? What "useable" or "practical" things do they say with regard to "ethics"?

Readers of Le Guin's essays can gain some insight into the books from her own writing about them. In her 1973 essay "Dreams Must Explain Themselves," she gives a quick summary of the "subject" of all three books in the *Earthsea* trilogy. She describes *A Wizard of Earthsea* as a "coming of age" story. There is almost an apologetic tone in the way she admits this, saying the subject is "the most childish thing" about the books. And yet the subject of "being grownup," as she puts it—or more accurately the process of *becoming* grown-up—is ultimately not something to be ashamed to write about. To the same extent that it is the subject of *A Wizard of Earthsea,* it can also be said to be the subject of *The Hobbit,* though it is perhaps more obvious in Le Guin's book: Ged begins the tale as a boy of seven years, leaves home, goes off to school, endures rivalry with classmates, and as a young adult must face the shadow of his own darker side (Le Guin, 50).

Regarding the subject of *The Tombs of Atuan*, Le Guin is also blunt. "If I had to put it in one word, sex." She explains that "there's a lot of symbolism in the book, most of which I did not, of course, analyze consciously while writing; the symbols can all be read as sexual." This is also easily discernible in the book. Ged, the male hero of the trilogy, must enter into and rob the maze of dark, hidden tunnels guarded by the virgin priestesses. The heroine, Tenar, a virgin, is charged with protecting these tunnels. When Ged penetrates these tunnels, the two ultimately go from protagonists to partners, and only thus do they conquer the real enemy: the *Dark Ones,* or *Old Powers,* who consume (and destroy) the identities of those who serve them. Le Guin also adds, however, that *The Tombs of Atuan* is also a coming of age story, but it is a "feminine coming of age. Birth, rebirth, destruction, freedom are the themes" (50).

Lastly, "*The Farthest Shore* is about death." Here again the subject is apparent in the reading. An evil wizard has sought to prolong his life—or avoid death—by opening up a gate from death to life so that he is able to return, at will, back to the realms of the living. There are two problems with his plan. The first is that he must sacrifice his very name in order to regain life. The second is that the gate becomes a "dry river" by which all of the life and power and magic of Earthsea, including even the stories of the Raft-Folk, is being sucked away. The Archmage Ged and future king Arren must journey into death in order to block the river and close the door. "That's why it is a less well built, less sound and complete book than the others," Le Guin admits. "They were about things I had already lived through and survived. *The Farthest Shore* is about the thing you do not live through and survive." Of course even this book, ultimately, is about "coming of age again, but in a larger context" (50).

So what do we make of this? In writing "coming of age" books, Le Guin is not doing anything unique. Some might argue that most fantasy literature fits that category—not only *The Hobbit,* but even *The Lord of the Rings,* if we take seriously Gandalf's words to the four Hobbits just before they return to the Scouring of the Shire just before the trilogy's end.[3] But there are other important themes in Le Guin's works as well: themes that run through all three books in the trilogy and convey a relatively consistent underlying worldview. It is the discovery of this underlying worldview that is most significant in understanding Le Guin's works, and what they can do in the hearts and minds of her readers. It is not enough to know that she wrote about coming of age, sex, and death. What does she say about these topics, through fantasy? What brings them together? To return again to Le Guin's quote: how are they "profoundly meaningful, and usable—practical—in terms of ethics; of insight; of growth"?

One theme that runs through all the books is the importance and power of words and language, and especially names. This is not surprising. As we have discussed in this book, particularly with respect to Owen Barfield and J. R. R. Tolkein, the importance of word and language and names all ties closely with the importance of story. An author such as Le Guin who is serious about story will also be serious about words and language. Like the wizards of Middle-earth, the wise of Earthsea (mages in particular) always take language seriously; no passing word is taken lightly. Late in the first book, when Ged makes a casual joke about a possible bad fate that might befall him on his quest, his best friend Vetch (also a mage) immediately reacts in a way that shows he takes these words with great seriousness. "'Avert!' said Vetch, turning his left hand in the gesture that

---

3. "I am not coming to the Shire. You must settle its affairs yourselves; that is what you have been trained for. Do you not yet understand? My time is over: it is no longer my task to set things to rights, nor to help folk to do so. And as for you, my dear friends, you will need no help. You are grown up now" (VI/vii).

turns aside the ill chance spoken of" (*Wizard,* 159). Le Guin is in good company. Or, rather, Vetch is in good company: the company of heroes. In *The Lord of the Rings,* both Aragorn and Gandalf make similar comments when the Hobbits jest lightly about the Ring. When Frodo jokes, "I hope the thinning process will not go on indefinitely, or I shall become a wraith," Aragorn replies quickly, "Do not speak of such things!" (I/xi). Likewise, just two chapters later, when in Rivendell Pippin jokingly calls Frodo the "Lord of the Ring," Gandalf immediately orders him to hush, adding that evil things *should not even be named* (II/i). This is not in any way to suggest that Le Guin was imitating Tolkien, but (as with other similarities) to suggest that the underlying ideas are very important to myth, and that both writers drew from the same Cauldron.

Indeed, the very power of a mage in Earthsea comes from his knowledge of names, and of the Old Tongue. Again, early in the story we already begin to glimpse that to know the true name of something is to have power over it. One of the first things Ged's aunt, a village witch, teaches Ged is "the true name of the falcon, to which the falcon must come" (*Wizard,* 5). And when the hero himself is named—that is, he is given his true secret name *Ged* by the wizard Ogion—we read, "Thus he was given his name by one very wise in the uses of power" (15). To know the true name of a thing is to have power over it. "For magic consists in this, the true naming of a thing. . . . Magic, true magic, is worked only by those beings who speak . . . the Old Speech" (46–47).

When Ged first comes to Roke, the School for Wizards, he must speak his own name to be admitted. Then the Gatekeeper, whose job it is to know all names, admits him, and he gets a glimpse of the power in names and words:

> In that moment Ged understood the singing of the bird, and the language of the water falling in the basin of the fountain, and the shape of the clouds, and the beginning and end of the wind that stirred the leaves: it seemed to him that he himself was a word spoken by the sunlight. (35)

It may be that the moment of revelation comes from the power of the place, or from the power of the Gatekeeper. But it may be that the power is invoked in Ged himself by his true naming, that his true naming somehow awakens in him something of his own being. In any case, the epiphany is associated with the speaking of a true name.

This is one reason why a wizard's school at Roke is needed: to give the knowledge and understanding of names and words. "Need alone is not enough to set power free: there must be knowledge" (8). At the wizards' school, the students gain one very particular and important type of knowledge: the true names of things in the Old Speech. And, perhaps more importantly, they learn how to discover for themselves the true names of things (and people). In *The Tombs of Atuan*, Ged explains this very succinctly to the heroine, Tenar.

> When Segoy raised the isles of Earthsea from the ocean deeps, all things bore their own true names. And all doings of magic, all wizardry, hangs still upon the knowledge—the relearning, the remembering—of that true and ancient language of the Making. There are spells to learn, of course, ways to use the words; and one must know the consequences, too. But what a wizard spends his life at is finding out the names of things, and finding out how to find out the names of things. (*Tombs*, 107–8)

In saying what he says about names and language, and in making the association with the myth of Segoy and the raising of Earthsea, Ged is also making the connection between words, language, and myth, suggesting that the three arise together: behind every word is not only a meaning, but a story, and story and its meaning go together. This relates closely to a view that Tolkien held about language, with one implication summarized succinctly by Shippey, who writes that Tolkien "believed that it was possible sometimes to feel one's way back from words as they survived in later periods to concepts which had long since vanished, but which had surely existed, or else the word would not exist" (Shippey, xiv).

Power and Balance

Even as Le Guin explores the importance of language and names, she also explores the nature and meaning of power. What is the purpose of power? What is its use? In the first chapter of *A Wizard of Earthsea*, young Ged, known then as Duny, discovers that he has magical power. "Untaught and knowing nothing of the arts and powers," he is nonetheless able to call in some goats using "words he had heard" even though he did not know "their use or meaning or what kind of words they were." Duny's aunt, a petty village sorceress known as the Witch of Ten Alders, observes Duny's considerable power. She begins to teach him spells, partly in an effort to control him for her own ends. But even though her knowledge is greater than his, and he is only seven years old, his inborn power is too great for her to fully control him. When she puts a spell of silence on him, he is unable to speak *words* but is still able to *laugh*. "Then his aunt was a little afraid of his strength, for this was as strong a spell as she knew how to weave: she had tried not only to gain control of his speech and silence, but to bind him at the same time to her service in the craft of sorcery" (*Wizard*, 2–5).

So power, as we saw in the previous section, comes from knowing the true names of things. But power is also an inborn thing in Earthsea, much as it is in Middle-earth. Gandalf, Aragorn, Galadriel, and Elrond all have power. Denethor has power. It is not something that can be purchased, or explained, or earned; one is born with it (or not). When Gandalf speaks a word of command, part of the power comes from the word itself—Gandalf is a master of words and languages—but some of the power comes from Gandalf's innate strength. When Aragorn gains mastery of the Palantír, or calls back Éowyn, Faramir, and Merry from death, it is not through knowledge of any spells but through his inborn power and might. So it is with Duny, who will become Ged. Ged was born to power. Another person without that inborn wizard's power could speak the same spells, and yet accomplish nothing. Knowledge is not enough. This is why Ged's witch aunt could not control Ged; even though she had greater knowledge, he had far greater inborn power.

Still, inborn power must be trained. And it has a purpose. Much of what Le Guin has to say in the trilogy has to do with the proper use of power. Early on in the story, Ged is enamored with power. When he goes to study under the wise and patient (but also very powerful) mage Ogion, it is with the desire to "enter at once into the mystery and mastery of power." He is frustrated when Ogion instead seeks to teach him patience and self-control (a more important type of power), saying, "You want to work spells. You've drawn too much water from that well. Wait. Manhood is patience. Mastery is nine times patience" (16–17). (This, as Le Guin knew, is a lesson that all her readers would do well to learn.)

Unfortunately, Ged is slow to learn the lessons Ogion wants to teach him. As the narrator describes it, Ged is too interested in *doing*, and not enough concerned simply with *being*. In many ways, he bears too much the mark of his first teacher (the witch), and hasn't yet begun enough to resemble his second (Ogion). This is true in more ways than one. Almost at the same time we learn of the limited power of the Witch of Ten Alders, we also learn of her even greater shortcoming: though she knows something of power ("she had a spell for every circumstance, and was forever weaving charms"), and though she has some small amount of inborn power, she knows "nothing of the Balance and the Pattern which the true wizard knows and serves" (16–17). Thus we begin to see that the ultimate end of power, in Le Guin's work, is to serve something called the "Balance" or "Pattern."

It is not until Ged comes to Roke that the reader begins to learn more about this balance and about the meaning of power. If one purpose of the wizards' school at Roke is to teach knowledge—knowledge of names and spells—another more important purpose is to teach wisdom. The particular wisdom is the wisdom to understand the balance: "Press a mage for his secrets and he would always talk ... about balance, and danger, and the dark" (44). By the end of the trilogy, Ged has become a model of being and not merely doing—so much so that he frustrates his young companion Arren, who is eager for action. He is also put forth as a model in understanding the Balance and Pattern.

Part of Ged's understanding of balance comes from his accomplishing of his central task in *A Wizard of Earthsea,* which is to overcome the horrible Shadow that he has loosed. For much of the book, the Shadow is pursuing him, and he is mortally afraid. Following the guidance of Ogion, however, he finally stops running from the Shadow and turns instead to face it. The Shadow then turns and flees, and Ged becomes the pursuer. When he finally catches it, he calls it by its name: *Ged.*

> And he began to see the truth, that Ged had neither lost nor won but, naming the shadow of his death with his own name, had made himself whole: a man: who, knowing his whole self, cannot be used or possessed by any power other than himself, and whose life therefore is lived for life's sake and never in the service of ruin, or pain, or hatred, or the dark. (180–81)

Le Guin seems to be suggesting that life is not about victories or defeats, but about finding balances. For Ged, there is a balance between what are apparently two different sides of himself. In that final sentence, Le Guin gets a little didactic, and overtly spells out a philosophy of life in the narrator's own voice (and not the voice of a character within the tale).

What is perhaps more important, however, than the explicitly stated philosophy is what lies behind this philosophy. When Ged realizes that the shadow is really just a part of him, it is a hint of one of the most important tenets behind Le Guin's books: in the *Earthsea* trilogy, evil is really just a part of good. Good, Le Guin seems to be saying, cannot exist without evil, and vice versa. To broaden this tenet, opposites aren't so much opposites as just two parts of the great balance. As the poets of Earthsea tell in the *Creation of Éa*, "Only in silence the word, only in dark the light, only in dying life: bright the hawk's flight on the empty sky" (181).

Good and Evil

This, of course, leads to one of the great questions that must be asked about any work of fantasy if we are to understand what its author is really suggesting about the nature of the universe. What does the work say about ultimate questions of morality? What are the definitions of good and evil? To put this another way, we wrote earlier that one of the hallmarks of modern fantasy is the existence of some significant cosmic battle that gives such important meaning to the actions of the heroes. In this particular work, what defines the two sides of the conflict?

There are certainly suggestions in Le Guin's work of some objective morality—some absolute definitions of good and evil that transcend time, place, and culture. We read, for example, that "even in the kingless centuries, the Archmages of Roke kept fealty and served the common law" (*Shore*, 14). This comment seems not unlike Tolkien's comment about the Hobbits of the Shire in the prologue to *The Lord of the Rings:* "For they attributed to the king of old all their essential laws; and usually they kept the laws of free will, because they were The Rules (as they said), both ancient and just" (*FOTR*, 18). This is an appeal to the existence of objective moral laws that transcend one particular king or culture; laws that can be said to be "ancient and just" according to some higher standard of judgment. Even the worst tyrants in the history of Earthsea have some knowledge of the existence and sanctity of this moral law, and a fear of breaking it. This is why the old couple whom Ged meets on an otherwise deserted island had not been put to death by their enemies in Kargad: "A tyrant or usurper who feared to shed kingly blood had sent them to be cast away" (*Wizard*, 142). Like the taboos discussed in the chapter on fairy tale, there was a moral taboo against shedding kingly blood, and so strong was this taboo that the tyrant refused to break it.

Indeed, we see the language of good and evil throughout the *Earthsea* trilogy, *seemingly* used as though these were objectively defined. For example, certain characters are described as evil, as are various actions and even the intents behind those actions. The Archmage Gensher tells Ged not only that the Shadow called up by Ged is "evil," but that "it wills to work evil through you" (*Wizard,* 66). Prince Arren says to Ged of the slave traders who captured them, "But you knew them to be evil men" (*Shore,* 66). And as Archmage Ged grows to a deeper understanding of the nature of his quest in the third book, he tells Arren, "I think we must come not only to a place, but to a person. This is evil, evil, what passes on this island: this loss of craft and pride, this joylessness, this waste. This is the work of an evil will" (87).

Along the same lines, we also see in Le Guin's *Earthsea* writings some echoes of another fundamentally important idea in Tolkien's writing—and in biblical Christianity: that each person is ultimately responsible for his or her own choices, and that there is the possibility of both good and evil choices. "Why is your face downcast?" the Lord says to Cain, early in the Genesis myth. "If you do what is right, will you not be accepted? But if you do not do what is right, sin is crouching at your door; it desires to have you, but you must master it" (Gen. 4:6–7). This message of moral responsibility and accountability is an even more important lesson that Ogion teaches (or tries to teach) Ged. "Have you never thought how danger must surround power as shadow does light? This sorcery is not a game we play for pleasure or for praise. Think of this: that every word, every act of our Art is said and is done either for good, or for evil" (*Wizard,* 23). Even as we get another glimpse that power is dangerous, and is not a toy, we are told more importantly that there are good and evil, and that every act (at least of wizardry) falls on the one side or the other. This bespeaks of an objective morality, and of a battle—a battle fundamental to the majority of modern fantasy, and touched upon earlier in our discussion of the Bible—in which there are no disinterested characters. In that way, the words Le Guin gives to Ogion are very similar to those given by Tolkien to Aragorn, and spoken to Éomer. "You may say this to Théoden son of Thengel: open war lies before him, with Sauron or against him." Aragorn is placing clear moral choice before the Rider of Rohan, and connecting the significance of his moral choice to the great battle that is being waged that is at the center of this work of fantasy. And when a short time later Éomer questions, "How shall a man judge what to do in such times?" Aragorn replies: "As he has ever judged. Good and ill have not changed since yesteryear; nor are they one thing among Elves and Dwarves and another among Men" (III/ii).

Later, when Pippin steals a look in the Palantír and then tries to make an excuse that he didn't know what he was doing, Gandalf tells him in no uncertain words, "You knew you were behaving *wrongly* and foolishly" (III/xi, emphasis ours). This is why Gandalf does not *excuse* Pippin but rather *forgives* him: to excuse him would be to remove from him any moral responsibility for his actions; to forgive him is to acknowledge that he has done wrong but to choose not to punish him. The Archmage Gensher treats Ged in a similar way when the young student, in haughty pride, tries to call up a spirit of the dead and thereby releases the Shadow upon the world. "You have great power inborn in you, and you used that power wrongly" (*Wizard*, 66). At another time, Ged also takes responsibility for the morality of his own actions, and confesses a wrong deed with wrong motives done earlier in life: "I should have known by that that I did wrong. I was possessed by anger and by vanity. For he was very strong, and I was eager to prove that I was stronger" (*Shore*, 75).

Ged is also quick to point out to Arren that each person must take responsibilities for his or her actions, and not to let those actions be ruled by another. In particular, they must not respond to evil with more evil. Thus, when Arren speaks to him of the evil of the slave traders, Ged replies, "Was I to join them therefore? To let their acts rule my own? I will not make their choices for them, nor will I let them make mine for me!" (66).

Despite the surface similarities in language, however, the careful reader of Le Guin begins to see that at some deeper level Le Guin is actually saying something very different from Tolkien or Lewis with respect to morality and any possible ultimate definition of it. For when Archmage Gensher chastises the young Ged for his prideful act, he goes on to explain just *why* it was wrong. "You used that power wrongly to work a spell over which you had not control, not knowing how that spell affects the balance of light and dark, life and death, good and evil. And you were moved to do this by pride and by hate" (*Wizard*, 66). Certainly part of the "wrongness" of Ged's actions had to do with his motivation—he was acting in pride and hate—but the real reason, the first reason, is that he had no knowledge of how his actions would affect the balance. And the reader is left to assume that his actions did upset the balance. Maintaining the balance is the ultimate goal. According to Gensher—and, it would appear, according to Le Guin, as least as she expresses her philosophy in the *Earthsea* trilogy—good is not supposed to triumph over evil, but rather the two are supposed to remain in balance, like light and dark, life and death. In this, Le Guin could not be much further in opposition to Tolkien and Lewis.

This is such an important underlying distinction that it must be explored. While both Le Guin and Tolkien speak of an objective good and evil, or ill, their definitions of these things are very different. In fact, as we see in the *Earthsea* trilogy, despite her use of the word "evil," Le Guin would ultimately deny any objective right and wrong. In "The Child and the Shadow" she writes:

> In the fairy-tale, though there is no "right" and "wrong," there is a differ-
> ent standard, which is perhaps best called "appropriateness." . . . Evil, then,
> appears in the fairy-tale not as something diametrically opposed to good,
> but as inextricably involved with it, as in the yang-yin symbol. Neither
> is greater than the other, nor can human reason and virtue separate one
> from the other and choose between them. The hero or heroine is the
> one who sees what is appropriate to be done, because he or she sees the
> *whole,* which is greater than either evil or good. Their heroism is, in fact,
> their certainty. They do not act by rules; they simply know the way to go.
> (Le Guin, 62)

The point here is not to comment on fairy tale, but to comment on Le Guin's understanding of fairy tale. She sees no objective good or evil—at least not any evil, like the evil of Sauron or Morgoth in Tolkien's Middle-earth, that is ultimately opposed to good. In Le Guin's view of fairy tale, evil and good are just two sides of the same thing, neither one being greater. In fact, she argues, human reason can't even separate the two or choose between them. Contrary to the fundamental definition of heroism in Tolkien's Middle-earth or Lewis's Narnia, for Le Guin heroes are not heroes for doing what is good or right, but simply for doing what is "appropriate." The language of morality has been replaced by the language of appropriateness. Appropriate to what standard or cultural norm? We are not told. What we are told is that there is some "whole" that is "greater than either evil or good."

This is where, in Earthsea, we return to the notion of balance. For Tolkien, good is ultimately defined as that which is done in obedience or service to the Creator, God, known in Middle-earth as Eru Ilúvatar; evil is that done in opposition to God. To obey Ilúvatar is good. To serve the enemy, Melkor or his servant Sauron, is evil. Thus good and evil are defined with respect to a personal being outside of nature. In Le Guin's trilogy, by contrast, the ultimate definition of good *is keeping the balance* (including, we are told, the balance between good and evil) and the ul-timate evil is defined as *upsetting the balance.*[4] Ged learns this at Roke

---

4. In this way, despite our earlier praise of her work, Le Guin might actually be said to be inconsistent or perhaps incoherent, in the sense that this definition is almost self-contradictory: if it is good to keep the balance between good and evil, and evil to break the balance, is there also a balance between *keeping*

from the Master Hand, who describes the difference between illusion and real changing:

> To change this rock into a jewel, you must change its true name.... It is the art of the Master Changer, and you will learn it, when you are ready to learn it. But you must not change one thing, one pebble, one grain of sand, until you know what good and evil will follow on that act. The world is in balance, in Equilibrium. (*Wizard*, 44)

Note the force of the Master Hand's warning: the wizards-to-be *must* not change "one grain of sand" without understanding of the good and evil that will follow. But who defines what good and evil are? Who or what defines that whole that is above them both? It is not so much that the young wizards in training should act only if their actions will bring about "good," but rather that they should act only if their actions don't upset the balance, and in particular if they have *knowledge* of what the effects will be. If their act will accomplish both good and evil, but keep them in balance, then it is okay. The "whole" over both good and evil, apparently then, is balance. Ged's shortcoming—his evil—is that he thinks being a wizard will make him "powerful enough to do what he [pleases], and balance the world as [seems] best to him, and drive back darkness with his own light" (44). Why is such thinking evil? Obviously Ged's plan is wrong, but does Le Guin have the resources within her world to say *why* it is wrong? Le Guin extols love and patience and condemns pride and violence. But when pressed for a reason why she prefers the former to the latter, she makes a rather unsatisfying and evasive appeal to Equilibrium.

One objection that might be raised to Le Guin's version of good and evil is that it places a burden on people without giving them any means to lift that burden. How can we ever know all the consequences of our actions in order to weigh the balance of them? To do so requires divine knowledge. Christianity shows a very different picture of moral judgment. We cannot know the consequences of our actions, but we can know that we are attempting to do what is commanded of us. This is why Luther says that we should "sin boldly." He recognizes that some bad (or "sin") might come of what we do, but this is not for us to control. If we intend to obey boldly, then we can leave the outcome of our actions to God.

---

the balance and *not keeping the balance*? In order to keep the balance, we must break the balance—but only half the time.

When Aragorn, at the start of *The Two Towers,* chooses to head west and pursue the orc-band that has captured Pippin and Merry, rather than heading east to help Frodo and Sam or south to bring his sword to Gondor, it is not because he can foresee the consequences. At the time of his decision, it would seem that either of the other two choices would have better consequences. He seeks to help Merry and Pippin because he believes it is the morally right thing to do, and he must leave the consequences in the hands of a higher power. But Le Guin will not admit God or knowledge of God into her world, and so her characters are left with an impossible moral burden to carry. Of course, she cannot excise morality entirely from her world, and so she is left with a fundamental inconsistency. She apparently was aware of this inconsistency, as her sci-fi works often wrestle with this explicitly. *The Left Hand of Darkness* and *The Dispossessed* both revolve around the clash of cultures and their moralities. In each case, she writes in an attempt to see if there can be any rapprochement between conflicting moral systems. The results are, in each case, ambiguous, and the problem winds up being skirted by unfounded dogmatic assertions.

Note that to say that there is no divine source of morality in Le Guin's work is not to say that there are no personal powers in Le Guin's work. Her work is populated by semidivine dragons, wizards, and Old Powers. Wizards are generally good powers, though some do turn to evil. Dragons are traditional enemies of Earthsea, but in some sense they are not *evil* powers, for they understand the balance and don't upset it. The Old Powers are certainly portrayed as powers of evil. In the first book, Ged explains to Serret something of the nature of one of the Old Powers.

> My lady, that spirit is sealed in a stone, and the stone is locked by binding-spell and blinding-spell and charm of lock and ward and triple fortress-walls in a barren land, not because it is precious, but because it can work great evil. . . . You who are young and gentle-hearted should never touch the thing, or even look on it. It will not work you well. (*Wizard,* 116)

Earlier in the book, when Ged, taunted by the daughter of an enchantress, tries to show off and gets into trouble playing with these powers, Ogion warns him, "The powers she serves are not the powers I serve: I do not know her will, but I know she does not will me well" (23). There is, however, no great power—no God or creator—that underwrites moral goodness. Ged grows into great power, but not only is his power limited, it is also used for evil early in his life. And by the same lights, even the Old Powers, ultimately, must be part of the same Balance, or Equilibrium.

All of this has direct implications to how one should live. Early in the first book, while Ged is still at Roke, the Master Summoner tells him, "You thought, as a boy, that a mage is one who can do anything. . . . The truth is that as a man's real power grows and his knowledge widens, even the way he can follow grows narrower: until at last he chooses nothing, but does only and wholly what he *must* do" (*Wizard,* 71). So despite the language of morality that Le Guin hints at from time to time, ultimately one's task is not to choose good, but rather to choose nothing at all. We are to make no moral choices, but only to do what we "*must* do."

Ultimately, the only reason that people are capable of doing evil—that is, of breaking the balance—is that they are capable of making choices. The rest of nature, creatures who merely act on instinct and not in free will, are not capable of evil. As we said before, for Le Guin evil is breaking the balance, and as Ged explains to Arren, only humans can do that.

> "A pestilence is a motion of the great Balance . . . this is different. There is the stink of evil in it. We may suffer for it when the balance of things rights itself, but we do not lose hope. . . . Nature is not unnatural. This is not a righting of the balance, but an upsetting of it. There is only one creature who can do that."
>
> "A man?" Arren said, tentative.
>
> "We men."
>
> "How?"
>
> "By an unmeasured desire for life."
>
> "For life? But it isn't wrong to want to live?"
>
> "No. But when we crave power over life—endless wealth, unassailable safety, immortality—then desire becomes greed. And if knowledge allies itself to that greed, then comes evil." (*Shore,* 35)

Both the hero Ged and the villain Cob agree on this fact, if nothing else. "Let all stupid nature go its stupid course," Cob says in defense of his choosing, "but I am a man, better than nature, above nature. I will not go that way, I will not cease to be myself!" (179).

It is not surprising, then, that Le Guin ultimately tries to get away altogether from the language of good and evil, right and wrong. At one point in *The Farthest Shore,* Arren asks Ged, "Is it a wicked thing, then [to call up dead spirits]?" Ged's reply is telling. "I should call it a misunderstanding, rather. A misunderstanding of life. Death and life are the same thing—like the two sides of my hand, the palm and the back. And still the palm and the back are not the same. . . . They can be neither separated, nor mixed" (74). There is no good or evil, only understandings and misunderstandings—quite the contrast to what Gandalf told Pippin, or even what Gensher earlier told Ged.

Life, Death, and Meaning

We are now very close to the heart of understanding the underlying worldview that governs the *Earthsea* trilogy. Ged explains something central to this understanding in his conversation with Yarrow, the younger sister of his close friend Vetch.

> All power is one source and end, I think. Years and distances, stars and candles, water and wind and wizardry, the craft in a man's hand and the wisdom in a tree's root: they all arise together. My name, and yours, or an unborn child, all are syllables of the great word that is very slowly spoken by the shining of the stars. There is no other power. No other name. (*Wizard,* 164)

Rather than Tolkien's theism, Le Guin's wise mage is suggesting a monism.[5] Everything is one. Her use of the yin yang brings to mind Eastern philosophy. Though she avoids any particular religion, this rings strongly of the sort of Westernized Eastern mysticism that George Lucas would later make famous in his first *Star Wars* trilogy: the existence of a single impersonal force that the emperor and Darth Vader as well as Luke Skywalker can all draw upon equally. And though the *viewer* of the *Star Wars* films is invited to choose sides, there is no objective criterion *within* the mythology to lead the viewer to call one side "good" and the other "evil." The closest we are given as grounds for making such judgment is that the empire's forces kill off the mothers of cute little furry Ewoks. "There is no other power," as Ged says. "No other name."

This—along with the impossibilities of knowing the outcome of all our actions—explains the emphasis in Le Guin's work on *being,* rather than *doing.* On the one side, if everything derives from one source, then there is no reason to *do* anything; all is One already. Again, from another

5. The Nameless Ones, or Old Powers, are a type of ancient gods, and thus the worship of them by the priestesses of Atuan would be a form of paganism. However, though paganism exists within *Wizard,* it is shown to be a false religion; as Ged tells Tenar, these old gods should not be worshiped. Le Guin is not, therefore, promoting this paganism as true or valuable religion.

point of view, if the highest meaning or power or purpose that transcends good and evil is equilibrium, then we are better off not acting at all. As we have seen, this is what Ged preaches to Arren throughout the third book.

> On every act the balance of the whole depends. The winds and seas, the powers of water and earth and light, all that these do, and all that the beasts and green things do, is well done, and rightly done.... But we, insofar as we have power over the world and over one another, we must *learn* to do what the leaf and the whale and the wind do of their own nature. We must learn to keep the balance. (*Shore*, 66)

In other words, we should deny the human nature of free will, and choose instead the nature of animals and leaves and winds, which is to choose not to choose.

Of course a fairy-tale hero is one who acts heroically. Ultimately, Le Guin cannot escape that, and so she still gives us fantasy heroes. Both Ged and Arren do act, and both act heroically and unselfishly, even self-sacrificially. It is also clear that they *choose* to act. In the final conflict of *The Farthest Shore*, most of the inhabitants of Earthsea, including many of the mages, choose inaction. What sets apart Ged and Arren—and what makes them heroes—is precisely the fact that they choose to act, and that they persevere in their action against great odds. Arren's climbing back from the land of the dead is ultimately an act of perseverance, described in a way very reminiscent of the journey of Frodo and Sam across Mordor, especially when Arren lifts Ged and carries him up the mountain. Thus, Le Guin's story perhaps speaks a truth that her philosophy does not.

Nonetheless, Le Guin's philosophy dictates that she defend Ged's philosophy against action. At one point Arren expresses his need to act. "'But then,' the boy said, frowning at the stars, 'is the balance to be kept by doing nothing? Surely a man must act, even not knowing all the consequences of his act, if anything is to be done at all?'" Again, Ged's answer captures the essence of Le Guin's message. "Never fear. It is much easier for men to act than to refrain from acting.... Do nothing because it is righteous or praiseworthy or noble to do so; do nothing because it seems good to do so; do only that which you must do and which you cannot do in any other way" (67). Ged is speaking almost the opposite of what Gandalf or Aragorn would say.

And this, not surprisingly, relates back to the Balance. For Le Guin, the purpose of life, we have seen, is to keep the balance: to make no choices, but to act only as we must. But what of the purpose of death? Le Guin's answer, in a single word: *acceptance.* All is one. Light and dark. Good and evil. Life and death. We must accept it. This, too, Ged explains to Arren.

> There are two . . . that make one: the world and the shadow, the light and the dark. The two poles of the Balance. Life rises out of death, death rises out of light; in being opposite they yearn to each other, they give birth to each other and are forever reborn. And with them all is reborn, the flower of the apple tree, the light of the stars. In life is death. In death is rebirth. What then is life without death? Life unchanging, everlasting, eternal?—What is it but death—death without rebirth. (*Shore,* 137)

Thus, we must accept death. Hence, the "first lesson and last of all," which is the most important lesson of lore taught by the Master Herbal at Roke, was "Heal the wound and cure the illness, but let the dying spirit go" (*Wizard,* 80).

What, then, is evil? Not to accept death is to upset the balance. That is evil. One of the things we learn about the Old Powers—the evil Nameless Ones—is that "they do not die. They are dark and undying, and they hate the light: the brief, bright light of our mortality" (*Tombs,* 107). The greatest evil ever done in Earthsea—and the greatest threat ever to its existence—was the efforts of the powerful wizard Cob to escape death.

This relates, of course, to one of the important questions to ask of a work of fantasy: what does it say about life and death and ultimate meaning—including the meaning of life and death? We wrote in an earlier chapter that the longing for something spiritual and eternal—including the longing for a life after death—seemed to be at the heart of the human condition, and also at the heart of Faërie. Death and mortality, Tolkien claimed, was one of the great themes of Faërie, including of his own work. The same can be said of Le Guin, but what Le Guin says about death through *Earthsea* is almost the opposite of what Tolkien suggests in his *Legendarium.* In Middle-earth, the longing for the eternal is not only natural, but good and healthy. The death of the body, whether for Elf or for Man (or for Dwarf or Hobbit) is not the end of life. The spirit lives on even when the body dies. And with the spirit lives the self. Granted that it would be wrong in Middle-earth to try to preserve a *bodily* life indefinitely. The Númenóreans seek to do this, and that effort is one of the evils responsible for bringing the downfall of Númenor, in the Akallabêth. An evil of the One Ring is that it preserves the bodily life but doesn't add any more life, so that the possessor becomes thin and stretched out. The body is being kept alive beyond what its nature calls for. Again, in Tolkien's Catholic-Thomistic-Aristotelian view, the nature of the body is written in its soul. To keep the body alive beyond what its nature calls for is to make body and soul repugnant to each other. The Ringwraiths are the rough equivalent of Mary Shelley's Dr. Frankenstein's monster.[6] But the spiritual life is another thing. Elves, should they die in Middle-earth, are promised an earthly resurrection in the paradise of Valinor. And though the promises for Men are not made quite as clear or repeated as often, there is a similar promise of an eternal life outside of the confines of the created world. When time ends, all of the Children (both Elves and Men) will take part along with the angelic Ainur in a great music in heaven. Here is the key feature; while the physical body ends, the soul or spirit endures and is given a new incorruptible body. In particular, selfhood, the individual, continues. This is a good promise in Tolkien's mythology.

In Earthsea, it is otherwise. Our selfhood is the very thing that is supposed to end when we die. Ged tells Arren:

> You will not live forever. Nor will any man nor any thing. Nothing is immortal. But only to us is it given to know that we must die. And that is a great gift: the gift of selfhood. . . . That selfhood which is our torment, our treasure, and our humanity, does not endure. It changes; it is gone, a wave on the sea. (*Shore*, 123)

We are not, according to Le Guin, eternal beings. Our "selfhood" and our "humanity," the things that define us as individuals, are what we lose. They are fleeting, like a wave. The longing for the eternal, even if universal, is false and misleading. According to Le Guin's worldview, all of Tolkien's promises of Valinor and the Second Music of the Ainur are false and misleading. The one thing—the only thing—that we ever know, according to great hero of Le Guin's *Earthsea* trilogy is that we must die, and that death is final.

Certainly, this may be true, but if so we cannot know it, and Le Guin's assertion comes across as unfounded dogmatism. This is ironic, of course, since so much of her writing seems calculated to oppose what she takes to be the dogmatic view that there is objective good and evil. (She seems

---

6. And, of course, the subtitle of Shelley's *Frankenstein* was *The Modern Prometheus*, invoking the Greek myth of the man who sought to steal immortal knowledge from the gods.

to want to say that there is no good, that it is good to believe so, and that balance is good.) In the end, her antimoralizing narrator's voice occasionally falls flat through its self-contradiction, but Le Guin's *stories* and her characters are believable and compelling, though her underlying worldview is decidedly in opposition to the Christian worldview of J. R. R. Tolkein and C. S. Lewis on many fronts.

8

THE DARKNESS
OF PHILIP PULLMAN'S MATERIAL

Too late. You haven't any choice: you're the bearer. It's
picked you out.

Philip Pullman's character
Dr. Grumman, *The Subtle Knife*

The books of Philip Pullman's *His Dark Materials* trilogy received
a surprising amount of attention when they were first released.
Pullman certainly has some instincts about what makes fantasy literature.
He understands, for example, that fantasy literature takes place near the
border of our world and the world of Faërie. The preface to the trilogy,
found in the first book, *The Golden Compass* (1995),[1] indicates that the
story will start in another world (similar to ours), continue in our world in
book 2, and then move between worlds. At times in the next two books,
The Subtle Knife (1997) and *The Amber Spyglass* (2000), the characters are
jumping back and forth between worlds, some of which—for instance,
the World of the Dead—are very unlike ours.

1. Originally published in England under the title *Northern Lights*.

One of the first things we learn about the world in which the story begins is that all humans of that world have dæmons.[2] Dæmons are something like human souls except they take external, visible forms as animals, and in fact can carry on conversations with other dæmons as well as with their humans. For adults, the animal form is fixed and relates to the nature of the person. The dæmons of children, however, can continue to change shapes. As expected, the lives of humans are intimately connected with those of their dæmons. If the human dies, their dæmon dies with them, and vice versa. And (with only a few exceptions) dæmons cannot go far from their human. Essentially, Pullman is making use of the notion of a *familiar,* or *familiar spirit.* At one point early in the *Earthsea* trilogy, when Ged takes a small animal called an Otak as a companion, his adversary Jasper teases him that he has a "familiar" (*Wizard,* 49–50). Le Guin was aware of the concept from mythology, but did not make much use of it. For Pullman, it is central to his story. His exploration of this concept is interesting and consistent enough with the construction of his world to be believable within that world. In another context, it could make for a very interesting fantasy novel or collection of novels.

Of Tolkien's three faces of Faërie, the Magical toward Nature is also evident in some of the magical devices that appear in Pullman's trilogy, such as those that provide the titles of the three books. Pullman also pulls from the Cauldron some important and potent elements of myth and legend. His *Armored Bears of Svalbard* bear a striking resemblance to the Old Norse were-bear (or bear-human) figure Bjarki and Tolkien's Beorn. Tom Shippey's description of Beorn and his literary predecessors could almost be a description of Pullman's Iorek Byrnison: "that strange combination of gruffness and good-humour, ferocity and kind-heartedness, with overlaying it all a quality which one might call being insufficiently socialized" (Shippey, 31–32).

Problems with Prose and Plot

Nonetheless, we say the amount of attention (including various awards) Pullman's trilogy has received is surprising. Despite some interesting concepts, the books overall are severely flawed. The most important ob-

2. Pullman's use of *daemon* is quite different from most of the classical understandings of daemons as the demigod progeny of gods and mortals (as we mentioned in chapter 4), and the early Christian theological notions of demons, or fallen gods/angels, but not wholly unlike the ancient Greek notion of a daimon, that is, a helpful spirit or even the locus of thought.

jection is simply that the writing and the story are not particularly good. A second problem—one that is related in that it may be the cause of the first—is that Pullman seems to have a metaphysical axe to grind, and he didactically champions a peculiar but inconsistent sort of materialism. Like too many other authors, he uses familiar notions from classical mythology and fantasy without any apparent sense of what these words and names mean. The result is a piecemeal collage of ideas that hang together tenuously at best. Before discussing the phenomenon of the books' success, it may be illuminating to discuss some of these flaws.

As mentioned, the greatest flaw is the quality of the prose, especially the dialogue. One example nicely illustrates Pullman's unrealistic, overly ornamental, and sentimental prose. The following dialogue takes place between the two main characters, Lyra and Will, toward the end of the final book:

> "Oh, Will," she said, "what can we do? Whatever can we do? I want to live with you forever. I want to kiss you and lie down with you and wake up with you every day of my life till I die, years and years and years away. I don't want a memory, just a memory . . ."
>
> "No," he said, "memory's a poor thing to have. It's your own real hair and mouth and arms and eyes and hands I want. I didn't know I could ever love anything so much. Oh, Lyra, I wish this night would never end! If only we could stay here like this, and the world could stop turning, and everyone else could fall into a sleep . . ."
>
> "Everyone except us! And you and I could live here forever and just love each other."
>
> "I *will* love you forever, whatever happens. Till I die and after I die, and when I find my way out of the land of the dead, I'll drift about forever, all my atoms, till I find you again." (*Spyglass*, 496–97)

We might find this passage at best passable (though by no means strong) writing, if the two characters involved weren't twelve years old. As such, the word *impoverished* comes to mind. Of course, even some reasonably good writers have weak passages, and so judging an entire trilogy by one dialogue is dangerous. There are some very good passages in Pullman's work, too, but much of the prose is difficult to digest.

Not only is the prose lacking, but the story itself is flawed. It lacks coherence and internal consistency. The next big concept after the dæmon familiars is *Dust*, which turns out to be the central subject of the whole trilogy. Dust is mysterious, even mystical. Lots of people try to deny its existence. Few (if any) mortals know what it is, though Lyra's father,

Lord Asriel, comes the closest among humans. Yet everybody in Lyra's world, and many in Will's world (which is our world), from theologians to scientists, wants to know more about it. Initially, the presentation of Dust is a seemingly good example of the first face of Faërie: the mystical toward the supernatural. Dust seems to point beyond this world to something marvelous and transcendent. Before long, however, Pullman's presentation of Dust becomes not mysterious but simply confusing, inconsistent, and also more scientific than Faërie.

In some places, Dust is explained as both the source and the product of conscious thought. "Dust is only a name for what happens when matter begins to understand itself. Matter loves matter. It seeks to know more about itself, and Dust is formed" (31–32). In Pullman's mythology, Angels themselves evolved out of Dust. We are also told, through Lyra's father, that Dust is what makes Lyra's *alethiometer* (her Golden Compass that functions not so much as a truth-meter as it does a truth-finder, or question-answerer) work (*Compass*, 370). And we later learn that Dust (known in our world as *shadow particles*) communicates with the third hero and the only other main character from our world, Dr. Mary Malone, through her computer. But then the Dust identifies *itself* to Dr. Malone as "ANGELS," admits that it intervened in human evolution, and gives "VENGEANCE" as a reason for intervention (*Knife*, 220–21; the use of all capital letters here is Pullman's). Vengeance against whom, we ask? Presumably against the *Authority*, who rules the Kingdom and has been trying to destroy Dust.

So after the first explanations of Dust prove false or incomplete, we are told that Dust is a very personal force, and that it associates itself with the rebel angels of the Republic who wish to overthrow the Kingdom. But that doesn't fit either. The forces of the Kingdom also have alethiometers. Which force of angels is it? If it is the Republic force, then why do they give true information to the alethiometers of their enemy? And vice versa? We also learn that the great battle is over what to do about Dust. The Kingdom tries to suppress Dust, while the Republic tries to defend it. However, both sides seem dependent upon it, and the Authority who rules the Kingdom himself evolved from Dust (was formed from it, or condensed from it). Pullman is obviously exploring, trying in vain for some consistent explanation. At times, however, it feels that he is making stuff up as he goes along.

Another illustration comes from the aforementioned war and the Subtle Knife that Will comes to possess. Throughout much of the trilogy, the narrative seems to be leading toward a great battle between the

Kingdom (established by the cruel and deceitful Authority) and the Republic (led by Lord Asriel, Lyra's father). These forces are wrestling for the future of the universes (uncountably many parallel universes, some of which are very similar to ours and to one another). Numerous different societies all have prophecies that such a great battle will take place. One of the most influential witches, Ruta Skadi, learns a seemingly important piece of information when she overhears a wise old grandfather cliff-ghast (another of the fantasy characters inhabiting Lyra's world). The cliff-ghast, speaking of the great battle to come, suggests that Lord Asriel won't be able to defeat the Authority because he hasn't got the Subtle Knife (*Knife*, 241). Will's father also sees the knife as the key weapon to defeat the enemy. "They had no idea that they'd made the one weapon in all the universes that could defeat the tyrant. The Authority. God" (283).

The battle eventually happens, but it turns out to be relatively unimportant to history—or at least much less of a significant event than all of the hype leading up to it. The Subtle Knife isn't even used in the battle in any significant way. The Authority over the evil powers of the Kingdom dies during the battle, but it is almost by accident; it is not the knife that kills him. His lieutenant and replacement, Metanon, is also destroyed. But so is Lord Asriel. There is no clear victor in the battle, and the whole thing proves to be almost irrelevant; we learn that a new leader will emerge to replace Metanon and will take over that kingdom.

The Subtle Knife and the Power of Death

What the whole trilogy hinges on—we discover at the very end—is the very existence of the Subtle Knife. Most of what happens in the trilogy serves merely to inform the young protagonist Will (who comes into possession of the knife shortly after the knife is introduced) that the knife must be destroyed in order to save the universes from the loss of Dust. En route to this discovery, Will and Lyra also accomplish two other important tasks. First, they open up the doors of the land of the dead so that ghosts can escape from endless torment into nothingness (an end of their existence). This is certainly a significant accomplishment. But this task really just proves to be one more difficulty for a couple of tenacious preteens who have already accomplished dozens of seemingly impossible feats through a combination of Lyra's ability to lie and Will's innate instinct as a fighter.

The other thing that the twelve-year-old Will and Lyra need to do—in addition to destroying the knife—is to fall profoundly in romantic love with each other. For some reason, the author associates their falling in love with the temptation of Eve in the Garden of Eden, and inserts into the story a former nun, Mary (Dr. Malone), in order to "tempt" Lyra to love Will (as if any such tempting was needed). In fact, a huge part of the whole trilogy is the prophecy that Lyra will be the new Eve, and that the future of the universes will depend on how she responds to this temptation. It was also prophesied that she would commit some great betrayal, but when the big betrayal happens—Lyra separates herself from her dæmon—it is so difficult to discern that *this is the big betrayal* that the narrative has to tell the readers that it has happened! Readers later learn that some of the inhabitants of Lyra's world (ones who are portrayed as heroic in the tales) have been committing this supposed act of betrayal for centuries.

In the model of many Disney films, most of the significant parental figures in the lives of Lyra and Will are killed. Will's father, Dr. Grumman; both of Lyra's parents, Lord Asriel and Mrs. Coulter; Lyra's surrogate father-figure, Lee Scoresby; and their later protectors, Lady Salmakia and Chevalier Tialys, all die (as does Lyra's closest childhood friend, Roger). The trilogy, however, ends more or less where it began. The knife has been destroyed, but this only restores the status quo. The boy Will must return to his own world, where he and Mary will have a big mess to clean up, but at least they'll have their friendship. The girl Lyra ends where she started, except a little more mature and wiser. In that sense, with the deaths of so many parental figures and the growing into adulthood of the two child protagonists, one can read the trilogy as yet another coming of age story. (Perhaps this is what some critics had in mind in giving the books some of the awards they received.)

Coming of Age?

Certainly the author very clearly symbolized this coming of age—the step from childhood into adulthood—by showing how Dust (a symbol of consciousness) begins to be attracted to Will and Lyra. (One of the central tenets of the book is that Dust is not attracted to children.) But, though this coming of age is certainly influenced by their difficult trials, the real coming of age (the final movement) happens when these two twelve-year-olds get romantically involved with each other. The night they spend together in each other's arms is the big climax of the trilogy, and for some unexplained reason helps stop the flow of Dust out of the cracks of the universe. The description of this meeting comes off the cover of a cheap romance:

> The word *love* set his nerves ablaze. All his body thrilled with it, and he answered her in the same words, kissing her hot face over and over again, drinking in with adoration the scent of her warm, honey-fragrant hair and her sweet, moist mouth that tasted of the little red fruit. (*Spyglass*, 466)

(Remember that the characters are twelve years old, and then digest the prose: "honey-fragrant hair" and "sweet, moist mouth.") To the author's credit, sex is only hinted at. Still, their final encounter, the next night, is even harder to accept as realistic.

> Will put his hand on hers. A new mood had taken hold of him, and he felt resolute and peaceful. Knowing exactly what he was doing and exactly what it would mean, he moved his hand from Lyra's wrist and stroked the red-gold fur of her dæmon.
> Lyra gasped. But her surprise was mixed with a pleasure so like the joy that flooded her when she had put the fruit to his lips that she couldn't protest, because she was breathless. With a racing heart she responded in the same way: she put her hand on the silky warmth of Will's dæmon, and as her fingers tightened in the fur she knew that Will was feeling exactly what she was. . . .
> So, wondering whether any lovers before them had made this blissful discovery, they lay together as the earth turned slowly and the moon and stars blazed above them. (499)

Adult readers (especially parents) must wonder what message a twelve-year-old child would take from the book.

A Sermon in Thin Disguise

Perhaps the books' greatest flaw, however, is how didactic they are. And this, ironically, may also be the reason for their cultlike success. Author Pullman has a very large chip on his shoulder, and it is evident in nearly every page of the book. The "chip" is an unrelenting animosity toward God, church, religion in general, and especially Christianity. Every dialogue, every moment of revelation, every speech from a wise character, and every portrayal of an evil character becomes yet another chance for Pullman to rail and preach against the evils of the church. Everything that has ever gone wrong in any of the universes, it seems, is the fault of the church or of those who believe in God. Will's father, Dr. Grumman, whom Pullman portrays as one of the wisest and most powerful human characters in the book, says of the Authority (God) and the Church: "We've had nothing but lies and propaganda and cruelty and deceit for all the thousands of years of human history" (*Knife*, 282). A little later, he adds:

> There are two great powers, and they've been fighting since time began. Every advance in human life, every scrap of knowledge and wisdom and decency we have has been torn by one side from the teeth of the other. Every little increase in human freedom has been fought over ferociously between those who want us to know more and be wiser and stronger, and those who want us to obey and be humble and submit. (283)

Those who "want us to know more and be wiser and stronger," of course, are those rebelling against the church and the Authority, who only want us to obey and submit. To continue his preaching, Pullman has one of the angels—also portrayed as wise and good—give the following history:

> The Authority, God, the Creator, the Lord, Yahweh, El, Adonai, the King, the Father, the Almighty—those were names he gave himself. He was never the creator. He was an angel like ourselves . . . formed of Dust as we are. . . . He told those who came after him that he had created them, but it was a lie. One of those who came later was wiser than he was, and she found out the truth, so he banished her. (*Spyglass*, 31–32)

Pullman's view of God, conveyed here, needs no explanation; it is already a sermon.

To further criticize the church, we are told that "every philosophical research establishment, so he'd heard, had to include on its staff a representative of the [church], to act as a censor to suppress the news of any heretical discoveries" (*Knife*, 110). The angel Balthamos tells us that the land of the dead—a hell to which all humans go when they die—is merely "a prison camp. The Authority established it in the early ages. . . . Even the churches don't know; they tell their believers that they'll live in heaven, but that's a lie" (*Spyglass*, 33). And the final summary indictment is the dismissive comment coming from Dr. Mary Malone:

"The Christian religion is a very powerful and convincing mistake, that's all" (441).

If Pullman were trying to write a story told from a Luciferian perspective, this is the sort of thing we might expect. C. S. Lewis's *Screwtape Letters* does just this to brilliant effect. In interviews, Pullman has made it plain that this is not his intent, however. It seems that a lot of the book is Pullman's thinly veiled expression in the form of fiction of his own religious beliefs.

> I don't know whether there's a God or not. Nobody does, no matter what they say. I think it's perfectly possible to explain how the universe came about without bringing God into it, but I don't know everything, and there may well be a God somewhere, hiding away.
>
> Actually, if he is keeping out of sight, it's because he's ashamed of his followers and all the cruelty and ignorance they're responsible for promoting in his name. If I were him, I'd want nothing to do with them.[3]

Expressed as personal essay, one can read this and consider it intelligently. However, such didactic and dogmatic writing is difficult to take in fantasy. Still, Pullman has obviously found an audience of readers who share his antireligious obsession and are willing to overlook the constant preaching and other flaws because they are cheerleaders for the same cause, or simply because Pullman is piping the jangling tune they want to dance to.

Given what we have said in this book about fantasy literature not being an appropriate venue for didacticism, one might ask whether the *His Dark Materials* trilogy should even be categorized as fantasy. Pullman himself questions the categorization, though his reasons are unusual. In the same interview on his web page, Pullman responds to the comment: "You once said that *His Dark Materials* is not a fantasy, but stark realism. What did you mean by that?" His response is:

> That comment got me into trouble with the fantasy people. What I mean by it was roughly this: that the story I was trying to write was about real people, not beings that don't exist like elves or hobbits. Lyra and Will and the other characters are meant to be human beings like us, and the story is about a universal human experience, namely growing up. The "fantasy" parts of the story were there as a picture of aspects of human nature, not as something alien and strange. For example, readers have told me that

3. Interview with Philip Pullman, from the official Philip Pullman website: www.philip-pullman.com/about_the_writing.asp.

the dæmons, which at first seem so utterly fantastic, soon become so familiar and essential a part of each character that they, the readers, feel as
if they've got a dæmon themselves. And my point is that they have, that
we all have. It's an aspect of our personality that we often overlook, but it's
there. That's what I mean by realism: I was using the fantastical elements
to say something that I thought was true about us and about our lives.[4]

That last sentence shows a very good understanding of fantasy, making
us wonder how Pullman misses his own point when he condemns other
fantasies as "unreal." All good fantasy authors trust their fantasy to "say
something . . . true about our lives." The phenomenal success of *The
Lord of the Rings* is due in part to the fact that Elves and Hobbits do say
something true about our lives (contrary to Pullman's opinion). Part of
the reason that the dæmons work as fantasy (as we mentioned above) is
that he does make them believable within his world. Ideally, however,
with Pullman the story exists to serve the message rather than the other
way around. Probably, then, what Pullman refers to as "stark realism" is
his portrayal of the church.

Confusion of Science Fiction and Fantasy

On deeper examination, however, the books indeed do bear as much
or more in common with science fiction than with fantasy. Consider the
dæmons, which Pullman considers central to his work. There are elements
of the portrayal of dæmons that are from Faërie and relate to the world
of the unseen. A similar comment can be made about Dust, which is
another central image of the trilogy. But then Pullman does something
similar to what George Lucas does with his second *Star Wars* trilogy,
which is that he tries to explain or control these mysterious elements
with science. One character in the book discovers a metal alloy that can
separate a human from his dæmon. Others discover scientific ways of
measuring Dust. Lord Asriel explains it to his daughter, Lyra:

> Some years ago a Muscovite called Boris Mikhailovitch Rusakov discovered
> a new kind of elementary particle. . . . Well, this new kind of particle was
> elementary all right, but it was very hard to measure because it didn't react
> in any of the usual ways. The hardest thing for Rusakov to understand

4. Ibid.

was why the new particle seemed to cluster where human beings were, as
if it were attracted to us. . . .

The energy that links body and dæmon is immensely powerful. When
the cut is made, all that energy dissipates in a fraction of a second." (*Compass*, 370–75)

Thus the mystical element—the element of Faërie—becomes simply
another part of the scientific world. At one point, the Dust itself even
tells Dr. Malone that Spirit and Matter are one and the same! The third
book of the trilogy especially could fit at home in a sci-fi catalog, and in
fact has some passages of strong speculative sci-fi writing; for example,
Mary's discovery of the world of the *mulefi* is reminiscent of some similar
writings where characters explore new worlds and meet new creatures.
The ease with which Mary learns their language seems a little unrealistic,
and there is a dramatic change in narrative voice when Mary Malone
comes into this land in the third book, but some of the other speculative
aspects of this world are creative and interesting.

Truth in Story

Despite all of the flaws, and the author's confusion about whether
he is writing fantasy or sci-fi, the books still contain Story. In our book
we have contended that all stories must contain some grains of truth, or
they cannot stand as story. This is true of Pullman's work, though the
basic Truth that the story conveys is, oddly enough, one that the author
seems opposed to.

One such truth is that there is a battle going on, and that everybody
is a part of it, whether they wish to be or not. The heroic witch Serafina
points this out to Lee Scoresby: "All I can say is that all of us, humans,
witches, bears, are engaged in a war already, although not all of us know
it" (*Compass*, 308). These words are not unlike those of Aragorn to Éomer
when they first meet on the Plains of Rohan (quoted earlier in this book),
and they ring true. It is the reality of this battle that makes the story (and
all stories) interesting.

Pullman's story also suggests that the battle involves moral choices,
and that this morality is not defined subjectively but exists in the fabric
of the universe. When discussing the war, Serafina also tells Scoresby, "If
there is a war to be fought, we don't consider cost one of the factors in
deciding whether or not it is right to fight" (308). In other words, Sera-

fina is saying that one must do what is right, and not what is convenient. Even young Will acknowledges that objective nature of morality. When he discovers a door to another world, we read that he knew it was such a door "at once, as strongly as he knew that fire burned and kindness was good" (*Knife*, 13).

We say that Pullman's *story* suggests this; Pullman himself might disagree. Here is the inconsistency we mentioned at the beginning of this chapter: the story that keeps trying to make the books interesting is repeatedly contradicted by the pseudophilosophical screed the author often substitutes for dialogue. Dr. Malone explains to Lyra and Will:

> But I stopped believing there was a power of good and a power of evil that were outside us. And I came to believe that good and evil are names for what people do, not for what they are. All we can say is that this is a good deed, because it helps someone, or that's an evil one, because it hurts them. People are too complicated to have simple labels. (*Spyglass*, 447)

Pullman's denial of external "powers" of good and evil seems odd, in that much of his book has conveyed an argument that the Kingdom of God (the Authority) is evil. This may not be inconsistent. Since God and the angels are merely other beings of Dust, like humans, Dr. Malone may not consider the Authority an external evil. Indeed, Dr. Malone's view that "good and evil are names for what people do" is not inconsistent with Tolkien's Christianity, and her comment that "People are too complicated to have simple labels" is entirely Christian. What Malone is lacking, though, is a reasonable definition of what good and evil are. What defines evil in her view (and in Pullman's)? She can say nothing beyond the shallow comment that a good deed is one that helps someone, and an evil deed is one that hurts somebody. One problem is simply that some actions might hurt some people and help others. How, then, do we define the action? If people are too complicated for simple labels, so are our actions. As we mentioned in the previous chapter, we can never see all the consequences of our choices, so Pullman's implicit consequentialism leaves us morally blind. More centrally, though, one has to ask *why* helping somebody is good and hurting somebody is evil. This assumes an objective morality. Why shouldn't we hurt people if we can get away with it? Pullman's ill-conceived system has no reply to this question, and no argument against perfect criminals or tyrants; it has no room for thinking about justice and virtue; and it can never lead to altruism or self-sacrifice.

In the end, one of the most important "messages" told by the story is in direct contradiction to the "messages" the author attempts to tell us through many of the wise characters in the story. Throughout the book, the angels, the witches, Dr. Malone, Lord Asriel, and Dr. Grumman all seem to say that life exists in making our *own* choices and *not* submitting to anybody else's will. This is what the Dust is all about: people making conscious choices. One of the supposed evils of the church and the Authority is that they try to impose some moral order on the universes—telling people what they ought and ought not to do. The church wants to destroy Dust, because by destroying Dust it will destroy free will and the ability to disobey.

In the end, however, Will and Lyra must give up their personal desires—their freedom—and submit to a moral good, because it is the right thing to do. When Will is trying to decide what to do with the knife, Dr. Grumman, Will's father, tells him: "Too late. You haven't any choice: you're the bearer. It's picked you out" (*Knife*, 283). Again, this message is not unlike what Gandalf tells Frodo about the Ring. The angel tells Will and Lyra something similar. Will and Lyra agonize, and end up deciding to do what is right—that is, they obey the moral obligation upon them rather than their own personal desires. They do (and are praised for doing) exactly the opposite of what the trilogy has been preaching from the start. When this happens, the trilogy comes as close as it can to true story.

9

GRACE ACROSS THE WHOLE
OF FAËRIE

Walter Wangerin Jr. and The Book of the Dun Cow

The writings of Walter Wangerin Jr. have encompassed as much of the broad spectrum of Faërie as those of any author alive. Exploring Wangerin's fiction, one can find illustrations of nearly everything we have written about in this book. In *The Orphean Passages,* he explored ancient Greek myth, alternating between a retelling of the tale of Orpheus and Eurydice, a sermon on faith that is also a commentary on this myth, and a novel that is something of a modern version of Orpheus's tale. In *The Book of God,* he presents or re-presents the Bible as a single historical narrative drawing upon its mythical power to communicate truth through story. His novel *The Crying for a Vision* is set in North America before European settlement and is inspired by early Native American legend. And the more recently published *Saint Julian* is set in medieval times, during the Crusades, and draws upon some of the tradition of medieval romance in telling the tale of the famous saint. All of these works succeed wonderfully as stories, and all are also worthy of exploration. The professor, author, and former pastor Wangerin has thought long and deeply about myth, fantasy, and fairy. He has written about it and taught it, and the profundity of his thinking is evident throughout the body of his creative works.

In this chapter we focus on *The Book of the Dun Cow,* Wangerin's first published novel, which is noteworthy not only for the beauty of the writing (the cadence of the narrative, the richness of the dialogue, and the economy of language are wonderfully poetic) and for the depth of meaning (it is the sort of book where one finds oneself underlining or highlighting more lines than not, and it rewards endless rereading), but also in another very interesting regard: *The Book of the Dun Cow* somehow manages to span the entire spectrum of Faërie discussed in chapter 1. It contains elements of classic fairy tale, connecting it to the stories recorded by the Grimms or those told by Hans Christian Andersen and George MacDonald. It contains elements of romance and epic fantasy more common in far longer works. It even encompasses cosmogonic and cosmological mythic elements taken from the farthest end of the spectrum from fairy tale. And it manages to do all three successfully, holding the three forms in balance.

The Book of the Dun Cow as Fairy Tale

The Book of the Dun Cow was first published in 1978 and was followed by a sequel, *The Book of Sorrows.*[1] It won several awards, including the American Book Award in 1980 for "Best Science Fiction Paperback." It contains many elements of classic fairy tale—so many, in fact, that many reviewers and readers who mistakenly associate all fairy tale with children have labeled the book as a children's book. The year it was published, it was also named "A Best Children's Book of the Year" by *The New York Times,* and "A Best Book for Children" by the *School Library Journal.*

Of course, as readers of our book are hopefully well aware by now, the connection between fairy tale and children is accidental, and often wrong. Thus, though these awards were well deserved with respect to the quality of Wangerin's writing, for the *New York Times* and the *School Library Journal* to label *The Book of the Dun Cow* a "children's book" is as erroneous as it is for the American Book Award to call it a work of science fiction. (See our discussion of the distinctions between fantasy and science fiction in chapter 2.) As has also been pointed out, however, the misguided association with children and the nursery is an issue that has plagued many great writers of fantasy and fairy tale, putting Wangerin in the company of Tolkien, Lewis, L'Engle, and Le Guin. In any case,

1. Walter Wangerin Jr., *The Book of Sorrows* (San Francisco: Harper and Row, 1985).

however misguided the notion, it is still a common association, and thus the "children's literature" categorization by reviewers emphasizes the presence of fairy-tale elements.

Probably the clearest aspect of the book that places it on the side of fairy tale is the setting. The realm of fairy story, as we wrote earlier, is usually very localized: the peasant's hut, the cottage in the woods, or the forest out the back door on the edge of the field on one side of the castle. In *The Book of the Dun Cow*, almost the entire novel takes place in a single barnyard—the domain of the rooster Chauntecleer—or in the adjacent wood on the one side, or the land between the barnyard and the river on the other. There is no great quest to take the heroes to distant lands. The only two scenes that take place elsewhere do so in another barnyard many miles upriver, where the rooster Senex first succumbs to evil and his land is taken over by the serpent rooster Cockatrice. This certainly places the book more in the genre of fairy tale than in epic fantasy or myth.

Just as there is an association with the traditional "where" of fairy tale, so there is also an association with the traditional "when." The classic fairy-tale beginning is "Once upon a time." Nearly every story in *The Complete Fairy Tales of George MacDonald* begins thus, or with the similar "There was once." So do many fairy tales of the Grimms' collection. In doing so, the fairy tale makes both a connection and a distinction between the long-ago fairy-tale time and the modern time. The main distinction between then and now, of course, is that in those days the realm of Faërie was ever so much closer, and thus day-to-day life was more likely to be influenced by its strangeness. The fairy tale must play to this strangeness to capture the reader's imagination, while simultaneously drawing the reader in by familiarity; however different those times were from today, some things never change, and the lessons we learn from that once-upon-a-time era still apply to our lives.[2] This is precisely what Wangerin accomplishes. At the start of chapter 4, he gives a similar time frame for *The Book of the Dun Cow:* "In those days, when the animals could both speak and understand speech, the world was round, as it is today." Thus, the book is set in the long ago before animals lost the power of speech when everything was different ... except for all the things that were just the same. Wangerin makes this point explicit. "These things were

2. Another potential advantage of setting a story in the vague long ago of fairy-tale time, as opposed to in the specific historical period of the present, is that the lack of specificity allows the reader to imagine the tale taking place *any* time. In specifically placing his story before the time of humans, Wangerin might lose out on this advantage. However, by making the strange familiar enough to us today, he gains that back.

no different from the way they are today," the story continues. "But yet some things were very different" (*Cow,* 22).

Even more important than the "where" and "when" of fairy tale, is the "who" that Wangerin draws upon. Three of the four main characters of Wangerin's tale are the rooster Chauntecleer, the Dun Cow of the title, and a dog named Mundo Cani. It is worth remembering that these are three of the four characters of one of the Grimms' most famous tales: "The Bremen Town-Musicians." And of course Chauntecleer is an even older "bone in the Soup" as evidenced by his appearance in Chaucer.

Now at this point we must raise one interesting issue brought up by Tolkien in his famous essay. Tolkien argued that stories like "The Bremen Town-Musicians" or the Swahili tale "The Monkey's Heart" included in Lang's *Lilac Fairy Book*—stories in which "no human being is concerned; or in which the animals are the heroes and heroines, and men and women, if they appear, are mere adjuncts"—are not really fairy tales. He calls them, instead, "Beast-fables." His argument distinguishing the beast-fable from the fairy tale is not one of quality; he didn't say that beast-fables held no virtue, or that they couldn't be good. Rather, he claims that "one of the primal 'desires' that lie near the heart of Faërie" is "the desire of men to hold communion with other living things." The problem with the beast-fable is that in it "the speech of beasts . . . as developed into a separate branch, has little reference to that desire, and often wholly forgets it." Thus, the ancient desire is cheated, rather than fulfilled. Another problem is that in many such stories the "animal form is only a mask upon a human face," and as a result the animals are not really believable *as animals.* Nevertheless, Tolkien admits that even the beast-fable has "a connection with fairy-stories." One element of that connection is "their strong moral element," by which Tolkien means—and we have repeated often in this book—"not any allegorical *significatio,*" but rather an "inherent morality" (*Essay,* 19).

C. S. Lewis's *Chronicles of Narnia,* for example, is ultimately about humans, but it also has many animal heroes, including badgers, beavers, and bears—and a very brave mouse named Reepicheep. Though the animals of Narnia are talking animals, their speech is not true animal speech that humans learn, but rather human speech that animals have been given as a gift. Thus, Lewis's tales fit more closely Tolkien's description of beast-fables. Certainly the beavers of *The Lion, the Witch, and the Wardrobe,* with their sewing machines and locked doors, are much more like animal masks on human faces than they are real animals. Now, as Lewis's tales develop, the animals of his later books become more like real animals. After the first book, for example, we meet no more animals that have sewing machines. And when it comes to battle, as in *Prince Caspian, The Horse and His Boy,* or *The Last Battle*—though Reepicheep and the mice are exceptions and fight with swords—most of the animals fight with tooth and claw.

What of Wangerin's story? It has no human characters at all. His animals are more akin to the animals in the later Narnia stories—that is to say, a little bit more like animals and less like people with animal masks than are the beavers, but still bearing rather human traits. In any case, the story certainly fits Tolkien's description of a beast-fable rather than a fairy tale. Nevertheless, whatever one thinks of Tolkien's classification, it is still the case that many traditional collections of fairy tales have included beast-fables of a type close in kinship with *The Book of the Dun Cow:* stories where the main characters are animals, and where humans do not appear. In the Grimms' collection of so-called fairy tales, there are numerous such examples, usually among the shorter stories, including "The Cat and Mouse in Partnership," "The Wolf and the Seven Little Kids," "The Mouse, the Bird, and the Sausage," "The Wedding of Mrs. Fox," "The Wolf and the Fox," "Gossip Wolf and the Fox," "The Fox and the Cat," and many others.

The connection between Wangerin's tale and the Grimms' tales is even stronger when one considers the actions of some of these animals. In several of the Grimms' tales—both those of the type Tolkien refers to as true fairy tales and those of the type he calls beast-fable—animals accomplish important and difficult feats that help defeat the schemes of the evil enemy. Moreover, it is often the small or seemingly insignificant animals, especially insects, who perform the tasks, as with the bees in "The Queen Bee" or the ants in "The White Snake." In Wangerin's tale we see many similar examples, especially of insects. In the great battle against Cockatrice and Wyrm, it is the ant Tick-Tock and his ant workers who build the great protective wall surrounding the barnyard, turning it into a fortress and protecting it from the flood. It is Scarce the mosquito—"Scarce was a mosquito. Scarce was all mosquitoes; but then all mosquitoes are one" (*Cow,* 131)—who brings word to everybody of the coming council. It is the bees who seal the ground against the awful stench of Wyrm. Again, in this regard also Wangerin's work stands alongside the best of the fairy-tale tradition.

One last thing that often separates the fairy tale from the myth is its tone. Though myth and fantasy may contain humor, and fairy tales can certainly be dark and serious in tone, by and large the fairy tale is a lighter work. Thus the Grimms' tales, and C. S. Lewis's, also give us many rather humorous animals. In Lewis's Narnia chronicles, along with Reepicheep we have the slow-witted bears in *Prince Caspian* and *The Last Battle*, and a very comic scene with numerous animals surrounding the recently planted uncle in *The Magician's Nephew*. Wangerin also draws often on this same tone, in the many humorous animals and their antics in the barnyard of Chauntecleer. He gives us the Mad House of Otter, an extended family of otters, with their treacherous plotting. He gives us Tick-Tock, the busy and very businesslike ant with his "Hup, two, three, four. Games, two, three, four!" (108). He gives us the ridiculous turkeys with their "goo-goo-good!" and "Ge-ge-get a gallop on, my bubble-brother!" (137). And he gives us one very "marooooned" Mundo Cani Dog with a large, bulbous nose and immense self-pity.

And, of course, he gives us the rooster Chauntecleer himself: Chauntecleer who likes to strut, for "strutting permitted pride and a certain show of authority, whereas flying looked mostly foolish in a Rooster: lumpish, graceless and altogether unnecessary.... It is a mark of superiority when part of the body does nothing at all" (7). It is difficult to miss the many associations between Wangerin's work and the body of fairy tale that has come before him. Whether we call that work a fairy tale or a beast-fable, we must acknowledge "their strong moral element" and "inherent morality," and that these are works very close to fairy tale if not within its boundaries; the connection is very strong.

The Book of the Dun Cow as Fantasy and Myth

If we see in *The Book of the Dun Cow* many elements of the traditional fairy tale, we must also see many of the deeper elements of fantasy and romance. One such element we have addressed several times in this book is the importance of speech, word, and language. We have already made the connection to Le Guin, Tolkien, and the book of Job, and we needn't say more about its importance here. What we do point out is that Wangerin, also, like the greatest writers of fantasy, draws on the importance of speech and language. And the way he does so has strong resonances with great works of fantasy like *The Lord of the Rings* or the *Earthsea* trilogy.

Like Vetch, who says "Avert" to Ged's careless words, or like Gandalf and Aragorn, who chastise the Hobbits for carelessly uttered curses, *The*

Book of the Dun Cow has the prophetess hen, Beryl, who takes language, curses, and blessings very seriously.

> Beryl also had an abiding respect for words. . . . Therefore she never spoke frivolously what she did not mean to say; and she surely never put into words anything which she did not wish to happen. For the words themselves could trigger it, and then it would happen. (111)

That Beryl is a prophetess is shown when she draws "three fair eggs" in the snow at the wedding of Chauntecleer and Pertelote—counting the chickens before they hatch, as it were. Chauntecleer takes Beryl's prophecy so seriously that he names his offspring before they are hatched, and the reader is not surprised when the prophecy comes to pass.

Thus, the reader also has just cause to be concerned when Beryl gets upset at the ants for their careless words about these three young chicks, Ten Pin, Five Pin, and One Pin, after they are hatched. "They'll not be home for tea, for tea," sing the ants. "They'll never be home for tea." What the ants are doing is cursing the chicks. But they don't see it as anything more than a joke, and thus they are surprised at the fury of Beryl's response. "'Stop!' screamed a voice from within the Coop. 'Evil tongues! Evil tongues! Not another word from your evil tongues!' Beryl exploded from the door, spilling feathers everywhere in her fury" (*Cow*, 109). It is nothing to the ants, but Beryl continues:

> "Games? Disasters! Incantations! Children could drown, for all your games.
> "Words curse, don't you know? . . . No more sense in your tiny black brains than slugs—to be handling *words*, to be light with *words*, and at the children's expense! Oh, to be talking such things!" (110)

Alas that nobody takes Beryl seriously. None of the barnyard characters do, that is. The author certainly does, and the reader—warned in advance by the truth of Beryl's prophecy—also feels a certain dread with Beryl.

The reader also sees the importance of words and speech in the "canonical crows" of Chauntecleer. Early in the story we are told that the rooster's crows "told all the world—what time it was, and they blessed the moment in the ears of the hearer. By what blessing? By making the day, and that moment of the day, familiar; by giving it direction and meaning and a proper soul" (12). A little later, Wangerin adds, "When Chauntecleer crowed his canonical crows, the day wore the right kind of clothes; his Hens lived and scratched in peace, happy with what was, and unafraid of what was to be; even wrong things were made right, and the grey things were explained" (13). Like the words of Gandalf or Ged spoken in battle, or like the liturgical calendar and the daily office of prayer, Chauntecleer's crows—his Crows Potens—also carry tremendous power.

Where we really feel the connection to epic fantasy, however, is in the scope of the battle. Chauntecleer and the animals under his care are fighting an epic battle, and the rooster's entire realm is at stake. We learn this early in the tale—in the second chapter—before we even know anything specific about the enemy, when we are given the following foreshadowing hint: "For an enemy was gathering himself against this Rooster and his land. Within a year Chauntecleer would find his land under a treacherous attack; and then, in that war, this third kind of crowing would become his necessary weapon" (13). As in *The Hobbit* or *The Lord of the Rings,* the small and seemingly insignificant characters of the world will be called upon to fight this battle. But prior to the battle, they are wrapped up in their own little secluded and protected shires, sheltered from the big dangerous world outside. "For the time being Chauntecleer was busy about lesser affairs, though he himself would have called them important enough" (13).

Wangerin also writes in the novel form, most familiar to epic fantasy. Which is to say, most importantly, that there is real character development (unlike in the fairy tale form). Again the reader's expectations for this are developed early in the story. Though we later get the fairy tale "once upon a time," the book actually begins: "In the middle of the night somebody began to cry"—the somebody being Mundo Cani dog. Immediate questions are raised. Who is crying? Why? Why is it the middle of the night? Thus it is that we come to know the dog with no illusions.

We also soon get insights into the chief rooster's psychology.

"Sir" and "pleases you" are right and proper things to say to a Lord, of course. But they are also hindrances to clear speech: They keep someone, if there are enough of them, from ever getting to her point. They keep a certain lonely distance between the Lord and his subject. (15)

It crossed his mind for the second time in a day that it would be good to have just one person for simple friendship and for talk. (37)

Certainly, there are many characters undeveloped and left only in fairy-tale caricature, but some—like Chauntecleer, Pertelote, Mundo Cani, and John Wesley—are developed more fully.

And the development of these characters ties closely to another important theme in fantasy, which is heroism and choice. It is the making of right choices—most specifically the choice against evil, however great the cost of that choice might be—that is shown to be what ultimately defines heroism. "I choose against evil," Chauntecleer declares. "I can surely choose against evil" (104). His wife, Pertelote, despite all she has suffered at the hands of Senex, affirms the same choice. "I, too, can choose against evil" (105). Even the widow mouse shows tremendous heroism in her choice, though she is less able to articulate it.

But just as we get comfortable with the crossover from the localized, lighthearted fairy tale to the deeper epic fantasy, we must then realize that Wangerin has actually taken *The Book of the Dun Cow* all the way to the deepest end of the spectrum of Faërie: to the cosmological and cosmogonic myth. If there is any doubt about this, one need look only at the title of chapter 4: "A Cosmography, in Which Wyrm Is Described, and One or Two Things about Him." Whereas cosmogony deals with the *origin* of the universe, and cosmology with the *nature* of the universe, cosmography seeks to actually map out the entire universe—which for Wangerin entails dealing with both its origins and its nature.

We read in chapter 4 of the time in which Chauntecleer lived:

> For in those days the earth was still fixed in the absolute center of the universe. It had not yet been cracked loose from that holy place, to be sent whirling—wild, helpless, and ignorant—among the blind stars . . . and God still chose to walk among the clouds, striding, like a man who strides through his garden in the sweet evening. (22)

These are mythic statements. Wangerin makes it clear that this is a story that deals with the gods, or with God, and immediately thereby gives it a mythic context. The language describing God striding in the clouds has resonance with mythic language of the Greeks and the Norse as well as with Genesis; it *is* mythic language; it deals with the earth's place in the cosmos, stating—in contradiction to modern science—that the earth was still at the heart of all that happens, which also lends mythic significance.

It is also difficult to miss the many images and allusions from biblical myth and story. The rooster's "conversion" moment midway through the book bears a striking resemblance to the biblical conversion tale of the apostle Paul (known at the time as Saul; see Acts 9). As with the famous apostle who fell to the ground blinded when a light flashed around him, God appears to Chauntecleer in a "blinding light" that knocks him off his tree "stunned, full of terror." And in the blinding light the rooster sees himself as "a filthy piece of thing." Even God's words to Chauntecleer ("'Why do you hurt my creatures?' said the Lord out of his radiance" [*Cow*, 143]) are undeniably similar to the words spoken by God to Paul in Acts 9:4 ("Saul, Saul, why do you persecute me?").

More important, in terms of the mythical element, Wangerin's book is also full of prayer (symbolized in Chauntecleer's canonical crows), which is simply people speaking to God. Moreover, it is full of *answered* prayer, meaning that God speaks back; he hears prayers, and he answers prayers. God is involved in the tale. To see the importance of this, we need only contrast it with another contemporary work of fantasy: Stephen Donaldson's *Chronicles of Thomas Covenant,* book 1 of which was published in 1977 (*Foul*), the year before *The Book of the Dun Cow.*

In Donaldson's mythology of the Land—the fantastic realm to which the protagonist Thomas Covenant is called from our world—there is a Creator, and there is good and evil, but the Creator is impotent to act within his creation. Though the Creator desires good, he has no power to oppose evil. In fact, his impotence is one of the fundamental and most important facts about the Land that provides the basis for all six books. In Donaldson's mythology, the good Creator made the earth within the arch of time, and then in a battle he imprisoned his evil counterpart, the Despiser, inside the universe, within the arch of time. As the wise Tamarantha points out, "in his fury [the Creator] cast the Despiser down, out of the infinity of the cosmos onto the Earth" (*Foul*, 294). The problem is that if the Creator were ever to work directly within his creation, he would thereby destroy the arch of time and free his cosmic enemy. Thus, he is rendered impotent by his own actions. His enemy, the Despiser, is now free to wreak havoc on earth. Again Tamarantha explains:

> For the very Law of Time, the principle of power which made the arch possible, worked to preserve Lord Foul, as we now call [the Despiser]. That Law requires that no act may be undone. Desecration may not be undone—defilement may not be recanted. Therefore Lord Foul has afflicted the Earth, and the Creator *cannot* stop him—for it was the Creator's act which placed Despite here. (294, emphasis ours)

Thus, in Donaldson's mythology, there can be no incarnation.[3] Not only that, but prayer is ultimately meaningless and empty, because even if the Creator can hear the prayer, he is unable to respond. "If the Creator were to silence Lord Foul, that act would destroy Time—and then the Despiser would be free in infinity again, free to make whatever befoulments he desired" (294–95). This fundamental point is repeated in every book. Indeed, as is pointed out by Lord Mhoram, the wisest figure in the first trilogy, the Creator cannot even be known! (292). It is thus left up to Covenant—the protagonist who is also impotent (sexually) as a result of leprosy—to save the world for the Creator.

In *The Book of the Dun Cow,* by contrast, God hears prayers and answers them again and again. Some of the most passionate moments of the story are scenes of Chauntecleer crying out in his distress. Two of the chapters even have the phrase "Chauntecleer's Prayer" in the title. And the powerful eucatastrophic moments of the story are the images of God's grace in the answered prayers. Consider the title of the book. It is not the rooster in the title, but the Dun Cow, the messenger of God and a symbol of God's grace and involvement in his creation. God can be known. God makes himself known. "For in those days ... God still chose to walk among the clouds, striding, like a man who strides through his garden in the sweet evening" (*Cow,* 22). Among other ways, he makes himself known through the Dun Cow. And this truth is important at every level of the story, from the fairy tale through the romance and the myth.

Three Genres, Four Evils

So we see this book straddling the whole realm of Faërie, from fairy tale all the way through myth. It includes character types, linguistic elements, and plot devices from all three. Perhaps the clearest illustration of the breadth of this work is in the representation of evil. It is also in the representation of evil that we begin to get at the heart of the book, and of our understanding of what it accomplishes and what is its "strong moral element" and "inherent morality." In *The Book of the Dun Cow,* Wangerin gives us four very different presentations of evil, which together span the whole spectrum of Faërie, and while doing so also suggest something fundamental about the meaning of our existence.

3. This is further illustrated by the fact that the messianic figure in Donaldson's series is merely another human from another world, one who is supremely reluctant to play the savior, and whose sobriquet is telling: "the Unbeliever."

Of course, the great evil in this book—the mythic evil, the colossus evil behind all the other evils—is Wyrm. "He was in the shape of a serpent, so damnably huge that he could pass once around the earth and then bite his own tail ahead of him" (*Cow*, 23). Certainly, this evil is greater than any mere fairy-tale evil—greater even than an epic fantasy evil of a Sauron or Saruman or Voldemort. It is an evil that affects the entire earth and all of history. It is a mythic evil. This mythic evil image comes directly from the great serpent in Norse mythology, the Miðgarð Serpent. It is also an evil that relates to the biblical myth and the serpent of Genesis. As we mentioned earlier, from the third chapter of Genesis onward, all of earth's history can be (and ought to be) understood in the context of the war on earth between the evil serpent and God's creation, in which not only humans but also the animals are involved (Gen. 6; Rom. 8).

In this way, the mythic evil of Wangerin's Wyrm is an evil akin to that of Morgoth: an evil too great to appear directly in the daily affairs of earth, but one, rather, who works through lesser evil servants. Consider the magnitude and nature of Wangerin's description of Wyrm. "He stank fearfully, because his outer skin was always rotting, a runny putrefaction. . . . He was lonely. He was powerful, because evil is powerful. He was angry. And he hated, with an intense and abiding hatred, the God who had locked him within the earth" (23). It is an evil that wages war directly against God. In fact, it is an evil that is almost unconcerned with lesser mortals, except to the extent that they can be used in its war against God. Thus, *The Book of the Dun Cow* is about a mythic war between God and Wyrm, in which the animals serve as guardians—fighting their seemingly small battles that are shown to have significance to the larger mythic war, even though they themselves often know little about this war.

But the lesser battles must be fought, and Wangerin gives us not only the great mythic evil, but also the epic fantasy evil; in addition to Wyrm, there is Cockatrice. Cockatrice is a rooster, of sorts. He is the son of a rooster. Not of a hen. Of a *rooster*! He is also the child of Wyrm. Conceived by the spirit of the Wyrm. Born of rooster Senex. Thus, Cockatrice is in his very being a mockery of the Christ who was conceived of the Holy Spirit of God and born of the Virgin Mary.

More of the nature of Cockatrice begins to become evident soon after he hatches, when "on the seventh day, the Rooster chick began to grow a tail. The tail had no feathers on it and no hair. It was a serpent's tail" (31). That last line makes the imagery clear. What is Cockatrice but a variation of the archetype of all fantasy evils: the dragon. Cockatrice is kin of Smaug, Glaurung, Fafnir, and the Beowulf dragon. As Pertelote tells the animals of the barnyard, its name rhymes with "hiss," reminding us again of snakes and serpents (148). "COCKATRISSSSSSSS," Chauntecleer screams at the start of the first battle, drawing "out the hissing of the enemy's name like spitfire" (183). It is a "demon" (207). A lesser demon than Wyrm, of course, but a demon nonetheless.

The connection of this rooster chick to the dragon of fantasy and medieval romance is made even clearer in the book's next paragraph, when Cockatrice begins to grow not feathers, but scales: "grey scales underneath its body, from the throat to the tail; and the tail itself was covered all over with scales." Only its head and wings are those of a rooster. And though it does not breathe fire, even that association with the dragons of fantasy is made when the reader is told that the head and wings "were like fire, and its eye was red." While Wyrm's chief battle is against God himself, and it is God—through the Dun Cow and the dog—who must defeat Wyrm, Cockatrice's battle is against the story's great hero, Chauntecleer. Thus, we have both a mythic evil and a fantasy evil.

But just as Wyrm, the great mythic evil beast, has a lesser offspring, a minion named Cockatrice, so too does Cockatrice sire countless offspring of his own, the Basilisks. To what part of the spectrum of Faërie do they belong? With Wangerin, eventually all categorizations begin to fall apart. The book is too complex for them. It covers too much ground. The Basilisks are venomous serpents. In size, they are more in keeping with the denizens of the fairy tale than with those of myth. A Basilisk could barely wrap itself around a baseball, no less the entire world as does its grandsire Wyrm. One alone, perhaps, belongs on the fairy-tale end of the spectrum. In keeping with this, many of the lesser fairy-tale animals of Chauntecleer's domain are capable of fighting Basilisks. John Wesley Weasel kills them by the hundreds. Ah, but there *are* hundreds, thousands even. And the sheer horror of their numbers is enough to move them collectively along the scale from fairy-tale villains to fantasy monster.

These, then, are three of the views of evil—the visible forms—that Wangerin gives us. The fourth is far more insidious, and far more devastating, and gets closer to the heart of the book and to Wyrm's vicious plot against God. It is the evil we see in Senex's coop after Senex's death when Cockatrice takes over.

> After the failure of the committee, the animals of the land broke apart. Each began to make his own way in the world. Each family created its

own remedies against the terrible killing stench—but then kept those
remedies to itself and grew narrow eyed and suspicious over-against its
neighbors. Each family sought its own food, stored in its secret places . . .
every family blamed the next. (82)

This is not an external evil that can be fought with tooth and claw. It
is an evil that is manifest in petty bickering, selfishness, suspicion. It is
an evil that is temptation. It is the antithesis of community, fellowship,
love, and everything the coop is supposed to stand for. And it is far more
insidious than any of the external forms, because it is far more destructive. Once the animals of Senex coop have given in to this evil, it is not
long before they descend "from speech to snarls, barks, roars, and bleated
accusations" (82).

And this aspect of evil—this anticommunity—fits all three ends of the
spectrum. When (largely in his dreams) Chauntecleer curses the other
animals ("Hate them. Hate them. Hate them all. *Ingrati*" [102]), and
wrestles with God ("You, God, promise—then break promises" [*Cow*,
123]), and listens to the temptations of Wyrm ("we have become wise
as God" [102]), we see this evil at the high mythic level in a way that
carries resonances with the stories of Adam and Eve, Job, and Oedipus.
In the plotting of the Mad House of Otter that almost destroys the
defenses of Chauntecleer, this aspect of evil is manifest in a way befitting heroic fantasy. In the comic ridiculousness of the pouting turkeys
we have a pettiness befitting the genre of fairy tale, but one nonetheless
that is also a part of this great evil that destroys community because it is
the opposite of community.

Eventually, this evil leads to a land that has become comparable to
Mordor or Saruman's Isengard. "The wasted land, the shattered society,
the bodies dead and festering, were all Wyrm's triumphs" (89). Among
all these aspects of evil, however—along with the wasted land and dead,
festering bodies that appear so gruesome—it is really the destruction
of community, the shattering of society, that is most deadly. This evil
is rooted in Wyrm and brought about in part by Cockatrice and the
Basilisks, but it transcends all the visible forms. Only in the destruction
of community can the animals be defeated. No other physical defeat is
possible without that. When the animals live in true community, when
their society is strong, then Wyrm is powerless against them. For the
animals "were there for a purpose. To be sure very few of them recognized
the full importance of their being, and of their being *there*" (23). Their
being is their purpose: to live out community in the image of the God

who created them. "Dumb feathers made watchers over Wyrm in chains! It was a wonder. But that's the way it was, because God had chosen it to be that way" (24).

Before Wyrm can escape to wage war against God, he must defeat the animals who are his guardians, and before he can conquer them, he must destroy their love for one another. Indeed, it's not so much that he must destroy their love *before* he can defeat them. Rather, destroying their love for one another *is* his victory. This is one of the chief points of the book! This is why so much of Wyrm's attack is in the form of temptation—first to Senex and then to Chauntecleer—to hate, or despise, the animals under their care. "You fool," Wyrm says to Senex. "They ride you mercilessly in your old age. They take advantage of every good thing you ever did for them" (27). Senex succumbs to the temptation. Chauntecleer comes close. "Dear Chauntecleer," Wyrm says, "you should have learned how quicksilver are the hearts of those you serve. . . . They have forgotten you, lonely Chauntecleer" (100). That's when Chauntecleer hits his lowest. "Hate you! Hate you! Hate you all!" he says in his dreams to his creatures (101). But Chauntecleer, unlike Senex, repents.

Ultimately, then, in *The Book of the Dun Cow,* the real battle against evil is not so much a physical war as it is a battle to live out community and love. And Wangerin leaves no doubt that this *is* a real battle. Living out true community is the only way to wage war against an evil whose main purpose is to destroy community. The destruction of community is not simply a byproduct of the attack of Wyrm and Cockatrice; it is the very purpose of the attack. Likewise, living out true community is not merely a means to victory for Chauntecleer and the animals; it *is* the victory. When the animals come together at Chauntecleer's coop, and live and fight together, and don't give in (either to the complaining of the turkeys or to the plotting of the otters or to the fear or the pettiness that destroyed Senex's realm), they defeat Cockatrice and Wyrm. We see this community embodied in many ways. We see it when Chauntecleer speaks words of love and encouragement to Mundo Cani. We see it in the care that John Wesley Weasel gives to the widow mouse and her children. We see it in the relationship between Chauntecleer and Pertelote. We see it most clearly in the self-sacrifice of the animals for one another, when they give their lives fighting the Basilisks, and when Chauntecleer sacrifices himself to fight Cockatrice—and both the Basilisks and Cockatrice are thereby destroyed.

Eucatastrophe and Grace

And yet—just as in *The Lord of the Rings*, where all hopes rest on the quest of Frodo and Sam, yet Aragorn, Théoden, and their armies must still fight the military battles at Helms Deep, Gondor, and the Black Gate—the *physical* battle against Cockatrice and the Basilisks must still be fought. And the battle is not insignificant. Evil must be opposed in all its forms; to abdicate the responsibility of fighting the battle against Cockatrice would be, for Chauntecleer, to give in to the enemy. He has *not* been given the strength to defeat Wyrm. He has *been* given the strength to defeat Cockatrice, just as the animals collectively have been given the strength (though at great sacrifice) to defeat the attack of the Basilisks.

So how is the battle fought? What strength were the animals given? Much could be said about this, but probably the simplest and most obvious approach is to consider the words of the Dun Cow spoken to Chauntecleer to prepare him for battle.

> Rue, she said, protection.
> Rooster's crow, confusion.
> One thing else to end the deed—
> A Dog with no illusion. (175)

We begin with *rue*. The first and more literal meaning of the word is clear; rue is a smelly plant, and as the animals discover, thanks to Lord Russell the fox, the smell of the rue plant wards off the Basilisks. It is, quite literally, protection. An animal smeared with the scent of rue is safe from the Basilisks. "Every warrior should also be smeared with the stuff," Chauntecleer orders. "Every warrior should stink of it" (181).

But the word *rue* also has a second meaning, and it is difficult to believe that this second, less obvious meaning is an accident. *Rue* also means regret and sorrow, which are closely related to, though not quite the same things as, confession and repentance. Certainly this meaning of *rue* is also a sort of protection to Chauntecleer when it comes time for battle against evil. For sorrow and repentance are antidotes to pride and complacency. Chauntecleer's own repentance is vital to the victory. In another way, so is his sorrow—especially his sorrow for the animals who suffer under his care. This sorrow is form of compassion, and a part of what it means to live out the community discussed earlier. Thus, Wangerin, in the warning message from the Dun Cow, is giving important information in the battle that all of us fight against evil. We don't cover ourselves with a smelly plant, but in a more metaphorical sense we cover our pride and sin with sorrow and repentence.

As for the "Rooster's crow," we have already discussed the importance and power of words and speech. This reaches its fullness in the battle when Chauntecleer "made a whip out of his crowing, and lashed the serpents with it. The serpents withered, shrank back. They rammed their heads against the ground as if they would crawl into it" (179). Without Chauntecleer's crowing, Wangerin suggests, the battle against the Basilisks would have been lost. But again, Wangerin is also calling his readers to their own battles against evil, and making it clear how important our own speech is in this battle. Certainly, Jesus, and later his disciples, drove out evil spirits with words, much as Chauntecleer drove out the Basilisks. Yet one need not drive out evil spirits to see the importance of words in the battle against evil. "If anyone is never at fault in what he says," James writes, "he is a perfect man, able to keep his whole body in check" (James 3:2). And later he adds, "The tongue is a small part of the body, but it makes great boasts. . . . With the tongue we praise our Lord and Father, and with it we curse men, who have been made in God's likeness" (James 3:5, 9). When Chauntecleer in his dream uses his speech to curse his animals, he is doing the work of Wyrm; he is working on the side of evil. Had he given in to his dreams, as Senex did, and begun to curse his animals when awake, Wyrm would have defeated him, just as he defeated Senex.

Both of these battles against evil are important. They become the means of the animals' victory over Cockatrice and the Basilisks. Ultimately, however, in *The Book of the Dun Cow*, the solution to evil—the means to its defeat—is altogether beyond anything Chauntecleer, or any of the animals of his domain, can do. Yet it is a means befitting the vast realm of Faërie. The solution is grace. Or, in the word of Tolkien, *eucatastrophe*. This eucatastrophe is at work through Mundo Cani, the "dog with no illusion." What does it mean that he has "no illusion"? The most obvious answer is that he has no illusion of greatness. He doesn't think more highly of himself than he ought. He has no pride. He does not grasp any rights, but rather does quite the opposite—he relinquishes everything he does have a right to. We see this especially when pouting turkey Ocellata pecks its way up the dog's back. "There was nothing left for the Dog to do but to pretend that he was not there. So he pretended with all of his might that he was not there" (*Cow*, 162). In this way, at least, Mundo Cani is imitating Christ, fitting the description given in

Philippians 2:7: he "made himself nothing, taking the very nature of a servant."

Mundo Cani is also a dog of gentle compassion, another characteristic associated with Christ. We see the gentleness in the way he carries the rescued mice in his mouth from the river all the way back to the coop (without sneezing). And then does the same for the (unappreciative) weasel during the battle. The tears he sheds are not tears of pain or discomfort; they are tears of compassion. "Blessed are those who mourn," Jesus said, "for they will be comforted" (Matt. 5:4). Certainly, this applies to the dog. In any case, Chauntecleer sees the dog's gentleness, and when The rooster's sons are killed and he must care for their bodies, he entrusts his beloved Pertelote to Mundo Cani.

Mundo Cani is also oft misunderstood, as was Christ. And, like Christ, he does not come as a political reader; there is no attempt to usurp Chauntecleer's place (though Chauntecleer fears this at one point.) Rather, he comes as a suffering servant, much like the Messiah (or Christ) described in Isaiah 42:2–3: "He will not shout or cry out, or raise his voice in the streets. A bruised reed he will not break, and a smoldering wick he will not snuff out." And even more like the description of the Messiah in Isaiah 53:3–5:

> He was despised and rejected by men,
> a man of sorrows, and familiar with suffering.
> Like one from whom men hide their faces
> he was despised, and we esteemed him not.
> Surely he took up our infirmities and carried our sorrows,
> yet we considered him stricken by God,
> smitten by him, and afflicted.
> But he was pierced for our transgressions,
> he was crushed for our iniquities;
> the punishment that brought us peace was upon him,
> and by his wounds we are healed.

For ultimately, of course, Mundo Cani gives his very life to defeat the serpent Wyrm and save his people. Continuing the description of Christ in Philippians: "He humbled himself and become obedient to death" (Phil. 2:8). Chauntecleer summarizes this all when he says to the dog, "You have become *salvation* for a flock of fools" (emphasis ours). And then, "You have a great heart, Soul of Mine; and I need you" (*Cow*, 165).

This is not the only resemblance of Mundo Cani to Christ. As Christ receives wounds to his head prior to his death, so also does the dog—three wounds: one to the nose from the battle with the Rat; wounds across his back from the turkeys pecking (wounds that may remind one of the stripes on Christ's back from the scourging); and the wounds in his mouth from carrying John Wesley Weasel. Then he gives himself in a self-sacrificial death, taking the burden of the coop upon himself. And though he is not shown to rise from the dead as does Christ, the book ends with a promise of resurrection. "He is alive," Pertelote tells Chauntecleer. "Only the bravest will see him again. Perhaps you will" (240).

It is important then to note that Mundo Cani is a dog who is not part of the coop, but comes from the outside.[4] Where he comes from, or why he comes, is never explained. Chauntecleer never asks. But by the end of the story, the reader understands that the dog is a gift of God, given in a way befitting every element of the tale. Given, that is, as a gift of grace. "There was never any question about who would make the sacrifice," Pertelote explains to a grieving Chauntecleer at the end. "Leader or not, it just wasn't your place to go. Cockatrice was yours; but Wyrm's eye was his. So it was from the beginning. So it had to be. . . . He accepted it as destiny" (238). The dog was sent by God for the purpose of dying, and he went willingly to his death. "He was making ready to die," the rooster finally confesses. "And I despised him" (239). Just as the Christ was despised and rejected even as he gave his life.

Which brings us to the other figure of grace, the Dun Cow herself. She is grace, comfort, and strength. God's grace. God's comfort. God's strength. She is answered prayer. She is God's representative. God's agent. God's messenger. She gives herself up as much as does the dog, though in a different way. And she also is despised by the rooster. Yet she always shows up exactly when she is needed. *"Modicae fidei—it is all for you,"* are her last words to the Rooster (237). Exactly when everything is lost without her. When the proud rooster is at the end of his rope, without

---

4. When we consider closely the dog's name, the connection to Christ becomes clearer. At first glance, *Mundo Cani* might look like it has something to do with the Latin words for "world" and "dog." *Cani* is in fact the dative singular of *canis,* dog. *Mundo,* however, has another meaning. It is the dative of the adjective *mundus,* which means "clean" or "pure." (Cf. the first line of Ps. 73 in the Vulgate, for instance: "Attamen bonus est Israhel deus, his qui *mundo* sunt corde.") *Mundus canis* would mean "the pure dog"; the use of the dative suggests that the dog is the means for something else: "by the pure dog." In Wangerin's story, the world is saved by the sacrifice of the dog with no illusion. Dog, of course, is God backward. This dog is, in many ways, like God. But it does not look like God. Surely God is glorious? This dog has no stately form that we should honor him, however. His godliness is seen in his actions, not in his appearance, defying our expectations.

any other hope, and finally is willing to acknowledge his weakness and need—that is when the Dun Cow makes her presence known. For unlike in Donaldson's *Thomas Covenant* books, where the hero Covenant must act on behalf of an impotent God and defeat the Enemy, in Wangerin's myth it is ultimately not the hero Chauntecleer who must defeat Wyrm. Chauntecleer has no hope of doing this. It is God who defeats Wyrm through his messengers the Dun Cow and Mundo Cani. This is the message of grace and hope—a story in which prayer really does matter because God is powerful and active in the world—and it is communicated profoundly in this work of myth, romance, and fairy.

10

Harry Potter

Saint or Serpent?

Shortly before Christmas 2001, around the same time that the first of Peter Jackson's long-anticipated film adaptations of *The Lord of the Rings* was being released, another fantasy film was hitting the theaters and receiving no small amount of attention. The film was the highly popular adaptation of J. K. Rowling's first *Harry Potter* book: *Harry Potter and the Sorcerer's Stone*. The fact that any work of fantasy could even temporarily vie for popularity with Tolkien's work is a remarkable feat.

As of February 2005, Rowling had published five (of a promised seven) books in the phenomenally successful Harry Potter series. Many of the official releases were marked by wildly enthusiastic midnight openings of bookstores—even in small towns!—with hordes of kids and adults lined up, many in costume, to buy the book the moment it became available. According to Reuters, in the United Kingdom alone the fourth volume sold close to 400,000 hardcover copies *on the first day*. Amazon.com presold another 400,000 copies. Total sales of all volumes are numbered in the tens of millions—likely to top 100 million total—and the books have been translated into thirty-one languages.[1] At the time of this writing, the sixth book in the series had been announced, and though the release date was still one month away, it was already being viewed with

---

1. Reuters, July 11, 2000, as recorded at http://www.cesnur.org/recens/potter_048.htm.

great anticipation, and is also likely to result in midnight store hours across the country. Three of the books in the series have already been made into films.

The question, of course, is what to make of these books. Some see them as no more than another harmless passing fad, albeit a wildly popular one. Some critics have disdained the books and Rowling's writing as being of poor quality, and as appealing to the lowest common denominator. Others have praised the writing style as elegant, or profound, or at the very least highly captivating. Many schoolteachers have heralded the books as godsends for society, if for no other reason than that their pupils have actually read the books enthusiastically—multiple times, in many cases—when previously the same students had been completely unwilling to open a book. These teachers reason that any book that makes reading preferable to video games and TV must be good.

For many Christians, however, the books are anathema. Their children are forbidden to read them, and are even pulled from public school classrooms if the books are chosen for read-aloud times. Why such an uproar and reaction? What evil do some people in circles of evangelical Christendom see in these books? The answer is simple: the books are full of magic and witches. The characters, good and bad alike, deal in witchcraft. They even ride around on broomsticks. According to the reasoning of some segments of Christendom, therefore, this makes the book an occult work.

Witches and Magic in Christian Literature

Coming, as it does, from so many different sources, this attack on J. K. Rowling's work is well worth considering. The first thing to consider—and the primary focus of this chapter—is whether there is a place for witches and magic in Christian literature, and if so what that place is. In this context, it is interesting to note that many of the same Christians who condemn Rowling's work on the grounds that its heroes are witches and wizards who routinely make use of magic and witchcraft also praise the writings of C. S. Lewis. Lewis is one of the most famous and celebrated Christian writers of the twentieth century, if not of all time. The seven books of his *Chronicles of Narnia* are fixtures on the bookshelves of Christians across the country and world. And yet Lewis's Narnia books have numerous witches and magicians of some sort or another, including the title characters of two of the books. The most obvious and famous such character is the White Witch of *The Lion, the Witch, and the Wardrobe.* She is joined by the magician of *The Magician's Nephew* and the Emerald Witch of *The Silver Chair.*

At this point, opponents of Rowling will point out that in Lewis's work, the aforementioned witches and magician are all clearly portrayed as being evil. The same comment could be made about the Bible itself, and the spirit medium of 1 Samuel 27, or the sorcerer of Acts 8, or the magician of Acts 13, or the magicians of Exodus 7, who match Moses's first miracle with a magic trick of their own. These characters appear in the story, but they are depicted as being opposed to God or to God's people. The problem with Rowling, these critics say, is that she portrays wizards and magical characters—most notably Dumbledore and the three young protagonists, Ron, Hermione, and Harry himself—as being *good.* They are the heroes of the story, not the villains, like the White Witch or Emerald Witch of Lewis's tales.

Ah, but Lewis has *good* magicians as well, appearing in several of his Narnia tales. One notable example is the character Coriakin, who rules the island of the Dufflepods in *The Voyage of the Dawn Treader.* Coriakin is portrayed as both good and wise. He is also explicitly titled the *Magician.* He walks around with a "curiously carved staff"—a common prop for a wizard—and has a book of spells called "*the* Book, the Magic Book," and later "the Magician's Book." As Lucy learns, the spells are quite real and powerful. Coriakin rules his land by "rough magic and in doing so is approved by Aslan himself (*Voyage*/x).

In the same book, there is also Old Man Ramandu and his daughter, who are akin to Coriakin and live in a land of considerable enchantment, which includes Aslan's Table on which meals are magically renewed each day. There are numerous other instances of good magic in the tales—and not only the magic of Aslan, which is called the Deeper Magic from Before the Dawn of Time. Lewis also makes use of many magical beasts and creatures, such as centaurs, naiads, dryads, and the Greek demigods Bacchus and Silenus, who in *Prince Caspian* magically provide a wonderful feast and tear down the bridge of the evil Narnians. Even Father Christmas, when he appears in *The Lion, the Witch, and the Wardobe,* appears as something of a good magician figure in contrast to the evil magic of the White Witch—a connection accentuated by the fact that both are driving around on sleighs. Just as the witch had earlier provided by magic the hot drink and Turkish Delight for Edmund, Father Christmas provides by magic a meal for the beavers and three children. His very appearance is something of a victory in the battle of his magic against that of the witch. Thus, very much as with Rowling's Harry Potter books, C. S. Lewis gives us a battle of good against ill with magic being used on both sides. A similar comment could be made about Lewis's adult fantasy novel, *That Hideous Strength,* in which one of the central aspects of the victory of the Good (Logres, the community of St. Anne's) over the Evil (N.I.C.E.), is the reappearance of the wizard Merlin, who uses his magical powers to bring about the destruction of the enemy.

It is worth noting that we can see in Coriakin something of the biblical figure of Elijah, or his successor, Elisha, both of whom wander the countryside as wizened old figures. One time when enemies come to capture Elijah, he calls down fire from heaven to consume them (2 Kings 1:7–12). Another time, when he wants to cross a river, he strikes it with his cloak, and the waters part (2 Kings 2:8). In the second of these instances, there is no mention of Elijah praying or asking God to perform the miracle. He acts as though the power were in himself. Elisha shows similar authority, striking the same river with a cloak to make the waters part for his crossing (2 Kings 2:14), and causing a lost axhead to float to the top of water (2 Kings 6:4–7). There is also a comparison between Ramandu and Elijah. As Elijah was fed in the wilderness by ravens (1 Kings 17:2–6), so too is Coriakin fed by a large white bird (*Voyage/*xiv*)*. And we haven't even mentioned the connections between many wizard figures and the powerful, staff-carrying figure of Moses.

Lewis is not the only author widely accepted in Christendom whose books make use of good magic. One cannot ignore the wizard Gandalf in Tolkien's works, or the powerful magic of those like Elrond and Galadriel, and even Aragorn. To that list we could add George MacDonald's fairy tales and fantasy novels, many of the novels of Charles Williams, Madeleine L'Engle's *Time* series, and many of the books of Stephen Lawhead, all of which are widely acknowledged as profoundly Christian works. Of course, this doesn't mean that the use of magic is good and acceptable in a Christian worldview. But it does mean that a reader who rejects Rowling's *Harry Potter* on the previously described grounds—that the books are full of wizards and witches performing magic, and that such use of magic is portrayed as good—must also reject on the same ground the works of MacDonald, Lewis, Tolkien, Williams, L'Engle, Lawhead, and many others.

We suggest that such an approach would be profoundly foolish and would cut one off from some of the greatest works of literature in Christendom. A far wiser approach is not to blindly judge a book by such superficial considerations, but to ask the deeper and more profound and important questions about the magic as it appears in these books. Two questions in particular must be addressed. The first is the more obvious. To what end is that power used—what is its final purpose? Is the power used to do good or to do evil? The second question may be more subtle, but is no less important. What is the source of magical power—where does it come from? What is its essential nature?

The Purpose of Magic

The use of what is often called "magic" is a standard feature of fantasy literature, both modern and ancient.[2] In the context of Faërie, enchantment is altogether appropriate. It has the ability to cast a very good spell, one that foreshadows the great God Spell itself. In the same essay in which he describes the Gospels as containing elements of fairy tale, Tolkien comments at one point that "Faërie itself may perhaps most nearly be translated by Magic" (*Essay*, 15). This acknowledgment has run through this book from beginning to end. This does not mean, however, that *all* use of magic is good and appropriate. Magical power may be (and often is) put to evil use. Speaking simultaneously both of the artistic skill of the writer and of the enchanting skill of the wizard, Tolkien writes in his essay "On Fairy-Stories":

> The mind that thought of *light, heavy, grey, yellow, still, swift*, also conceived of magic that would make heavy things light and able to fly, turn grey lead into yellow gold, and the still rock into swift water. If it could do the one, it could do the other; it inevitably did both. When we can take green from grass, blue from heaven, and red from blood, we have already an enchanter's power—upon one plane; and the desire to wield that power in the world external to our minds awakes. It does not follow that we shall use that power well upon any plane. We may put a deadly green upon a man's face and produce a horror; we may make the rare and

2. Part of the confusion over what to make of magic in fantasy literature comes from the fact that the English *magic* is used to translate two very different meanings or concepts that are captured by the Latin *magia* and *goeteia*. In the *Oxford English Dictionary*, the English "magic" has the narrow meaning of "witchcraft or magic performed by the invocation and employment of evil spirits." A broader meaning is simply magic performed by the incantation of spells. Tolkien, in a draft of a letter written in 1954, seems to use these two words in yet a different way, meaning by *goeteia* the types of magic producing deceits and illusions, and by *magia* the types of magic "producing real results" in the world (see *Letters*, 199–200). Though in this chapter we stick to the single word "magic" as it is most commonly used in English, we deal with all of these forms of magic, including both the narrow and broad meanings of *goeteia*: the invocation of evil spirits and the invocation of impersonal magic powers in nature.

terrible blue moon to shine; or we may cause woods to spring with silver leaves and rams to wear fleeces of gold, and put hot fire into the belly of the cold worm. (*Essay,* 24–25)

At the most general level, then, we must ask, to what end is magic being used? Is it being used for good or for evil? And at a deeper level, does the author even distinguish between good and evil? If so, what objective grounds are given for such distinction? The later questions are far more important than the *vehicle* that is used for doing the good or evil: whether it is magical power, or human strength, or intellectual ability, or technology. A work of literature that suggests that good and evil are merely human constructs—that they are subjective categories, or just not categories at all—is in dramatic opposition to fundamental truths of Christianity, and the Christian should be far more concerned for that than whether or not the work has wizards, witches, mage, and magicians. To that extent, rather than asking whether a fantasy novel includes magic as a means to an end, we should ask to what end the magic is used, and then ask what defines the end toward which any abilities should be used.

This question is related to motive, but is distinct. Magic in fantasy literature has been used to produce art, to aid creativity, to enchant and delight, to heal the sick, and even to enhance and uphold physical structures like castles and walls and entire kingdoms. It has also been used to deceive and manipulate, to enslave, to wound, and to kill. It has been used in battle both to defend and to destroy. Some uses of magic, such as the making of beauty or the healing of the sick, seem altogether good. Some uses, such as building or upholding a kingdom or castle or the enchantments in a forest, or increasing one's might in battle, might be put to good use or to evil use. Some ends, like deceiving or enslaving, the Christian might understand as being forms or uses of magic having no good value and being altogether evil. Writing a personal letter in 1954 describing his own use of magic in *The Lord of the Rings,* Tolkien comments that there are two types of magic, and that "neither is, in this tale, good or bad (per se), but only by motive or purpose or use. Both sides use both, but with different motives" (*Letters,* 199–200). As hinted above, we will later argue that there is, in fact, at least one type of magic that may have no good use. Nonetheless, Tolkien's point is timely and important. The first thing to consider is the motive.

So varied are the ends to which magic can be put that Galadriel, one of the wisest beings in Tolkien's Middle-earth, and also one of the most powerful in a certain type of magic, questions whether the same word, *magic,* should even be used for different uses of power. When offering Sam the opportunity to peer into her magic mirror, she says to him:

> For this is what your folk would call magic, I believe; though I do not understand clearly what they mean; and they seem also to use the same word of the deceits of the Enemy. But this, if you will, is the magic of Galadriel. Did you not say that you wished to see Elf-magic? (II/vii)

Lewis must have had the same distinction in mind when Aslan says of the White Witch in *The Magician's Nephew* that she "has fled far away into the North of the world; she will live on there, growing stronger in dark Magic" (*Nephew*/xiv). In referring to the Witch's magic as "dark," such a statement surely implies that there are other kinds of magic that are not dark. There are both dark, or evil, magic and light, or good, magic. In a famous personal letter written in 1951 to Milton Waldman, Tolkien also described a difference between Elven magic and the magic of Sauron.

> The chief power (of all the rings alike) was the prevention or slowing of decay (i.e. "change" viewed as a regrettable thing), the preservation of what is desired or loved, or its semblance—this is more or less an Elvish motive. But also they enhanced the natural powers of a possessor—thus approaching "magic," a motive easily corruptible into evil, a lust for domination. (*Letters,* 152)

Again, there is a distinction between two types of magic, and here the distinction is based on motive. One possible motive is preservation. The other is domination. These different motives may result in very different types of magic.

Putting all of this together, we might see magic in Faërie—or in a work of fantasy—as symbolic of something in our real world. Some types of magic become, as suggested, symbolic of art itself. Isn't art an enchantment and a spell? *Most* forms of magic, however, more closely resemble what in our world is probably best summarized as technology, and to a lesser degree science and engineering. Most people have no idea how a refrigerator or a car or a television works. You put a can of soda into an electric fridge on a hot day, and take it out a few hours later to find it chilled. To the engineer, it works by well-known laws of physics. To the layperson who understands nothing of thermodynamics, it functions as magic. The same can be said for the automobile, and even more for many medical treatments. In his letters, Tolkien on more than one occasion associates magic with machinery. In the letter just quoted, Tolkien also remarks, "But at Eregion great work began—and the Elves came their nearest to falling to 'magic' and machinery." Later in the letter, he associates the power of the One Ring with both "mechanism" and "lies"—an association of magic as an allegory of machinery and also as a tool for deceit. But the clearest indication of what magic may be used to represent is suggested earlier in the letter. Writing about the main ideas of his book, he comments, "Anyway all this stuff is mainly concerned with Fall, Mortality, and the Machine." He then goes on to associate machinery with magic, saying that the "Machine (or Magic)" is a vehicle for the "desire for Power, for making the will more quickly effective." In other words, some types of magic function as a symbol of machinery, or technology. "The Machine is our more obvious modern form though more closely related to Magic than is usually recognized" (145–46).

Is technology fundamentally evil? Some would say so, but the harshest critics of magic in literature are usually not the ones to say this. Our houses are kept warm by many wonders of modern technology. Both authors of this book might be dead today were it not for the discovery of antibiotics and the developments of modern surgical techniques. Can technology be put to evil uses? Of course. Modern technology has made it much easier to kill larger numbers of people from greater distances. Ultimately, magic, like technology, can be a vehicle for power. Power to what end? To heal? To preserve? Or, perhaps, to enslave and dominate other wills. Through the symbolism of magic, a modern fantastist may explore the morality of modern technology, and more effectively imaginatively motivate her or his readers to make more moral use of their powers than is possible through cold rational discourse. Thus the presence in a fairy tale of one who performs magic—whether we call that person a wizard or witch, mage or magician—and the acknowledgment that such magic may be good, should not for the Christian suggest that the story is evil any more than the presence of any object of modern technology implies that the story is evil.

The Source of Magic

The second question is a little more subtle, but may be of equal or greater significance in assessing a work. What is the source of magical power for the witch, wizard, magician, mage, or sorcerer? There are several possibilities. It may be that the "magical" power is ultimately derived from an internal source, and is inherent in the individual. Or it may be that the power comes from some external source; it is conjured up, through a use of spells and magic invocations. That external source may be something inanimate, like nature, or something personal like a genie or powerful spirit. It may be something called into service of the magician.[3]

The first view toward magical power sees it as inherent in the magician or wizard himself or herself. This understanding of magic was explored earlier in the book, in the chapter on Ursula Le Guin. Tolkien's wizard Gandalf and Le Guin's mage Ged both are full of native power. They learn certain spells and words of power, but these act more to release their own powers than to conjure up some external force. This is what Gandalf is speaking of when he says to Frodo, "There are many powers in the world, for *good* or for *evil*" (II/i). Aragorn also has some native power, demonstrated when he claims and masters the Palantír of Orthanc. On several occasions in *The Lord of the Rings,* Aragorn is also called upon to heal somebody. Early in the tale he succors Frodo long enough so that Elrond can take care of him. Later he brings healing to Éowyn, Faramir, Merry, and later still to Sam and Frodo. In each case, Aragorn seems to draw upon some internal strength. This is most evident in the healings of Faramir and Éowyn. "Here I must put forth all such power and skill as is given to me," Aragorn says as he enters the house. And when he tends to Faramir, we read, "Now Aragorn knelt beside Faramir, and held a hand upon his brow. And those that watched felt that some great struggle was going on. For Aragorn's face grew grey with weariness; and ever and anon he called the name of Faramir." When he comes to Éowyn, he calls her by name and kisses her on the brow. "Then, whether Aragorn had indeed some forgotten power of Westernesse, or whether it was but his words of the Lady Éowyn," she is restored to health (V/viii). One of the ways that Aragorn is recognized as king is through his power to heal. *The hands of the king are the hands of a healer,* is an old proverb in Gondor, repeated by the old wife Ioreth, and soon heard around Minas Tirith.

Indeed, we see this view of power from the very start of Tolkien's *Legendarium,* when on the first page of *The Silmarillion* we read:

3. Readers may consider yet another possibility: that the power is not something called upon to serve the "magician," but rather something or someone that the magician is in service to. In which case the magician isn't wielding the magic as a tool, but offering himself as a vehicle. This, however, is not magic; it is best called a "prayer," and the result (if the prayer is answered affirmatively and the gift of power is granted) is probably best called, simply, a "miracle."

> Then Ilúvatar said to them: "Of the theme that I have declared to you, I
> will now that ye make in harmony together a Great Music. And since I
> have kindled you with the Flame Imperishable, ye shall show forth your
> powers in adorning this theme, each with his own thoughts and devices,
> if he will." (*Silm*, 3)

Ilúvatar, the Creator in Tolkien's Middle-earth mythology, has endowed
his creative beings, the angelic Ainur, with various powers, and they are
invited to use those powers to serve their Creator. Father Christmas's
power in *The Lion, the Witch, and the Wardrobe* seems to be of this sort.
He doesn't have to conjure any spells to provide the magical meal for the
beavers and three children.

Having addressed this earlier, we needn't explore this concept of magical power much further. There is, however, one aspect worth thought. As
the wizard figure was earlier compared with the biblical figures of Elijah,
Elisha, and Moses, this type of power can also be seen as a close analogy
to the Christian notion of the gifts of the spirit (see, for example, 1 Cor.
12–14). These spiritual gifts are not natural or fleshly; they are not merely
talents that are developed through practice. Rather, they are spiritual and
supernatural. The gift of healing especially, and the gifts of prophecy and
tongues, would also be very much at home in a fantasy novel. Could it
be that magic in a fantasy novel—at least the type of magic that functions as an internal power—often functions as a symbol of spiritual gifts?
The spiritual gifts can be used well. They can also be misused and put
to selfish or prideful purposes, as when the person speaks in tongues to
gain attention, or uses the gift of preaching to bolster pride, or exercises
any spiritual gift without love (see 1 Cor. 13:1–2).

Regardless of the explicit religious views of the author, it seems not
only possible but likely that the ancient longing for and knowledge of
an internal magical power is a reflection of some spiritual truth in the
universe, or of a cultural memory of figures like Elijah. In any case, the
use of this sort of power is, for the mage or wizard, simply a being of
what they were intended to be. It is, to that extent, a joyous manifestation
of their nature. It is a true reflection of the being of the one using the
power, and a magic the Christian need not react against.

Of course, not all magic in fantasy novels functions as internal power.
Some portrayals of magic place its source in something external: something called upon or used by the magician. This type of magic leans more
toward the popular ideas of witches brewing potions and speaking complex spells. This is not to say that even this type of magic is of necessity

evil. Here again, we must further divide the magic into two possibilities. Does the external power being drawn upon have as its source something inanimate: a part of the nature or the natural world, a belief in the magical properties of the earth, which will be released when potions are brewed according to various laws? Or is it something personal and supernatural? There are numerous examples in fantasy literature representing the first of these two cases: magicians drawing upon the magical power of nature. Such power may be used to enchant or harm somebody. It may also be used to heal. In *The Lion, the Witch, and the Wardrobe,* Father Christmas gives to Lucy a vial of magical ointment that will heal any wound. This potion is used again in *Prince Caspian* and *The Voyage of the Dawn Treader.* In *The Magician's Nephew,* there is an apple tree whose fruit—the "apple of youth, the apple of life"—has the magical power to heal. It has such power that the Witch truthfully tells the hero, Digory, that "one bite of the apple would heal" his deeply sick Mother (*Nephew*/xiii). When Digory's mother does eat it, the doctor comments, "This is the most extraordinary case I have known in my whole medical career. It is—it is like a miracle" (*Nephew*/xv).

When Aragorn heals Éowyn and Faramir, he uses his native power as mentioned earlier, but he also uses the healing powers of nature. As we read, it is not only his power he must call upon, but his *skill* as well. Part of his skill is his knowledge of the magical healing powers of various herbs. In the aforementioned healings, he makes use of the athelas plant, *kingsfoil* in the common tongue. Aragorn understands that it has healing power to drive away the black breath. He uses his own power to draw forth the healing virtues of the plant, but it is equally true that he draws on the healing powers of the plant itself.

Although one could certainly make evil use of the power of nature, Tolkien would argue that there is nothing *inherently* evil in magic such as this (any more than there is evil in extracting salicylic acid from willow bark to cure headaches). As we discussed earlier in the book, one of the three essential faces of Faërie is the Magical Face toward Nature. When the magician calls upon some power of nature, it only serves to build upon the perception of nature as magical. When rightly viewed, such a face toward nature only serves to bring to light how beautiful and wonderful and mysterious creation is. And so this type of magic, also, should pose no threat to a Christian reader.

It is the third type of magic—the third concept of magic, or source for magical power—that is most troublesome in a work of Faërie. It is when the witch or wizard draws his or her power from some external

personal supernatural or invisible source that the magic bears closest
resemblance to occult practices in our own world. This is the witch who
calls upon evil spirits to do her bidding, or the man who has the bottle
by which he controls the genie. If one believes in such invisible personal
powers—demons, or ghosts, or genies—then one may be tempted to
perform rites and ceremonies to call such powers to aid. Often, there is
a belief that such invisible powers are *bound* by laws *requiring* them to
give aid if a certain spell is said in a certain way, or a certain invocation
is spoken. When Aladdin possesses the bottle or lamp, the genie *must*
obey him.

There are two problems with this type of occult magic. The first is
that it functions by slavery and domination. The creatures being called
by the magician have no choice; they must obey. It has been argued that
the essential magical power of the One Ring in *The Lord of the Rings* is
the power to enforce one's will upon others.[4] The possessor of the Ring
has the right to rule the demonic Ringwraiths. This is powerful magic.
It is also magic that Tolkien argues has no good or proper use. "The
supremely bad motive," he writes, "is (for this tale, since it is specially
about it) domination of other 'free' wills" (*Letters*, 200). It is no accident
that Tolkien makes this comment in a context of a discussion of magic.
It is also no accident that the magic that has domination as a *purpose*
also works through the *means* of domination; the source of that type of
magic is the domination of powerful beings and the forcing of them
to the will of the magician. Not even the wisest and best powers of
Middle-earth—not Gandalf, not Elrond, not Galadriel—can use this
particular type of magic power to a good end. The Christian does well,
then, to be wary of any portrayal of this type of magical power as good
or acceptable. This doesn't mean that such magic should not be portrayed
in a work of fantasy, but only that *if* it is portrayed, then it ought to be
portrayed for what it is: evil. In this way, the tale of Aladdin might be
seen as a much more destructive story, in that Aladdin is portrayed as a
hero because he accomplishes his goals by magic through the enslaving
of a powerful genie.

A second problem with this type of magic is that the magician is
often deceived. When a man works a spell or uses a magic charm and
calls upon a demon to do his bidding, is the demon really obeying the
magician's will, or does the magician become a slave of the demon? The
Christian has good cause to believe the second possibility is far more

4. See Dickerson, 96–101.

likely. This also makes occult magic very dangerous, and it suggests that any representation of it ought to portray it for the evil it is.

Uses of Magic in *Harry Potter*

So far we have actually said nothing about J. K. Rowling's use of magic in the Harry Potter stories. This is because we wanted to establish the principles first, and to establish them with reference to examples that are older and less embroiled in debate. If we can see clearly enough that the questions we have posed above are the right questions to ask, then perhaps we can approach *Harry Potter* objectively and make a fair assessment. How is magic portrayed in Rowling's work? What is its source? What is its purpose? Does she really portray *occult* magic as good?

Our first observation is that the most important types of power used by good characters of the tale—those on the side of Dumbledore—are internal powers, inherent in the wizards and witches who wield the power. This is clearest in the case of the protagonist Harry Potter, and in the stories' greatest hero, the wizard Dumbledore. In the very first book, *Harry Potter and the Sorcerer's Stone,*[5] before Harry has learned a thing about magic or wizardry—before he has even heard of Hogwarts, much less been there—we begin to see his inherent power in the incident with the boa constrictor at the zoo. First, Harry begins speaking with the snake. Then, when Dudley punches Harry in the ribs to get a closer look, Harry's power gets the better of him, and—without knowing how he does it, or even that he has done it—he makes the glass disappear, releasing the snake. That Harry is responsible can be seen both from the fact that the snake hisses "Thanksss, amigo" to him and that Aunt Petunia punishes him with "his longest-ever punishment" (*Stone,* 27–31). There are other similar incidents as well, which Harry remembers in his conversation with Hagrid: mysteriously escaping the pursuit of Dudley's gang, making his hair grow back overnight after a "ridiculous haircut," and the boa constrictor episode. Even the very way Hagrid asks the question indicates that the power is in the wizard himself, more than in any spells. "Not a wizard, eh?" Hagrid asks. "Never made things happen when you was scared or angry?" (58). Harry can make things happen

---

5. Originally titled *Harry Potter and the Philosopher's Stone,* but retitled in the United States, perhaps because the publishers presumed U.S. readers were too ill informed to know what the famed philosopher's stone was.

without knowledge of spells because he is a wizard, and being a wizard means one has some sort of internal power.

What we see of Harry's possession of some inherent or internal power is true of all wizards, from the most bumbling like Neville—who at the age of eight shows his magic powers for the first time by saving himself from falling out the window by bouncing "all the way down the garden and into the road" (125)—to the most powerful like Voldemort and Dumbledore. A central theme in the book is the difference between wizards (those with power) and muggles (those without power): the native possession (or lack thereof) of power is what separates them. Even if muggles went to the wizards' school at Hogwarts and learned all the spells, it would avail them nothing. And even among wizards, there are varying degrees of power. Some spells require more power than others. "*Avada Kedavra*'s a curse that needs a powerful bit of magic behind it," Professor Moody tells his class at one point in book 4, *Harry Potter and the Goblet of Fire*. "You could get all your wands out now and point them at me and say the words, and I doubt I'd get so much as a nosebleed" (*Goblet*, 217). It is not only his wisdom, but his great internal power that makes Dumbledore the greatest wizard of his day. Dumbledore often performs magical feats without any noticeable use of spells, sometimes with nothing more than "a little flick" of his wand (*Stone*, 127).

There are not many glimpses of the extent of his power early in the series, but they grow as the series progresses. Finally, in *The Goblet of Fire*, when Dumbledore rescues Harry from the imposter Mad-Eye Moody, Harry and the reader see some of the capacity of this wizard.

> At that moment, Harry fully understood for the first time why people said Dumbledore was the only wizard Voldemort had ever feared. The look upon Dumbledore's face as he stared down at the unconscious form of Mad-Eye Moody was more terrible than Harry could ever have imagined. . . . There was cold fury in every line of the ancient face; a sense of power radiated from Dumbledore as though he were giving off burning heat. (*Goblet*, 679)

One can see a close comparison with the power Gandalf exhibits when he faces Saruman at Isengard after the battle of Helm's Deep, shattering Saruman's staff with a single sentence. It is a duel of internal power, and this time Gandalf, who has passed through death, is greater. Headmaster Dumbledore's great internal power is most clearly seen in these confrontations with other wizards. Later in this book, he squares off against Cornelius Fudge, the minister of magic, in the hospital wing where Harry is recovering. He takes a step toward Fudge, "and once again, he [seems] to radiate that indefinable sense of power that Harry had felt after Dumbledore had Stunned young Crouch [the imposter Mad-Eye Moody]." And Fudge, though certainly powerful himself as evidenced by his position, takes a step back (705–6).

In book 5, *Harry Potter and the Order of the Phoenix*, Dumbledore finally comes face to face with the Death Eaters and with their master, Voldemort. Though the Death Eaters have been shown to be very powerful in their battle with Sirius, Lupin, Moody, Tonks, and Kingsley—the good wizards from the Order of the Phoenix—their confrontation with Dumbledore makes it very clear where the greatest internal power is.

> Dumbledore was already at the foot of the steps when the Death Eaters nearest realized he was there. There were yells; one of the Death Eaters ran for it, scrabbling like a monkey up the stone steps opposite. Dumbledore's spell pulled him back as easily and effortlessly as though he had hooked him with an invisible line. (*Order*, 805)

This is not to say that all exhibitions of magical power in the Harry Potter books are of this sort. It is not surprising, given that the series is about wizards, that we see examples of all of the types of magic discussed at the start of this chapter. For example, there is no shortage of magical potions that are brewed to accomplish some task. There are: the Draught of Living Death (*Stone*, 138); the potion to cure boils, botched by Neville in Snape's class (138–39) and various other healing potions used by Madame Pomfrey in the hospital wing at Hogwarts; and Polyjuice Potion, to change temporarily into somebody else's shape, used by Harry, Hermione, and Ron (*Chamber*, 164ff), and the list goes on—numerous other potions are used through all of the books. It is a horrible potion that Wormtail uses to bring Voldemort back to full life (*Goblet*, 641–43). Many of these potions are based on the magical properties of nature. Which is to say, it is not only the power of the wizard that makes the potion, but the ingredients themselves, whether common things from our world, like porcupine quills, or stones taken from the stomachs of goats, or real plants like the poisonous asphodel, wormwood, monkshood, wolfsbane, and aconite (*Stone*, 138–39), or fictitious plants found only in Fairy. As discussed earlier in the chapter, the use of potions made from the magical properties of nature is one example that fits the category of Tolkien's Magical face toward Nature. This does not mean that all such uses are good. Rowling makes it clear within the stories that this magic—which can best be compared with modern pharmaceutics—can be used for either good (as is the case with Madam Pomfrey's healing) or evil, as when Wormtail cuts off his own hand and spills Harry's blood to make the potion that restores Voldemort to life.

To repeat our point in the context of Harry Potter, the presence of this type of magic in a tale should not be cause for alarm to the Christian, any more than the presence of chemistry or pharmaceutics or just plain herb lore in any other type of novel should be cause for alarm. The question is what the author does with it. If heroes are portrayed as virtuous for using plant lore to make hallucinogenic drugs to distribute to teenagers, or for creating a poison to kill innocent victims or a drug to enslave other people, then the Christian should be concerned—not that such "magic" is used, but that the evil use of it is portrayed as good. If the same things happen, but are shown to be evil, or if heroes use their knowledge of potions to heal, then the underlying moral message of the tale is completely consistent with Christian teaching.

Yet another type of magic is the magic of words. Spells work because words have power. We see this throughout Rowling's books. And it is a teaching not only consistent with, but *fundamental to* Christian scripture. God created the world, we are told in Genesis 1, through language. He spoke and it happened. He is a God of language, and for him language is power. If humans are created in God's image, as the author of Genesis so clearly states, then we must assume that humans also are endowed with the power of words. The Bible speaks so strongly against cursing, and so favorably toward blessing, and in general about the importance of speech, precisely because words and language are potent. (See, for example, Lev. 20:9, Luke 6:28, Rom. 12:14, Col. 4:6, and James 3:9–10, as well as chapter 3 of the present work for our discussion of words in the book of Job.) To use the symbolism of Faërie, blessings and curses are a sort of magic—a power that the Creator endowed the created beings with. Rowling illustrates this clearly through the power of spells. We must be careful what we say—and indeed, since even the thoughts of a wizard are powerful, what we think.

To this end, it is somewhat disturbing that students of Hogwarts are taught certain curses. Though God at times curses nations, people, or things (e.g., Gen. 3:14, 12:3), the Bible tells us not to curse. The few biblical instances where humans are right to curse involve prophets who are not so much casting their own curses as they are passing on the curses that God has pronounced, or at least warning that they will come (e.g., Jer. 42:18; Mal. 4:6). Thus, the critique of Rowling is not that she takes the power (or magic) of words (spells and curses) too seriously, but that she might not take the magic seriously enough. To answer this charge, we make just a few observations. The first is that although the Hogwarts teachers do teach some spells that are curses, they do this rarely and with many warnings, and they refrain from teaching the worst curses. The one curse intended to kill is called, simply, an Unforgivable Curse. That Rowling would label it thus is an important moral pronouncement on curses, or at least on curses meant to do permanent harm.

Second, the curses that are taught are generally taught only as a means of self-defense. And here we might note that even the word *curse* is used in a somewhat different way. Though the worst curses in Rowling's books are akin to the biblical notions of curses—words intended to bring great evil upon somebody—the common "curses" taught to Hogwarts students have the purpose not of doing evil to another, but simply of binding the power of an enemy to prevent him or her from doing evil. For example, one of the first spells taught Hogwarts students is the spell to disarm an enemy. Though this might be *used* for evil, it is certainly not a curse, in that it is not its inherent purpose to do evil; it *may* be used for good. We might again see a biblical parallel with the power given to apostles to cast out or bind evil spirits, through the use of words, so that the spirits cannot do further harm.

Our third observation is that the wisest and greatest hero, Dumbledore, is never seen to be cursing anybody. Even when he comes face to face with Voldemort at the end of *Order of the Phoenix,* and something of his full might is displayed (not only against Voldemort, but moments later in yet another confrontation with Fudge), we learn from none other than Voldemort himself that Dumbledore is not trying to kill his enemy.

> Dumbledore flicked his own wand. The force of the spell that emanated from it was such that Harry, though shielded by his stone guard, felt his hair stand on end as it passed, and this time Voldemort was forced to conjure a shining silver shield out of thin air to deflect it. [. . .]
>
> "You do not seek to kill me, Dumbledore?" called Voldemort, his scarlet eyes narrowed over the top of the shield. "Above such brutality, are you?" (*Order,* 813–14)

Whatever spell Dumbledore was trying, it was not a curse intended to slay his enemy. This comes as a shock to Voldemort, for though he recognizes the Unforgivable Curse as an act of brutality, he is completely willing to be brutal. The difference between them makes clearer Rowling's views on cursing.

We might summarize what we have seen of magic so far as follows. Spells are used, of course. Potions are brewed. One of the main purposes of the school of Hogwarts is to teach the knowledge necessary to use these spells. Another, at least from Dumbledore's viewpoint, is to train the pupils in the wisdom necessary to use them well—which, among other things, means never performing curses that will cause death, damnation, or real injury to another. Nonetheless, the essential power resides in the wizard. Without the wizard's inborn power, the spells mean nothing. This point is probably made most clearly by the simple fact that not everybody is a wizard. Some have power. Some do not. Hence the considerable distinction between wizards and muggles.

So what of the other type of magic: the magic that comes from conjuring other powers and coercing them to one's will, the type of magic we associated with the occult and suggested is altogether evil? The answer is simple. Such magic is used in the Harry Potter books, but it is used only by the enemy: by Voldemort and his Death Eaters, or by the more villainous Hogwarts students (namely, Draco Malfoy, whose father, Lucius, is a Death Eater) and occasionally by misguided officials in the Ministry of Magic. In *The Chamber of Secrets,* for example, young Draco uses a Serpensortia spell and conjures a snake to attack Harry (*Chamber,* 194). While this example may seem trivial and merely misguided, rather than purely malicious, other instances get closer to occult magic as described earlier, and to what makes it so evil. One of the issues that runs continuously from book 2 onward is the enslavement of house elves. House elves are, as we learn, very powerful, and one who controls a house elf has access to its power. Death Eater Lucius Malfoy thinks nothing of this sort of enslavement. To him, it is just another means to power. He rules over the house elf Dobby just as one who owns a genie's lamp rules over the genie and has access to its power. One of the victories that Harry wins in *Chambers of Secrets* is the freedom of Dobby from his enslavement to Lucius. And just how powerful the house elves are is revealed an instant later when Lucius tries to take revenge on Harry.

> Lucius Malfoy stood frozen, staring at the elf. Then he lunged at Harry.
> "You've lost me my servant, boy!"
> But Dobby shouted, "You shall not harm Harry Potter!"

There was a loud bang, and Mr. Malfoy was thrown backward. He crashed down the stairs, three at a time, landing in a crumpled heap on the landing below. He got up, his face livid, and pulled out his wand, but Dobby raised a long, threatening finger.

"You shall go now," he said fiercely, pointing down at Mr. Malfoy. "You shall not touch Harry Potter. You shall go now."

Lucius Malfoy had no choice. (*Chamber*, 338)

Until that moment, Dobby had been a mistreated slave at the command of Lucius. Now he is free. "Harry Potter freed Dobby!" he shouts. From that point on, Hermione sets out to free all the house elves. And Dumbledore, we are led to believe, is in full support of her plan. Hogwarts becomes a refuge for freed house elves. Because the power to enslave—or, more specifically, the occult power that comes through enslavement of a powerful being—is an evil in Rowling's world.

Even when one tries to use this sort of power for good, Dumbledore believes, it turns out to be evil. Such is the case with the extremely powerful *dementors*, which Fudge tries to use for the supposedly good purposes of the Ministry of Magic. First, he limits their use to being guardians of the prison at Azkaban. But later (in *The Prisoner of Azkaban* and *The Goblet of Fire*), he uses them to track down fugitives and to guard Hogwarts against escapee Sirius Black. Dumbledore is against all such use. He tells Fudge in clear terms that "the first and most essential step is to remove Azkaban from the control of the dementors." Part of Dumbledore's reasoning is given; he says that the dementors are loyal to Voldemort and will "join him the instant he asks them," because Voldemort can offer them "more scope for their powers and their pleasures" (*Goblet*, 707). In other words, the demonic forces that Fudge thinks he is ruling will soon be ruling him. But Dumbledore seems to have other reasons as well. One is that he is opposed to the cruel Azkaban prison altogether, because it dehumanizes the prisoners. Yet another probably relates to his opposition to any magic that works by enslavement or manipulation of other powers—powers beyond the internal power of the wizard—to do one's bidding. Thus, J. K. Rowling shows this occult magic to be evil, or at least to be associated with evil. She suggests no good use of it. It is with considerable significance that we note this: while both sides use the other forms of magic, only the side of Voldemort and the Death Eaters use the type of magical power that comes by dominating or manipulating another's will.

J. K. Rowling and Objective Morality

This brings us to a final issue with regard to the Harry Potter books. Where do they stand with respect to objective morality? Do they give a transcendent or objective basis for judging good and evil? Here again, Rowling's works stand consistent with Christianity. Rowling makes it clear that there is a cosmic battle going on. By book 5, we can name both sides: the Order of the Phoenix, and the Death Eaters; those who stand with Dumbledore, and those who stand in service of Voldemort. There is no question in the books that this is a battle between good and evil. This issue is treated more lightly in book 1, where Voldemort is portrayed as not very nice because he killed the hero's parents, and Dumbledore's goodness is seen more as gentleness and kindness. Yet even in the first book, the groundwork is laid. It is Quirrell, the servant of the enemy, who denies the existence of good and evil. "A foolish young man I was then, full of ridiculous ideas about good and evil," he tells the hero, Harry, when he has captured him toward the end of the book. "Lord Voldemort showed me how wrong I was. There is no good and evil, there is only power, and those too weak to seek it" (*Stone*, 291). That such thinking is associated with Quirrell and Voldemort immediately discredits it for the reader and serves to suggest the very opposite: good and evil are real categories, and those who refrain from using power may be acting in goodness rather than weakness.

Later on, when Harry talks with Dumbledore at the end of the book, he sees that there really are objective values. Though Dumbledore does not use the words *good* or *evil* in the conversation, he communicates much about them by the example of his friend Nicolas, who willingly destroys the Stone because it is the right thing to do, and not because it is convenient or will gain him power. Doing the right thing will cost him his life, but he does it anyway. In the context of this discussion, Dumbledore also points out that "the Stone is not such a wonderful thing." It can provide money and life, "the two things most human beings would choose above all—the trouble is, humans do have a knack of choosing precisely those things that are worst for them" (*Stone*, 297). Here Dumbledore is echoing a maxim of biblical morality that can be found many places, not the least of which is Jesus's Sermon on the Mount, in Matthew 6:19–24.

As we move through the series, the presentation of good and evil becomes more profound. By book 4 the definitions are getting clear. It is at the end of *The Goblet of Fire* that Rowling begins to paint the picture most clearly. All of chapter 36 ("The Parting of the Ways"), where we read the debate between Dumbledore and the powerful political leader Cornelius Fudge, is critical in clarifying the issues—critical in a way reminiscent of similar debates in *The Lord of the Rings* between the wizard Gandalf and the political rulers of his time, Théoden and Denethor. Neither Théoden nor Denethor are servants of Sauron, and yet both require convincing by Gandalf to do what they can to fight the enemy. In Théoden's case, Gandalf succeeds. Denethor, however, falls into despair. What about Dumbledore and Fudge? Throughout their conversation, Dumbledore continues to return to one fundamental issue: the enemy Voldemort has returned, and he must be fought. If Fudge takes the steps necessary to fight him, he "will be remembered . . . as one of the bravest and greatest Ministers of Magic we have ever known." But if he fails to act, history will remember him "as the man who stepped aside and allowed Voldemort a second chance to destroy the world" (*Goblet*, 708). Unfortunately, some of the steps Dumbledore calls him to take are unpopular, such as removing the dementors from the prison and making peace overtures to the giants. But popularity isn't the issue with Dumbledore. For that matter, neither is Cornelius Fudge's legacy, though Dumbledore appeals to it. Dumbledore calls people to do what is right for no other reason than that it is the right thing to do. Rowling's Dumbledore is in the same company as the heroes of Lewis and Tolkien when he says that there is a battle and that everybody is on one side or the other. "'The only one against whom I intend to work,' said Dumbledore, 'is Lord Voldemort. If you are against him, then we remain, Cornelius, on the same side'" (709). Rowling's point couldn't be made any clearer. There are sides, and they are not arbitrary. "Remember," Dumbledore tells his students after the death of Cedric, "if the time should come when you have to make a choice between what is right and what is easy . . . remember Cedric Diggory" (724). Moral right is not defined by personal convenience. It is a choice that must be made.

We see, then, a wonderful illustration of a point made by T. S. Eliot in his introduction to Charles Williams's *All Hallows Eve*. Eliot sees Williams as in accord with St. Augustine, who held that our freedom consists only in choosing with whom our hearts will be aligned.

[Williams] sees the struggle between Good and Evil as carried on, more or less blindly, by men and women who are often only the instruments of higher or lower powers, but who always have the freedom to choose to which powers they will submit themselves. (Eliot, xvi)

Dumbledore is also clear that those who are fighting against evil must work together. "You are on the same side now," he says to Snape and Black, who have a long history of dislike for each other (*Goblet,* 712). And later he says something similar to the gathering back at Hogwarts:

> I say to you all, once again—in the light of Lord Voldemort's return, we are only as strong as we are united, as weak as we are divided. Lord Voldemort's gift for spreading discord and enmity is very great. We can fight it only by showing an equally strong bond of friendship and trust. Differences of habit and language are nothing at all if our aims are identical. (*Goblet,* 723)

At this point, Dumbledore might well be speaking to the Christian church, and his message is one the church would do well to hear. The church may have a different external culture from the world, with different habits and language, but it means nothing if at the roots the church is full of the same internal discord and distrust.

And here Rowling seems to be making an even more profound point. Why does Fudge refuse to acknowledge Voldemort's return? Because to accept the truth, "to believe that Voldemort could have risen," would cause a "disruption in his comfortable and ordered world" (707). In other words, some wish to ignore the battle—to ignore the reality of evil—because it is inconvenient and will interfere with their comfortable lives. Only a few are willing to engage in the struggle against evil. This is teaching that could have come directly from Jesus. Add this observation to the numerous similarities between aspects of books 4 and 5 and the apocalyptic vision of John recorded in the book of Revelation, including that the Death Eaters all have marks indicating that they are servants of Voldemort (see Rev. 14 and 19), and that Voldemort, like the Antichrist, has recovered from a fatal wound (see Rev. 13), and it becomes difficult to believe that the Harry Potter books could have been written by anybody who was not a Christian, or at least deeply steeped in and sympathetic to Christianity and its literature! (The Cauldron contains many Christian bits and bones, and Rowling ladled them out liberally.)

Indeed, if there is one thing that should trouble Christians about the view of good and evil in the Harry Potter books, it is the way that certain acts of the heroes are blithely overlooked. Harry, Hermione, and Ron are often deceiving and rule-breaking, and this seems to be acceptable because the end toward which they are working is justified. There is some validity to this charge, especially in the early books where Harry succeeds in defeating Voldemort precisely because he (Harry) disobeys rules—with a knowing wink from Dumbledore. In the later books, however, it gets more serious. In *The Prisoner of Azkaban,* Professor Lupin, one of the wiser Hogwarts professors, who was a good friend of Harry's father and becomes a good friend of Harry's, chastises Harry for his flagrant disrespect of rules and his flaunting of his powers. "Your parents gave their lives to keep you alive, Harry," he tells him. "A poor way to repay them—gambling their sacrifice for a bag of magic tricks" (*Prisoner,* 290). The outcome of book 5 and the result of some of Harry's choices might also raise some doubts about the tactics of the three young heroes. Though Harry's forming of Dumbledore's Army is certainly against the rules, it might be seen in the same light as Christians secretly meeting underground during times of persecution. As for Harry's other rebellions stemming from his pride, however, they result in the death of somebody very close to him. So despite what might be seen as failings in the first three books, Rowling challenges her readers to take even this issue seriously. Harry's life is not his own to spend as he will. He has been bought with a price—in his case the price of love paid by his mother—and he bears on his forehead the visible scar, marking him by love and by a power greater than his own. Christians, too, have been bought with a price (1 Cor. 6:20, 7:23) and set apart for a purpose, and like Harry need to be reminded of that divine calling (1 Thess. 4:7).

A more serious concern arises with Dumbledore, for his actions cannot merely be written off as youthful foolishness. Dumbledore, as mentioned, is the great hero of the books. At the end of *The Goblet of Fire,* he tells the gathered students "the truth is generally preferable to lies." By saying "generally," he seems to be implying that there are times when lying is preferable. Even the use of the word "preferable" suggests that truth is a personal subjective preference as distinct from an objective moral law. Of course, it is a statement that might appear in any novel, fantasy or otherwise, and has nothing to do with magic or witchcraft. Still, the Christian reader is left to wonder why, after so many other illustrations of clear objective moral principles, Rowling would choose this wording. A single line buried in one of the books, it might be overlooked except for one thing: at a critical juncture in book 5, Dumbledore himself chooses to lie. When Dumbledore's Army is discovered at Hogwarts, and Fudge blames Harry Potter and threatens to take him off to Azkaban, Dumbledore takes responsibility. "You organized this?" Fudge asks him. "I did," Dumbledore replies, in full knowledge that his words are untrue. And he continues the lie, claiming that the meeting was "supposed to be the first meeting," even though they have been going on for some time. Other than the fact that the ensuing scene when Fudge tries to arrest Dumbledore is one of the most enjoyable moments in any of the first five books, the lie itself is deeply disturbing. Depending on the translation of Exodus 20:14, many Christians would see Dumbledore's words as a breaking of the ninth commandment. However, no apology is given. Readers may be led (or misled) to accept Dumbledore's model, and to see lying as acceptable and justified, especially in light of his earlier words.

In defense of Rowling, three points should be made. The first is perhaps the most significant. If we are to judge Dumbledore's actions against the objective standard of the Ten Commandments, we should realize that most modern translations of Exodus 20:16 read like the NIV: "You shall not give false testimony *against your neighbor*" (emphasis ours), rather than the simpler "You shall not lie." In fact, Dumbledore is not bearing false testimony against anybody but himself. If this is the correct translation, then, he is not breaking the commandment. This still does not mean that lying is acceptable. There are other passages that speak against lying (e.g., Eph. 4:25; Col. 3:9), and Hebrews 6:18 tells that it is impossible for God (in whose image man is created) to lie. These passages must also be taken seriously. Nonetheless, this first point relates to the second: there are few who would criticize Christians who, in Nazi Germany in the 1930s and 1940s, lied in order to protect Jews from concentration camps. To the contrary, many Christians who worked during this time to hide and protect Jews are viewed as heroes for their courageous stands. Now, if speaking untruth is at all times morally wrong, then the real heroism of these Christians does not justify their lying. They might have chosen other paths, such as a refusal to give *any* information to the secret police, either truthful or untruthful. In other words, the heroism of their self-sacrifice should be understood as a separate question from the morality of their choice to lie. Nonetheless, in such circumstances it is easy to understand their choice. And that is precisely the circumstance Dumbledore is in when he lies to protect Harry. Fudge had come to arrest Harry to take him to Azkaban, a prison camp at least as horrific as the Soviet Gulags if not the concentration camps of Nazi Germany. In telling his lie, Dumbledore was acting unselfishly, risking himself to keep Harry from an unjust and horrible fate.[6]

6. Given Dumbledore's considerable power, it may not actually have been any risk at all. Nonetheless, he still sacrifices his current position and status, and something of his freedom.

Finally, the necessity placed on Dumbledore to make such a sacrifice was a consequence of Harry's own flagrant breaking of rules, and so Rowling really is challenging the reader to consider whether the end toward which Potter and his friends work in the various books justifies the means; bad means, Rowling is telling us again, may have bad consequences. Had Rowling invited the reader to wrestle with any of these issues, especially the first and second—even raising the possibility that Dumbledore's lie *might* have been wrong—then the whole passage would be wonderful fare for Christian reading. Even as it is, it has much to offer. Putting aside the issue of the headmaster's lie, we note that Dumbledore's sacrifice for a sinful Harry is Christlike as well, giving himself not for the righteous but for an impudent boy who at the time neither appreciates nor understands it.

11

Once upon a Time . . . The End

Novelist Walker Percy made the comment that we live our lives in yearning. Although counseled on every hand to "stay in the moment," the mind is predisposed to cast forward, seeking to snare the future and bring it close. That's why stories engage us, because the space between "Once upon a time . . ." and "The End" is where we live our lives.

Harold Fickett, *Conversations with Jesus*

Theories lie more readily than stories. That is why our psychologists tell us we are good but our novelists tell us we are evil.

Peter Kreeft, *A Turn of the Clock*

We ended this book with a look at J. K. Rowling's Harry Potter books in part because these books have been so controversial. (We argued in the previous chapter that the uproar, though in many cases well-intentioned, has been at some level misguided.) But there was another good reason for ending with Harry Potter, and that is the central place given to magic in Rowling's work. For many critics, the main issue at stake is the use of magic, which some suppose to be irreducibly wicked. What we pointed to in Rowling was a strong connection or relationship between magic, ethics, and transcendent longing. Even to say that magic is central to Rowling's work is an incomplete statement; one ought to say rather that a central idea is the relationship between magic, ethics, and meaning, for Rowling weaves them all together, using magic as a vehicle for exploring questions of meaning.

Recall what we said about the Bible in part 1. There are two foolish ways to read the Bible with regard to its mythic elements. One is to deny that the Bible contains mythic elements, and the other is to claim that the Bible contains little other than myth, meaning that it contains little truth. Ironically, both of these positions rely on the same jaundiced view of myth, namely, that what is mythical is untrue. There are two analogous poor ways of thinking about magic. One is to identify all magic with evil, and the other is to think of all magic as nonsense. There is yet a third poor way to think about magic—not just poor, but very dangerous—and that is to be drawn to the practice of it as a means of gaining power. But the fact that magic can be treated poorly in literature does not mean that all treatments of it are bad; we ignore magic and its literature at our peril. Magic, as Tolkien argued, is at the root of Faërie and fantasy. We earlier quoted him saying, "Faërie itself may perhaps most nearly be translated by Magic." Now, an instant after he makes this statement, he immediately amends it, adding, "but it is magic of a peculiar mode and power, at the furthest pole from the vulgar devices of the laborious, scientific, magician" (*Essay*, 15). *Enchantment* might be an even better word than *magic*. But whichever word we use, the idea behind it is at the heart of Faërie. Yes, it is a magic that can make "heavy things light and able to fly," but more importantly it is a magic whose very nature is to work as a "spell or incantation" over the reader. Of course, Tolkien's statement about the peculiar magic of Faërie is also true of the magic of Dumbledore (even if not in general true of the magic practiced by others at Hogwarts), and of Tolkien's Gandalf and Galadriel, and Lewis's Aslan and Father Christmas, and Le Guin's Ged, and Stephen Lawhead's Taliesin and Merlin—and, dare we say, of Elijah and Elisha; their magic is natural and internal, though rarely effortless, and is very unlike the popularized laborious (and laboratory) magic that Tolkien contrasts it with.

To be clear, the authors of this book are not in any way advocating the practice of magic, any more than we are suggesting that our readers try to walk through the backs of wardrobes into other worlds, or fly in hearses to distant planets (as Lewis's character Ransom does in *Perelandra*). We (both the authors of this book and our readers) are right to reject occult magic, and all its dangers, both in its source and in its effects. We are right to reject the lust for power, which may in Faërie also be expressed through a grasping for magic, even as in our world it may be expressed through attempts to dominate others through technology or wealth, or through a desire to gain political influence for its own sake. We do well to reject any works of fantasy that portray such desires as good. But if we reject fairy tale because it contains magic and enchantment, then we must reject Faërie itself in all its varied forms, from the high and cosmogonic myth all the way to the romantic fairy tale. And if we reject this all, we are bankrupt.

Some Summary Questions

At this point we might do well to stop and take stock of where we have been. Is it possible to give a summarizing list of principles that will wrap up our discussion? Possibly. But before doing so, we return once again to J. R. R. Tolkien, and a warning he issued in his essay on *Beowulf.*

> The significance of a myth is not easily to be pinned on paper by analytical reasoning. It is at its best when it is presented by a poet who feels rather than makes explicit what his theme portends; who presents it incarnate in the world of history and geography, as [the poet of *Beowulf*] has done. Its defender is thus at a disadvantage: unless he is careful, and speaks in parables, he will kill what he is studying by vivisection, and he will be left with a formal or mechanical allegory, and, what is more, probably with one that will not work. For myth is alive at once and in all its parts, and dies before it can be dissected. (*Monsters,* 15)

We have tried in this book to be defenders of myths. In trying to guide our readers to a better understanding of fantasy literature, we have also argued for the tremendous value to society of the whole spectrum of the literature of Faërie (or at least of the better works of the kind). And we have done so, it must be admitted, through a certain amount of analytical reasoning. We hope that in doing so we have not thereby killed through vivisection the very thing we were hoping to bring to light. We hope that what we have done is encouraged our readers to turn to those mythopoets who feel the material and present it incarnate. At the very least, it was in that hope that we wrote the book as we did, pointing to examples, making connections, and drawing the modern reader back to the great stories of the past—even in the midst of admittedly analytical exploration at times—rather than simply trying to explain the meanings of a plethora of modern works (as if such a thing could be done even if we wanted to).

We have, therefore, a certain hesitancy to try to summarize the principles of the book in a neat and tidy little list. We do, however, think that a handful of the most important questions we have posed bear a summary repeating, because they are the right questions (at least the right starting questions) to ask about a work of the genre we have been exploring. Of the various questions we posed, there are three groups of related questions whose answers will usually bring one closest to the heart of a work of Faërie. We begin this list of questions where the book left off, with magic. We assume that magic and enchantment will play some role in a work of fantasy. The important concern is not whether there is magic, but the nature of the magic.

> What is magic used for? Is its goal the domination of wills? What is its end?

> What is the source and means of magic? Does it work through internal power, through nature, or through the domination of wills, occult or otherwise?

We also must ask, in any work of fantasy, what is the nature of good and evil, and how that relates to the heroic.

> Are good and evil defined? Are they subjective or objective? What or who is the ultimate arbiter of what is good?

> Is moral virtue shown to be heroic? What makes a hero a hero?

A somewhat related question has to do with the human condition, and is connected to our discussion of the differences between science fiction and fantasy.

> What does the work say about the human condition? Are humans fundamentally good, and merely in need of better technology to improve our

lives, or are we in need of moral redemption beyond any technological aid? And is life inherently valuable and worth redemption?

Once we begin to speak of redemption, of course, we must also speak of grace, and whether the work of fantasy points toward grace. And this leads to the last group.

The final list below has to do with meaning: the meaning of life and death, the meaning of the universe, and the meaning of one's own existence. Ultimately, these questions will lead toward both the source and end of the universe and of life. We saw, for example, that a main difference between Le Guin's Earthsea and Tolkien's *Legendarium* is the view of death. And we saw that one of the things separating Walter Wangerin Jr.'s *Book of the Dun Cow* from Stephen Donaldson's *Chronicles of Thomas Covenant* is how open or closed the universe is to an external power. In Wangerin's world, God can act, there is answered prayer, and this gives meaning to the creatures of Chauntecleer's domain. The creator of Donaldson's The Land, by contrast, is impotent, and this gives a very different meaning. This last list of questions is hardest to phrase, but perhaps most important and most worth the effort.

> What is the cosmogony of the fantastic realm in which the tale takes place? Does the world of the story have a personal and purposeful beginning that gives meaning to its history and to the lives of its inhabitants?

> What is the relationship between life and death? Is death an end or a beginning? Does one's personhood end at death?

These last two groups of questions return us to the notion of transcendence. Is there any transcendent meaning, value, and morality in the universe, or are these things only what the individual creates for himself or herself? For all of these questions, myth, heroic romance, and fairy tale can be profound means of exploring and communicating the answers—without ever giving a didactic list of answers.

Why We Read from Faërie: A Few Final Thoughts

We end by returning to the very question of why the reader should read the literature we have been speaking of. Why do we want mythic

and imaginative answers? Why not stay with the analytical? In answer
to this, philosopher Peter Kreeft once wrote:

> Myths are even prophetic, pointing to the truth from afar, as Greek phi-
> losophy is prophetic. For God has not left himself without witnesses even
> outside Israel, though none of these other witnesses is divinely guar-
> anteed and infallible. The human soul has intellect, will, and emotions;
> some knowledge of the truth, the good, and the beautiful. And God sent
> prophets to all three areas of the soul: philosophers to enlighten the intel-
> lect, prophets to straighten out the will, and myth-makers to tease and
> touch the emotions with a desire for himself. The philosophers have an
> analogue in the soul, a philosopher within: our understanding. The prophets
> have an analogue in the soul too, a divine mouthpiece called conscience.
> And the myth-makers too have an analogue in the soul, a dreamer and
> poet and myth-maker within. (*Kreeft*, 215)

The myth-maker, the teller of fairy tales, and the writer of fantasy all
may speak profoundly to the human soul. They do so through art, and
imagery, including the imagery of magic in many of its forms, and as
such they speak directly to the soul through the imagination.

It has always been the case that there are people who claim myth and
fantasy are outmoded, that the stories they tell are fantastic and therefore
not relevant and not true. What we hope we have shown is that myth
and fantasy are both perennially relevant and eternally true. Truth is not
limited to that which has been proven by scientific experiment or deductive logic. If it were, we would never know any truth at all. Scientists need
assumptions and logicians need premises to make their demonstrations
relevant to life. Assumptions and premises come from our experience;
they rest upon stories. We always have need of moral and other truth to
be expressed in universal story, story that we can relate to and which is
plastic enough to have relevance for our decisions. Bettelheim is right:
we store up stories that shape and mold our moral character. This is not
something we outgrow.

Ursula Le Guin provides yet another powerful summation.

> For fantasy is true, of course. It isn't factual, but it is true. Children know
> that. Adults know it too, and that is precisely why many of them are afraid
> of fantasy. They know that its truth challenges, even threatens, all that
> is false, all that is phony, unnecessary, and trivial in the life they have let
> themselves be forced into living. They are afraid of dragons because they
> are afraid of freedom . . .

> Children know perfectly well that unicorns aren't real, but they also
> know that books about unicorns, if they are good books, are true books.
> (*Dragons*, 40)

The same can be said of magic. It isn't factual, but it is true. What
Dumbledore says to Fudge at the end of book 4—and what Rowling
is saying to her readers, through the imagery of wizards and magic and
spells and enchantment—also challenges us. It challenges that which is
phony, unnecessary, false, and trivial. It challenges us to move past our
comfortable lives and to engage in a significant battle. Myth, fantasy, and
fairy at its best always do that. They challenge us to live lives governed
by the transcendent, eternal, moral, and unseen realities, and not by the
mundane, temporal things that seem so real and physical and common-
place. "The electric street-lamp may be ignored, simply because it is so
insignificant and transient. Fairy-stories, at any rate, have more permanent
and fundamental things to talk about" (*Essay*, 57).

Our hope, then, is that this book will not be a substitute for reading the
great stories that have shaped our world, but a provocation to go and read
them. We cannot pretend to have given anything like a comprehensive
survey of myth and fantasy. As we said at the outset, we have for the most
part written about the stories we know and like the best, but we know
there are other great stories out there. We have focused on the literature
that has shaped Western culture. We would be delighted to see others
do the same with the literatures of other cultures. To paraphrase Kreeft,
God is not without witnesses—in any place or time or literature. Even
in Western culture, we have left out much that is worth reading.[1]

We will conclude with a caveat, however, one we have mentioned
several times. Faërie is not a safe place to enter, and one should not enter
incautiously. Stories are enchanting. The stories we talked about in part
1 of this book have insinuated themselves into the fabric and seams of

---

1. In this regard, the living authors Madeleine L'Engle and Stephen Lawhead come to mind for
both authors of this book. Our omission of these authors and others in part 2 of this book should not
be read as a censure of their work. We heartily recommend both! Lawhead masterfully weaves together
multiple myths in his retellings of the Arthurian stories. The result powerfully illustrates what we have
been saying about the truth of myth. L'Engle's genius deserves greater treatment than we could give in
a single chapter. Her ability to weave medieval European myth from the *Mabinogion*, Native American
legend, science fiction, and biblical story into a consistent and enjoyable narrative is pure genius. In both
cases, we had to omit them because we found other authors enabled us to say more succinctly what we
had to say. If we have succeeded in provoking you to read more myth and fantasy, however, Lawhead's
Taliesin (first in his Arthurian trilogy) and L'Engle's *A Wrinkle in Time* (and its many companion volumes) are excellent places to start.

our culture. In some cases, they constitute the stitching that holds the cloth together. Where would Lewis and Tolkien be without MacDonald? Where would we be without the Grimms? What would our sense of law and the Constitution be like were it not for Homer? How impoverished we would be were it not for the story of Job. And has any story changed the world more than the *Gōd Spell*?

The stories in part 2 have their effects as well. We become like that which we admire, and it behooves us to choose our stories well. No one seriously doubts that reading builds our vocabulary. It is just as certain that stories build our moral vocabulary. They shape our life together. Stories become a part of us, and they change us. Mythic and fantastic literature, perhaps more than any other literature, reminds us of the relevance of our moral decision making. Our attention is focused on that which transcends our mundane experience of brute action in the world. We are reminded that the world is shot through with significance, that we ourselves are significant, no matter who we are. We are reminded as well that everything that signifies is a sign of something else. The whole world—ourselves included—points beyond itself to that which it signifies. We are signs, the world is a sign, a character in a story greater than our small tales can capture. That story is being told in our lives, in our decisions, in our every little choice, just as we see happening in the great myths. Reading the stories of Faërie is no escapism, no mere flight of fantasy. Read them aloud, with others, if possible. These stories are, after all, about us.

Appendices and Indices

For Further Reading

Nearly all of the works of myth, romance, and fairy tale referred to in the first part of this book were written in a language other than modern English—the fairy tales of George MacDonald being the notable exception—and many were written in languages no longer spoken today (e.g., Old English, Old Norse, classical Greek). Most modern readers will need to read at least some of these works in translation. Fortunately, good translations exist for all of them, and in most cases several exist, with varying motivations on the part of the different translators. Some translators make literalism their aim, while others try to capture the spirit of the text or the meter or alliterative scheme of the poetry. The following list should provide a starting place for the reader of modern English. In a few instances, we list multiple translations. For simplicity's sake, however, we usually list only one (even when several exist), suggesting texts that are accessible over those that are very literal but not as readable. Our reasons for this are two: these are, first and foremost, stories, and they should be enjoyed; the more readable the translation, the more likely it is to be read and enjoyed by more people. Second, this is not a definitive list, but a suggestion of a place to start enjoying these classic works; if you enjoy a story in one translation, find another translation and read that one, too, and you will likely find a different translator has brought out a different aspect of the original work. Of course, if you know the languages, you should read the texts in the original; the ability to do so is one of the chief motivations for learning these languages.

I. Recommended Translations

The Bible. We recommend starting with the New International Version (NIV) or the New Revised Standard Version (NRSV). The NIV is a popular translation, largely because it is very readable. Its chief weakness is that it sacrifices much of the original rhetoric and poetry in order to make it more accessible to the general reader. The NRSV is less popular than the NIV but also very readable, with perhaps a slightly better sense of poetry. The NRSV is also sensitive to instances of ambiguity in nouns and pronouns in the original text.

The Book of Job. Job is found in every Bible, but you may also want to read a separate translation. The single best translation and commentary is Robert Sacks's (University of South Florida Press, 2000). Stephen Mitchell's popular translation (HarperPerennial, 1987) is very readable, but Mitchell has edited out the Elihu passage, so it is incomplete.

The Heliand. G. Ronald Murphy, S.J., trans. (Oxford University Press, 1992). A very readable prose translation, with a helpful introduction and valuable appendices.

Homer, *The Iliad* and *The Odyssey*. There are good translations by Richmond Lattimore (University of Chicago Press, 1961), Robert Fagles (Viking, 1990), and Stanley Lombardo (Hackett, 1997). Lattimore's translations are especially good. Lombardo's are translated in a loose, very readable style. Be sure the edition you buy has a list of proper names in the back; Homer includes hundreds of gods, people, and places in his epics, so you'll want to have this list as a reference.

Greek Playwrights: Aeschylus, Sophocles, Euripides. After Homer, these are among our chief sources of information about the ancient Greek myths. We recommend the four-volume *The Complete Greek Tragedies,* edited by David Grene and Richmond Lattimore (University of Chicago Press, 1992).

Apuleius, *The Golden Ass.* Jack Lindsay, trans. (Indiana University Press, 1961). This is the main source for the Cupid and Psyche myth, as retold by C. S. Lewis in his *Till We Have Faces.*

Apollonius of Rhodes, *Jason and the Golden Fleece*. Richard Hunter, trans. (Oxford University Press, 1995).

Virgil, *The Aeneid.* Robert Fitzgerald (Vintage, 1990).

Beowulf. You might start with the *prose* translation by E. Talbot Donaldson, in the Norton Critical Edition (W. W. Norton, 2001). Although it is now acknowledged that there are a small number of errors—misglossed words—in Donaldson's translation, overall it is an excellent prose translation and does a very good job of keeping the tone and imagery of the original, while remaining readable. The edition also has helpful commentary, including an abridged version of Tolkien's famous essay. Probably the best translation in *poetry* is Seamus Heaney's version (W. W. Norton, 2001). Heaney's masterpiece is part translation and part interpretation. Heaney is a great poet, and at times trusts his poetic instinct more than literalism in the translation; he'd rather give the modern reader a feel for the poem than precise definitions of various artifacts. It reads as great poetry.

Snorri Sturluson, *The Prose Edda.* Jean I. Young, trans. (University of California Press, 1964).

Le Chanson de Roland / The Song of Roland. Dorothy L. Sayers, trans. (Penguin, 1957). (Sayers was also a contemporary and acquaintance of C. S. Lewis, as well as the author of the highly acclaimed Lord Peter Wimsey mystery novels.)

The Arthurian Legends: An Illustrated Anthology. Richard Barber, ed. (Boydell Press, 1996).

Gawain and the Green Knight / Pearl / Orfeo. J. R. R. Tolkien, trans. (Del Rey, 1988).

Wolfram von Eschenbach, *Parzival.* Helen M. Mustard and Charles E. Passage, trans. (Vintage Books, 1961). There is also a nice children's translation by Katherine Paterson, entitled *Parzival: The Quest of the Grail Knight* (Dutton Juvenile, 1998).

The Mabinogion. Gwyn Jones, trans. (J. M. Dent & Sons, 1991). A compilation of Welsh myths, and one of the main sources of Arthurian legend (and of Lloyd Alexander's very good *Prydain* series). This edition of the *Mabinogion* has a good introduction.

Dante, *The Divine Comedy.* Dorothy L. Sayers, trans. (Penguin Classics, 1950). Sayers's notes are very helpful for understanding obscure cultural and theological references.

Jacob and Wilhelm Grimm, *German Fairy Tales.* There are perhaps more translations, retellings, and editions of these than of any of the other works discussed in this book. Some notable versions include *The Complete Grimm's Fairy Tales* (New York: Pantheon, 1944), based on a translation by Margaret Hunt, revised by James Stern, and with an introduction by Padraic Colum and commentary by Joseph Campbell; also *German Fairy Tales*, vol. 29, Helmut Brackert and Volckmar Sander, eds. (Continuum, 1985). If you can find the Modern Library edition of *Tales of Grimm and Andersen*, Frederick Jacobi Jr., ed. (1952, now out of print), it's well worth it for the introduction by W. H. Auden.

II. Selected Modern Retellings

It's always best to read the originals rather than condensations, but we find the following reference works helpful from time to time.

Bullfinch's Mythology. Written in the 1850s, this is one of those very useful works that has been reprinted too many times to count. Bullfinch retells the myths of Europe from ancient times through the Middle Ages. Helpful indices bring the reader quickly to paragraph-length summaries of the stories. Pay attention to what edition you're getting. Look for an inexpensive edition that contains all the volumes in one book. The one published by Modern Library is good.

Edith Hamilton, *Mythology* (Mentor Books, 1940). A more recent condensation of the major myths of Greece and Rome.

Norma Lorre Goodrich, *Medieval Myths* (Meridian, 1994). An overview, presenting (in some cases abridged) medieval romances from nine different regions ranging from Scandinavia, Russia, and Ireland down to Spain. The book should have been titled *Medieval Romances,* and the commentary is only moderately interesting, but the choice of stories is appropriate and gives a broad survey of the times.

Ingri and Edgar D'Aulaire, *D'Aulaires' Book of Greek Myths,* **and** *D'Aulaires' Norse Gods and Giants.* These are excellent introductions to Greek and Norse mythology. Ostensibly children's books, these retellings and the D'Aulaires' masterful artwork make good reading for all ages. *Norse Gods and Giants* is currently out of print, but the New York Review of Books republished *Daulaires' Book of Norse Myths* in 2005.

Stephen R. Lawhead, *Arthur, Merlin,* and *Taliesin* (Crossway Books, 1987–89). Simply beautiful retellings of the great Arthurian myths, woven together with the Atlantis myth. All three were republished by Zondervan in 1996.

III. A Very Short List of Recommended Commentary on J. R. R. Tolkien and C. S. Lewis

This could easily be the longest section. There are, quite literally, scores of books in this category, with many new ones being added every year. We will make no attempt to list even the best few, but limit ourselves to just one good book on Tolkien and one on Lewis that we believe to be excellent starting places for a critical exploration of the writings of these authors.

Tom Shippey, *J. R. R. Tolkien, Author of the Century* (Houghton Mifflin, 2002).

Thomas Howard, *C. S. Lewis, Man of Letters: A Reading of His Fiction* (Wipf & Stock, 2004), originally published under the title *The Achievement of C. S. Lewis* (Shaw, 1980).

INDEX

Note: The names of literary works are italicized except in cases where the name of the work is the same as the name of the character, and references apply to both (e.g. Cinderella, Beowulf, Job, etc.).

INDEX

271